Changes

Readings for Writers

Changes

Readings for Writers

Second Edition

Jean Withrow

Borough of Manhattan Community College
City University of New York

Gay Brookes

Borough of Manhattan Community College
City University of New York

Martha Clark Cummings

Monterey Institute of International Studies

CAMBRIDGE
UNIVERSITY PRESS

PUBLISHED BY THE PRESS SYNDICATE OF THE UNIVERSITY OF CAMBRIDGE
The Pitt Building, Trumpington Street, Cambridge CB2 1RP, United Kingdom

CAMBRIDGE UNIVERSITY PRESS
The Edinburgh Building, Cambridge CB2 2RU, UK   http://www.cup.cam.ac.uk
40 West 20th Street, New York, NY 10011-4211, USA   http://www.cup.org
10 Stamford Road, Oakleigh, Melbourne 3166, Australia

First published by St. Martin's Press, Inc. 1996
Reprinted 1998

Printed in the United States of America

Library of Congress Cataloging-in-Publication Data Available

ISBN 0 521 65788 1 Student's Book
ISBN 0 521 657873 Instructor's Manual

ACKNOWLEDGMENTS

Helen Nearing, excerpt from Loving and Leaving the Good Life. Copyright © 1992 by Helen Nearing. Reprinted with permission from Chelsea Green Publishing Company, White River Junction, Vermont.
Maggie Mok, "Sometimes Home Is Not Really Home." Reprinted by permission of the author.
Edward P. Jones, "The First Day" from Lost in the City by Edward P. Jones. Copyright © 1992 by Edward P. Jones. Reprinted by permission of the author and William Morrow & Company, Inc.
Nicholas Gage, pages, 1–7, "Going to America" from A Place for Us. Copyright © 1989 by Nicholas Gage. Reprinted by permission of Houghton Mifflin Co. All rights reserved.
Jamaica Kincaid, excerpts from "A Walk to the Jetty" from Annie John by Jamaica Kincaid. Copyright © 1984, 1985 by Jamaica Kincaid. Reprinted by permission of Farrar, Straus & Giroux, Inc., and Pan Books Ltd. London.
Michelle Dominique Leigh, "Ancestral Oranges." From The House on Via Gombito, New Rivers Press, 1991. Reprinted by permission of the publisher.
Joe Klein, "The Education of Berenice Belizaire," from Newsweek, August 9, 1993. Copyright © 1993 Newsweek, Inc. All rights reserved. Reprinted by permission.
Lawrence Kutner, "Parent & Child: Misconceptions with Roots in the Old Days," from The New York Times, November 19, 1992. Copyright © 1992 by The New York Times Company. Reprinted by permission.
Barbara Mujica, "No Comprendo," from The New York Times Op-Ed page, January 3, 1995. Copyright © 1995 by The New York Times Company. Reprinted by permission.
Ecclesiastes 3: 1–8. From The New English Bible. Copyright © The Delegates of the Oxford University Press and The Syndies of the Cambridge University Press 1961, 1970, 1989. Reprinted by permission.
David Updike, "The Colorings of Childhood: On the Burdens, and Privileges, Facing My Multi-racial Son." Copyright © 1992 by David Updike, first published in HARPER'S, reprinted with the permission of Wylie, Aitken & Stone, Inc.

Acknowledgments are continued on pages 247–248.

Contents

To the Instructor xiii
To the Student xvi

Unit 1
Two Worlds 1

Before Reading 2

When One Door Opens *Helen Nearing* 2

After Reading 3   Topics for Writing 3   After Writing 3

Before Reading 4

Sometimes Home Is Not Really Home *Maggie Mok* 4

After Reading 4   How I Read It 5   How It's Written 5
Topics for Writing 6   After Writing 6

Before Reading 7

The First Day *Edward P. Jones* 7

After Reading 9   How I Read It 9   Topics for Writing 10
After Writing 10

Before Reading 11

Going to America *Nicholas Gage* 11

After Reading 16   How I Read It 16   How It's Written 17
Topics for Writing 17   After Writing 18

Before Reading 19

A Walk to the Jetty *Jamaica Kincaid* 19

After Reading 23   How I Read It 24   How It's Written 24
Topics for Writing 25   After Writing 26

Before Reading   27

Ancestral Oranges *Michelle Dominique Leigh*   27

After Reading   27   How It's Written   28   Topics for Writing   28
After Writing   29

Before Reading   30

The Education of Berenice Belizaire *Joe Klein*   30

After Reading   32   How It's Written   32   Topics for Writing   33
After Writing   33

Before Reading   34

Misconceptions with Roots in the Old Days *Lawrence Kutner*   34

After Reading   36   Topics for Writing   36   After Writing   37

Before Reading   38

No Comprendo *Barbara Mujica*   38

After Reading   39   How I Read It   39   How It's Written   40
Topics for Writing   40   After Writing   41

Before Reading   42

Ecclesiastes 3:1–8   42

After Reading   42   How I Read It   43   How It's Written   43
Topics for Writing   43   After Writing   44

Before Reading   45

The Colorings of Childhood: On the Burdens, and Privileges, Facing My Multi-racial Son *David Updike*   45

After Reading   47   How It's Written   48   Topics for Writing   48
After Writing   49

Before Reading   50

On Turning Fifty *Judy Scales-Trent*   50

After Reading   53   How It's Written   53   Topics for Writing   54
After Writing   55

Before Reading   56

Child of the Americas *Aurora Levins Morales*   56

After Reading   57   How It's Written   57   Topics for Writing   57
After Writing   58

About All the Readings in This Unit   59

Preparing for Writing 59   Writing 59   After Writing 59

Extra Readings   61

My Way or Theirs? *Liu Zongren   61*

**The Sacred Seed of the Medicine Tree: Can Indian Identity
  Survive? *Linda Hogan   64***

Stowaway *Armando Socarras Ramírez   66*

Snow *Julia Alvarez   70*

A Story of Conflicts *Yeghia Aslanian   71*

Chocolate Tears and Dreams: Summer 1953 *Evelyn C. Rosser   73*

I Stop Writing the Poem *Tess Gallagher   74*

Unit 2
Becoming/The True Self   77

Before Reading   78

Believing in the True Self *Gloria Steinem   78*

After Reading 79   How It's Written 79   Topics for Writing 79
After Writing 80

Before Reading   81

Becoming a Writer *Russell Baker   81*

After Reading 83   How It's Written 83   Topics for Writing 84
After Writing 84

Before Reading   85

Johnnieruth *Becky Birtha   85*

After Reading 90   How It's Written 90   Topics for Writing 91
After Writing 91

Before Reading   93

homage to my hips *Lucille Clifton   93*

After Reading 93   Topics for Writing 94   After Writing 94

Before Reading   96

Rekindling the Warrior: Gangs Are Part of the Solution, Not Part of the Problem *Luis J. Rodriguez   96*

After Reading   98   How I Read It   98   Topics for Writing   98   After Writing   99

Before Reading   *100*

Safe *Cherylene Lee   100*

After Reading   *101*   How It's Written   *101*   Topics for Writing   *102*
After Writing   *102*

Before Reading   *103*

I'm Working on My Charm *Dorothy Allison   103*

After Reading   *104*   How It's Written   *104*   Topics for Writing   *104*
After Writing   *105*

Before Reading   *106*

My First Job *Leticia Fuentes   106*

After Reading   *107*   How It's Written   *107*   Topics for Writing   *108*
After Writing   *109*

Before Reading   *110*

New-Collar Work: Telephone Sales Reps Do Unrewarding Jobs *Dana Milbank   110*

After Reading   *111*   How It's Written   *112*   Topics for Writing   *112*
After Writing   *113*

Before Reading   *114*

The Bread Shop *Studs Terkel   114*

After Reading   *116*   How I Read It   *117*   Topics for Writing   *117*
After Writing   *118*

Before Reading   *119*

A Scale of Stresses *Susan Ovelette Kobasa   119*

After Reading   *121*   How I Read It   *122*   How It's Written   *122*
Topics for Writing   *123*   After Writing   *123*

Before Reading   *124*

It's O.K. to Cry: Tears Are Not Just a Bid for Attention *Jane Brody*   *124*

After Reading   *126*   How It's Written   *126*   Topics for Writing   *127*
After Writing   *128*

Before Reading   *129*

Going Through the House   *Claire Braz-Valentine*   *129*

After Reading   *131*   How I Read It   *131*   How It's Written   *132*   Topics for Writing   *132*   After Writing   *133*   A Private Writing Activity   *134*

Before Reading   *135*

Falling Away, Here at Home   *Julia Aldrich*   *135*

After Reading   *137*   How It's Written   *137*   Topics for Writing   *138*
After Writing   *138*

About All the Readings in This Unit   *140*

Preparing for Writing   *140*   Writing   *140*   After Writing   *140*

Extra Readings   *141*

Hope Emerges As Key to Success in Life   *Daniel Goleman*   *141*

Poem [2]   *Langston Hughes*   *143*

Gravy   *Raymond Carver*   *143*

Homework   *Peter Cameron*   *144*

Unit 3
A Changing World   153

Before Reading   *154*

Father's Day   *Michael Dorris*   *154*

After Reading   *155*   How I Read It   *156*   How It's Written   *156*
Topics for Writing   *156*   After Writing   *157*

Before Reading   *158*

New York Finds Typical Family Being Redefined   *Sam Roberts*   *158*

After Reading   *159*   How I Read It   *159*   Topics for Writing   *159*
After Writing   *160*

Before Reading   *161*

Power *Donald McCaig*   **161**

After Reading   *162*   How It's Written   *162*   Topics for Writing   *162*
After Writing   *163*

Before Reading   *164*

Against PCs: Why I'm Not Going to Buy a Computer *Wendell Berry*   **164**

After Reading   *166*   How I Read It   *166*   Topics for Writing   *167*

Letters   **167**

After Reading   *168*

Before Reading   *169*

Wendell Berry Replies   **169**

After Reading   *169*   After Writing   *170*

Before Reading   *171*

Cyberhood vs. Neighborhood   *Editors,* Utne Reader   **171**

After Reading   *172*

Before Reading   *173*

Whiz Kid Anonymous: A 10-year-old's Take on the Internet *Michael Kearney*   **173**

After Reading   *174*   How It's Written   *174*   Topics for Writing   *174*
After Writing   *175*

Before Reading   *176*

Pockets of Paradise: The Community Garden *Editors,* Seeds of Change **176**

After Reading   *178*   How I Read It   *178*   How It's Written   *178*
Topics for Writing   *179*   After Writing   *179*

Before Reading   *181*

Take Two Bowls of Garlic Pasta, Then Call Me in the Morning: Or Try a Dose of Echinacea a Day *Suzanne Hamlin*   **181**

After Reading   *184*   How I Read It   *184*   How It's Written   *184*
Topics for Writing   *184*   After Writing   *185*

Before Reading   *187*

Taming Macho Ways *Elvia Alvarado*   **187**

After Reading   *189*   How It's Written   *189*   Topics for Writing   *190*
After Writing   *190*

Before Reading   *191*

Gays, the Military . . . and My Son *Roscoe Thorne*   **191**

After Reading   *193*   How I Read It   *193*   How It's Written   *193*
Topics for Writing   *194*   After Writing   *194*

Before Reading   *195*

Buzzard *Bailey White*   **195**

After Reading   *195*   How It's Written   *196*   Topics for Writing   *196*
After Writing   *197*

Before Reading   *198*

The Brave Little Parrot *Rafe Martin*   **198**

After Reading   *200*   How It's Written   *201*   Topics for Writing   *201*
After Writing   *202*

Before Reading   *203*

The Future Is Yours (Still) *Abbie Hoffman*   **203**

After Reading   *204*   Topics for Writing   *204*   After Writing   *205*

Before Reading   *206*

Keeping Quiet *Pablo Neruda*   **206**

After Reading   *207*   How I Read It   *207*   Topics for Writing   *208*
After Writing   *208*

Before Reading   *209*

Entering the Twenty-first Century *Thich Nhat Hanh*   **209**

After Reading   *210*   How I Read It   *211*   How It's Written   *211*
Topics for Writing   *211*   After Writing   *212*

About All the Readings in This Unit   **213**

Preparing for Writing   *213*   Writing   *213*   After Writing   *213*

Extra Readings   **215**
Haiku *Teishitsu*   **215**
Family Man: Three Is the Loneliest Number *Roger L. Welsch*   **215**

Need We Say More? Average Hours per Week Spent by Eighth Graders on Various Activities *U.S. Department of Education* *219*
How Flowers Changed the World *Loren Eiseley* *220*
The Earth Community *Thomas Berry* *221*

Appendix A
Gathering Ideas   223

1. Freewriting *223*   2. Clustering *224*   3. Making a List *225*   4. Cubing *228*

Appendix B
Responding to Readings   230

1. Response Questions *230*   2. Double-Entry Notebook *230*   3. Annotating *233*
4. Descriptive Outlining *233*

Appendix C
The Reading Process (How We Read)   237

Appendix D
The Writing Process (How We Write)   238

Appendix E
Suggestions on Writing (Beginnings, Endings, Being Specific, Showing Instead of Telling)   240

Appendix F
After Writing   245

Index 249

To the Instructor

Changes: Readings for Writers, second edition, is an interactive, developmental, and integrated skills book focusing on reading and writing. It is intended for adults at intermediate to advanced levels. The book helps ESL students develop all language skills, especially reading and writing, through reading and responding to selections in writing and through talking with their peers. This process leads to more writing, which students then share with their peers and instructor.

This new edition offers a choice of forty-four readings with related activities and sixteen extra readings, bringing the total to sixty. Within the overall theme of *changes*, the readings are grouped in three units (Two Worlds, Becoming/The True Self, and A Changing World). Most of the readings in this edition are new. While the texts still vary in difficulty, length, tone, and genre, we have increased the number of expository readings in order to help students develop academic English and learn to read academic texts. This edition also places more emphasis on revision than the first edition did.

Before and after each reading are a number of activities to choose from. These activities draw upon all language skills. The extra readings at the end of each unit focus on the same themes but have no accompanying activities, thus allowing you and your students the freedom to use these readings in any way you choose.

Changes has certain features that make it unique among other reading/writing texts:

- The readings, which encompass a variety of genres, voices, and moods, include stories, poems, essays, letters, myths, and folktales.
- The readings vary in length and level of difficulty.
- All readings are original, not adapted.
- The writers, both professional and student, represent many different nationalities.
- The activities are stimulating, thought provoking, and student centered.
- Most activities are structured so that students may collaborate and share their work in small groups, in pairs, or in whole-class discussions.

- The varied readings and activities allow for instructor and student choice.
- The appendices assist students in responding to readings and improving their writing.

The activities combine reading and writing in some interesting ways. Students progress from reading to recording the significance of the text for themselves in reading logs. Then, because reading and writing are seen as social events taking place in a community, students are asked to talk in collaborative groups in order to understand the significance of the text for others. Class discussion helps shape many diverse understandings into a common meaning (or meanings). Finally, students write once again, this time with a new context for their thoughts and understandings. Reading and writing are further connected by activities that help to raise students' awareness of reading/writing strategies.

This text is based on the theory that the meaning of a selection is enhanced as students interact with the selection and their peers. The meaning changes and develops further as students see the subject from different viewpoints, as expressed in further reading, or in the writings and thoughts of their classmates. In our view, meaning resides as much in the reader as in the text itself. This view of the act of reading has shaped the categories and nature of the activities in the text.

Changes is also based on our understanding of the writing process and its development in ESL writers. We know the writing process is a complex linguistic and cognitive one in which thought and language interact in abstract ways. It is fluid and open-ended. The development of certain abilities in the process is gradual and, yet, ungradable. Writing is also intricately linked to reading, and as a result, students' writing abilities are enhanced. These understandings inform our approach to teaching writing.

This text takes students through all the steps of the writing process, commonly defined as prewriting, revision, getting feedback, editing, and publishing. The readings and the Before and After Reading activities provide a basis for the early stages of the writing process: gathering ideas and getting started. The readings serve as a resource for ideas, topics, and viewpoints, as well as for countless examples of genres, structures, vocabulary, styles, usage, even punctuation and spelling. The writing (and reading) activities include ample opportunities for getting feedback leading to revision and the production of final pieces.

In this student-centered text, the role of the instructor is often implied. Some of your tasks will include the following:

- setting up groups or pairs
- answering questions about the activities, the readings, and the instructions for writing

- structuring and facilitating class discussion and sharing, helping to make sense and order out of the sometimes conflicting and disordered group reports
- adding the interpretations of the larger community
- referring students to various parts of the appendices as appropriate

One thing to remember is that we don't think there are right and wrong answers, responses, or interpretations to the readings or to students' responses and writings. We hope you will help to stimulate the construction and reconstruction of interpretations and the composition of students' own thoughts on self-selected topics. To this end, you may prod and encourage, suggest and question. But primarily we hope you will provide a student-centered classroom with appropriate interaction, so that there is a positive, tolerant, and supportive atmosphere for students' expression of honest feelings, questions, tentative propositions, and responses to what they read and to one another.

This book is a product of collaboration. We would like to thank those who have collaborated with us, knowingly or unknowingly. First, our students who teach us how to teach. Second, the many authors whose works appear in the book and who implicitly teach how to write. Third, our teachers whose ideas shine through *Changes* and instruct us in how to teach writing. Fourth, our colleagues who share their thoughts and experiences on teaching students. We especially thank our reviewers: Janie B. Burkhardt, Norwalk Community College; Patricia Chernoff, Borough of Manhattan Community College, CUNY; Alberta N. Grossman, Borough of Manhattan Community College, CUNY; Mara Hegedeos, Cuyahoga Community College; Lisa Heyer, San Francisco State University; Priscilla Karant, New York University; Andrea Kevech, San Francisco State University; and Maxine Steinhaus, Borough of Manhattan Community College, CUNY. Finally, we thank the St. Martin's editors and staff for their assistance and support. We are grateful to you all.

Jean Withrow
Gay Brookes
Martha Clark Cummings

To the Student

In *Changes*, you will do a lot of reading, and you will write a lot about what you have read. Sometimes it will seem like you have been writing forever, and you will turn the page and find that the next section of the chapter you are working on is called "Topics for Writing." There is a reason for this.

Changes is a book designed to help you see and work with the connections between your ideas and the ideas of other writers. You will be asked to read, to pay attention to what you feel and think as you are reading, and to write about your thoughts and feelings. Your understanding of and responses to others' writing, including that of your classmates, will become the basis of your own writing.

As you read this book, you will be writing your own "book," your *reading log* or reading journal, which can be a spiral or loose-leaf notebook. In it, you will write your thoughts about and reactions to what you read. When you look back at these thoughts and reactions, you will easily find ideas for writing pieces on related topics. We ask you to do this because this is what professional writers do. They spend a great deal of time reading, thinking, and writing down their ideas before they actually start writing a story or an essay or a poem.

One set of activities—Before Reading, After Reading, and Topics for Writing—asks you to write as a way of making connections. The Before Reading activities ask you to bring to mind what you already know about a topic. Once you have read the story or essay or poem, the After Reading activities ask you to respond to what you've read—to consider the text and to explore your feelings, thoughts, and interpretations—by writing in your log.

At this point, the writing you have done and the discussions you have had have prepared you for writing a more finished piece of your own. The activities in Topics for Writing offer you a choice of topics. But you are free to shape a topic to your own thinking in any way you want. This is the time to put your ideas in order, focus on a topic and the points you want to make, and come up with examples and reasons to "show" your thinking. A final activity, After Writing, gives you a chance to share your ideas with a group and get feedback on your writing.

Another set of activities is designed to help you become aware of your reading and writing processes. In How I Read It, you will look at your reading process in comparison to that of your classmates. In How It's Written, you'll do what accomplished writers do—that is, look at how a story, poem, or essay is written. In other words, you will read like writers. In After Writing, you will reflect on how you wrote. By becoming more aware of your own and others' reading and writing strategies, you will become a stronger, more flexible reader and writer.

Many activities in this book suggest that you work with a group. You can learn a great deal by working with others, sharing ideas and interpretations, comparing reactions, and solving problems. Working in groups also gives you an opportunity to talk, and good talk leads to good thinking. When you engage in collaboration and conversation, your thinking changes, and you are enriched.

As you read the various instructions in this book, you will often see a reference to an appendix. The appendices, located at the back of the book, contain many helpful ideas on how to use this book and how to improve your writing. Be sure to read the six appendices with care.

We hope the readings and activities in *Changes* will not only help you develop as readers, writers, and thinkers in English, but will also give you new ways of thinking about *change*.

Jean Withrow
Gay Brookes
Martha Clark Cummings

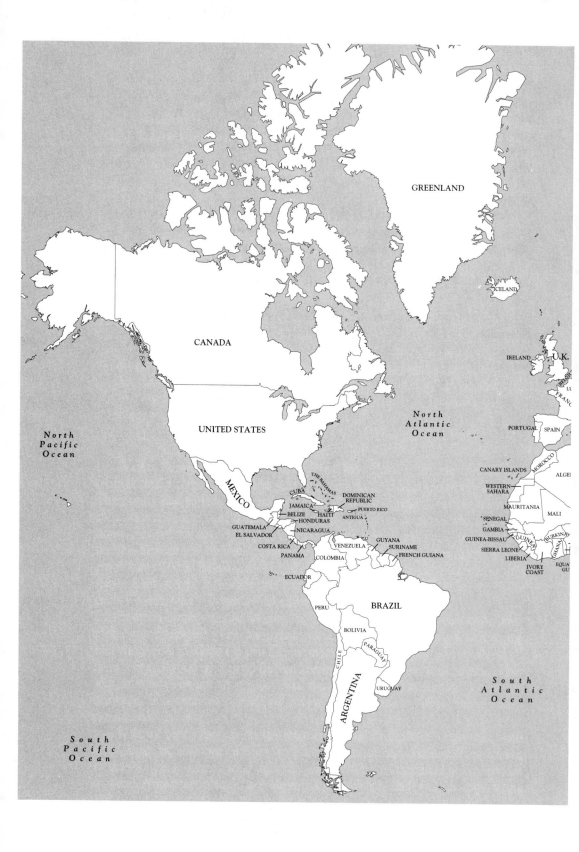

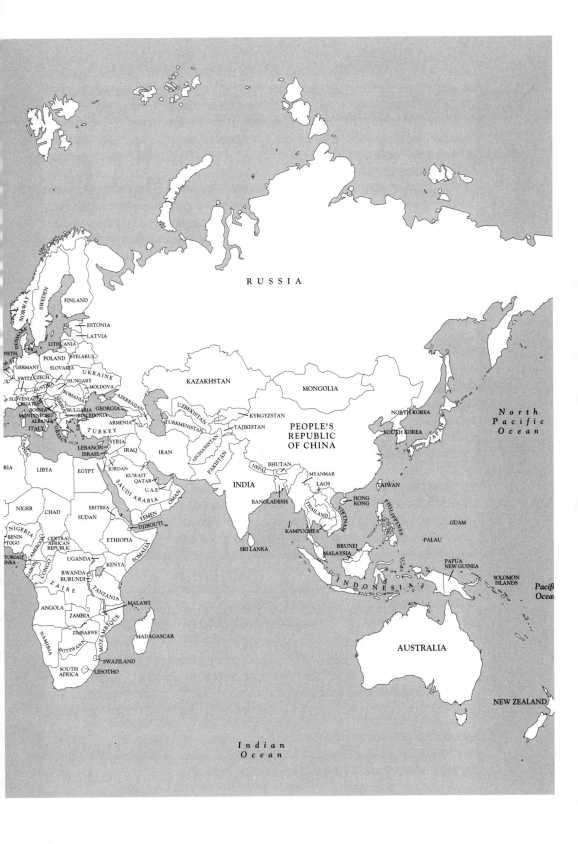

Two Worlds

One can learn nothing except by going from the known to the unknown.

CLAUDE BERNARD

1. Note the title of the unit, "Two Worlds." What does that mean to you? Read the quote. What connection do you see between the quote and the title? **Freewrite** for a few minutes about the title and the quote. (See Appendix A.1, pp. 223–224, for an explanation and examples of freewriting.)

   Share your freewriting with a partner. Did you and your partner write similar or different things? Explain.

2. On a separate, unlined sheet of paper, draw a map of your life. Represent the significant times in your life: when you made changes, the high points and low points, and when you were between two worlds (because of education, age, beliefs, or the known and the unknown). Start at the beginning and move to the present. Draw pictures or use graphic representations as you go along. Your life map may go up and down. Add words and color if you wish.

   Show your map to a group of classmates. Tell them about one or two important points in your life. Answer their questions. Use the map to give you ideas for things to write about.

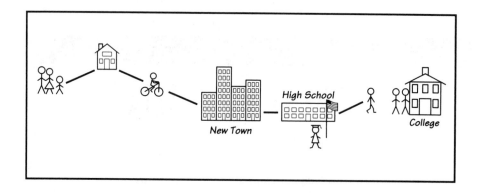

BEFORE READING

1. Look at the first six words of the following excerpt: "When one door closes, another opens." In your reading log, freewrite for three to five minutes about these words: what they mean, if they are true, whatever else comes into your mind.

   Share your writing with a partner.

2. Read the short excerpt.

When One Door Opens
Helen Nearing

Helen Nearing wrote these words after her husband of fifty-three years died. At that point in her life, she chose to live alone and to write about their life together. She and Scott Nearing had been devoted to homesteading, peace, and social justice. They considered it the "good life."

When one door closes, another opens . . . into another room, another space, other happenings. There are many doors to open and close in our lives. Some doors we leave ajar, where we hope and plan to return. Some doors are slammed shut decisively—"No more of *that!*" Some are closed regretfully, softly—"It was good, but it is over." Departures entail arrivals somewhere else. Closing a door, leaving it behind, means opening onto new vistas and ventures, new possibilities, new incentives.

AFTER READING

1. Add to what you wrote in your reading log.

2. Think of an experience you or someone you know has had that illustrates a sentence in the passage. You might, for example, think about this sentence: "There are many doors to open and close in our lives." Write about the experience in your log.

    Share what you wrote with your partner.

3. Think of a *saying* in your language that is similar to the thought expressed in the passage. Write it down and explain it.

    Share the saying with your partner and the whole class.

TOPICS FOR WRITING

Choose one activity.

Activity A: Choose one of the sentences from the passage and use it to begin a piece of writing. In your writing, tell the story or the experience that led you to choose it.

Activity B: Create a dialogue between two people using one of these two sentences:

  a. "No more of that!" or
  b. "It was good, but it is over."

Activity C: Explain a *saying* in your country, culture, and language that is similar to the thoughts expressed in this passage. Tell what the saying is, where it came from, and when people use it. Give a personal experience illustrating the meaning of the saying.

AFTER WRITING

Read your writing aloud to your group. Ask your listeners to tell you what they understand from your piece.

BEFORE READING

1. Look at the title of this story. With your class, make a **cluster** of the words you associate with this title. (See Appendix A.2, pp. 224–225, for an explanation and example of clustering.)
2. Now read the story.

Sometimes Home Is Not Really Home
Maggie Mok

Maggie Mok was a student at Hunter College of the City University of New York when she wrote this composition.

I was born in Hong Kong, but most of us in Hong Kong consider that our real homes are on Mainland China. It may be only a small village in China. With all my desires and hopes alive, I went back to my "real home," a village in Canton, five years ago. Afterwards, I felt like I had landed on another planet rather than back home.

The first moment I stepped off the train, the people in the village looked at me as if I were a foreigner. A man came forward to ask me if I wanted to buy this or that. A woman suggested many inns for my stay. A group of children followed me. I felt like I was "E.T., come home."

I met my relatives at the station. It seemed that all my relatives had come to receive me. All of a sudden, I felt I was very important. But the first question my uncle asked me was how much money I had brought with me. Then my aunt asked me if I had brought any presents for them. I thought that I had made a wrong decision to come back to my "real home." I really wanted to step on the train and go back to Hong Kong.

In fact, I had planned to stay in the village for a week. After the first day of my visit, I decided to stay for only three days. As a matter of fact, even during that time, I seldom went out.

AFTER READING

1. In your reading log, write answers to these questions: What do you understand or see in what you just read? How do you feel about what you understood or saw? What do you associate with your understand-

ing? (See Appendix B.1, p. 230, for an explanation and examples of **response questions**.)

Share your writing with your group. Choose one person's writing to read to the class.

2. Choose one activity.

Activity A: What did Maggie Mok learn from her experience? In your reading log, **make a list** of the things she learned and share it with a partner. (See Appendix A.3, pp. 225–227, for information on and examples of lists.)

Activity B: Do some research in the library to find out:

a. Where is Hong Kong located in relation to China?

b. What is the political status of Hong Kong now?

c. How did it become that way?

d. How will Hong Kong's relationship to China change in the future?

3. Tell your group what you learned.

HOW I READ IT

How did clustering words around the title help you prepare for reading the story? Write about this for a few minutes in your reading log. Share your writing with the class.

HOW IT'S WRITTEN

1. There are four paragraphs in Maggie Mok's composition. Make a **descriptive outline** of the composition. That is, describe what each paragraph *says* (What information does it contain?) and what each paragraph *does* (What is its function?). Here are some of the things paragraphs do:

introduce an idea	develop a reason
give an example	describe
list	compare
analyze	offer a hypothesis
explain	elaborate
synthesize	conclude

(See Appendix B.4, pp. 233 and 236, for more explanation and an example of descriptive outlining.)

2. What connections do you see between the four paragraphs? List the words or ideas that hold the composition together and make it easy for the reader to move from one paragraph to the next. Work with a partner.

3. Discuss your ideas with your group. Make a list of things to remember the next time you write a composition. Share your list with the whole class. Write a combined list on the chalkboard. Copy any new ideas you want to remember into your reading log.

TOPICS FOR WRITING

Choose one activity.

Activity A: Maggie Mok writes that when she saw all of her relatives waiting to greet her, she felt very important until she realized they were hoping she had brought them either money or gifts. Write about a time in your life when you arrived somewhere and were disappointed. What did you learn from this experience?

Activity B: Describe a situation in which people are living in a place they don't consider their home. Give the historical background of the place. Describe its relationship to the place people call home. Then tell what happens when someone travels from one place to the other, as Maggie Mok did.

Activity C: Maggie Mok writes that she was looking forward to going home, to her "real home." Do you feel that way about your country, that it's your "real home?" Or do you feel at home in another place? What place is your "real home?" Write a composition describing that place and tell why you feel the way you do.

AFTER WRITING

Read your composition to your group. As a group, tell what you like about each composition. (See Appendix F, pp. 245–246, for more explanation of sharing your writing and giving feedback to classmates' writing.)

On your own, look at the list of things to remember when you write a composition. Check your composition against the list.

BEFORE READING

1. What words come to your mind when you hear the phrase, "first day of school"? Write them down. Then share them with your partner. Put words from your combined list on the board, but don't repeat words already there.

    As a class, put the words on the board into categories and give each category a title.

2. Freewrite for a few minutes about one of your first days of school—your very first day, or the first day in a new school.

3. Read the following excerpt from "The First Day." Your teacher may read the first paragraph aloud.

The First Day
Edward P. Jones

Edward P. Jones grew up in Washington, D.C., and now lives in Virginia. His short-story collection, Lost in the City, *won the 1993 PEN/Hemingway Award for a first book of fiction.*

Walker-Jones is a larger, newer school and I immediately like it because of that. But it is not across the street from my mother's church, her rock, one of her connections to God, and I sense her doubts as she absently rubs her thumb over the back of her hand. We find our way to the crowded auditorium where gray metal chairs are set up in the middle of the room. Along the wall to the left are tables and other chairs. Every chair seems occupied by a child or adult. Somewhere in the room a child is crying, a cry that rises above the buzz-talk of so many people. Strewn about the floor are dozens and dozens of pieces of white paper, and people are walking over them without any thought of picking them up. And seeing this lack of concern, I am all of a sudden afraid.

"Is this where they register for school?" my mother asks a woman at one of the tables.

The woman looks up slowly as if she has heard this question once too often. She nods. She is tiny, almost as small as the girl standing beside her. The woman's hair is set in a mass of curlers and all of those curlers are made of paper money, here a dollar bill, there a five-dollar bill. The girl's hair is arrayed in curls, but some of them are beginning to droop and this makes me happy. On the table beside the woman's pocketbook is a large notebook, worthy of someone in high school, and looking at me looking at the note-book, the girl places her hand possessively on it. In her other hand she holds several pencils with thick crowns of additional erasers.

"These the forms you gotta use?" my mother asks the woman, picking up a few pieces of the paper from the table. "Is this what you have to fill out?"

The woman tells her yes, but that she need fill out only one.

"I see," my mother says, looking about the room. Then: "Would you help me with this form? That is, if you don't mind."

The woman asks my mother what she means.

"This form. Would you mind helpin me fill it out?"

The woman still seems not to understand.

"I can't read it. I don't know how to read or write, and I'm askin you to help me." My mother looks at me, then looks away. I know almost all of her looks, but this one is brand new to me. "Would you help me, then?"

The woman says Why sure, and suddenly she appears happier, so much more satisfied with everything. She finishes the form for her daughter and my mother and I step aside to wait for her. We find two chairs nearby and sit. My mother is now diseased, according to the girl's eyes, and until the moment her mother takes her and the form to the front of the auditorium, the girl never stops looking at my mother. I stare back at her. "Don't stare," my mother says to me. "You know better than that."

Another woman out of the *Ebony* ads takes the woman's child away. Now, the woman says upon returning, let's see what we can do for you two.

My mother answers the questions the woman reads off the form. They start with my last name, and then on to the first and middle names. This is school, I think. This is going to school. My mother slowly enunciates each word of my name. This is my mother: As the questions go on, she takes from her pocketbook document after document, as if they will support my right to attend school, as if she has been saving them up for just this moment. Indeed, she takes out more papers than I have ever seen her do in other places: my birth certificate, my baptismal record, a doctor's letter concerning my bout with chicken pox, rent receipts, records of immunization, a letter about our public assistance payments, even her marriage license—every single paper that has anything even remotely to do with my five-year-old life. Few of the papers are needed here, but it does not matter and my mother continues to pull out the documents with the purposefulness of a magician pulling out a long string of scarves. She has learned that money is the begin-ning and end of everything in this world, and when the woman finishes, my mother offers her fifty cents, and the woman accepts it without hesitation. My mother and I are just about the last parent and child in the room.

My mother presents the form to a woman sitting in front of the stage, and the woman looks at it and writes something on a white card, which she gives to my mother. Before long, the woman who has taken the girl with the drooping curls appears from behind us, speaks to the sitting woman, and introduces herself to my mother and me. She's to be my teacher, she tells my mother. My mother stares.

We go into the hall, where my mother kneels down to me. Her lips are quivering. "I'll be back to pick you up at twelve o'clock. I don't want you to go nowhere. You just wait right here. And listen to every word she say." I touch her lips and press them together. It is an old, old game between us. She puts my hand down at my side, which is not part of the game. She stands and looks a second at the teacher, then she turns and walks away. I see where she has darned one of her socks the night before. Her shoes make loud sounds in the hall. She passes through the doors and I can still hear the loud sounds of her shoes. And even when the teacher turns me toward the classrooms and I hear what must be the singing and talking of all the children in the world, I can still hear my mother's footsteps above it all.

AFTER READING

1. After you've read the story, write an entry in your reading log. Write about what you understand in the story, how you feel about it, and what associations you make. Save this entry.

2. Many emotions are evident in this piece. With a partner, go through the story, marking words or phrases that show positive feelings with a plus (+) and those that show negative feelings with a minus (−). Name the emotions.

   Talk with your partner about the various feelings that each character might feel all at once and how each character's feelings change.

3. With a partner, make a list of the characteristics of the mother and of the child telling the story. How are the mother and child similar? How are they different? What characteristics do you value in each of them?

   Are the mother and child going down the same road? Or are their lives taking different turns? Find evidence for your thoughts in the text. After talking with your partner, write an entry in your reading log.

HOW I READ IT

With your group, read aloud the sections where the characters are talking. Take the different roles (the child, the mother, the woman at the table, and the woman with the child). As you read, try to express the feelings of the characters. Practice several times, making the reading into a short drama. Perform your dramatic reading for the class.

TOPICS FOR WRITING

Choose one activity.

Activity A: Pick a sentence or a phrase from the story that connects to your experience. Write about how that sentence or phrase relates to the story, "The First Day." Then tell how it relates to your experience. Describe your experience. Write an ending that connects with the beginning of what you wrote but also opens up a new world. (For some suggestions on **beginnings** and **endings,** see Appendix E, pp. 240–241.)

Activity B: Both the mother and child in this story are opening a new door. Both are entering a new world, though perhaps not the same one. Using your reading log entries, write about these two people fifteen to twenty years from now. Imagine a future event or a future day in their lives. Tell what happens and what they say to each other.

Activity C: Write a one act play for several characters. Focus on a situation like the one portrayed in this story, an everyday occurrence in which one person needs something from another person in charge. The situation should include a conflict and a resolution. Before you start, think of several possibilities. (You may work with a coauthor.)

AFTER WRITING

1. Before you write your final draft, exchange your writing with one person. Show the person how far you have gotten. Ask for feedback on any part that you think needs work. Do the same for your partner.

2. After the students have finished their final drafts, spread the pieces throughout the classroom, putting each one on a separate desk or chair. Put a blank piece of paper beside each student's work. Allow time for individuals to move around the class, stopping for about five minutes to read each paper. On the blank piece of paper, write a positive one-sentence comment or a question. Sign your name. (Read as many as time permits.)

   When time is up, nominate one to be read by the author to the whole class (or to be published, posted on the wall, or acted out).

BEFORE READING

1. Look at the photograph. The two young women and the two children are about to sail for America. What might be in their minds? Write down what you think any one of the four might be thinking.
   Share your thoughts with your group.

2. In your group, what other things can you guess about the group from the picture? For example, what country do you think they are in, why are they leaving, what are their relationships to each other, and what is their background? Make a group list.

3. Look through the story. Note the breaks, marked by *. While reading, when you get to the break, stop and write in your reading log what you are thinking about (for example, where you guessed right or wrong, what you still want to know, or an association or thought).
   Now read "Going to America."

Going to America
Nicholas Gage

This excerpt is taken from the book, A Place for Us, *Nicholas Gage's powerful story of his family's immigration to the United States. He also wrote about his mother, Eleni, who was murdered. He lives in Massachusetts, where his family settled when they arrived here in the late 1940s.*

Exiles feed on dreams of hope.

AESCHYLUS, *Agamemnon*

The black-and-white photograph, like many others taken during the late 1940s, shows a group of refugees leaving their devastated homeland to make a new beginning in America. There are four travelers: two nearly grown young women in Greek peasant dress and two small children, a boy and a girl, who appear about eight years old. Behind them hover two men in stylish city clothes—relatives charged with seeing the orphans safely onto the ship that will carry them to their new country. In the background looms a huge naval vessel, and all around is the bustle of the Piraeus harborside.

But the four pilgrims stand still and solemn in the midst of the blur of activity, grimly facing the box camera of the street photographer who has been paid to record their last moments on Greek soil. The older girls, with long braids down their backs, are all in black, from their crude village shoes

and stockings to their bulky wool skirts and cardigans. They are in mourning for their mother, who died so that they could make this journey.

Her name was Eleni Gatzoyiannis. Eight months earlier, in June of 1948, she arranged her family's escape from their mountain village because the Communist guerrillas occupying it had begun gathering children to send to indoctrination camps behind the Iron Curtain. But at the last minute Eleni was forced to stay behind, and she told her children to flee without her. In a refugee camp later, they learned that she had been imprisoned, tortured, and finally executed by the guerrillas in retribution for their escape. They dyed their clothing black in boiling pots over the fire and prepared for the journey to America, for their mother had told them that whatever happened to her, that was where they must go.

The little girl in the photograph proudly clutches a tiny plastic purse and wears new clothes purchased in an Athens department store. The little boy fled the village barefoot, and for the voyage to America he has acquired heavy brogans made in the refugee camp. In the photograph one of his shoes is untied, but no one notices and ties it. He wears an ill-fitting suit of gray wool with short pants and a bulky jacket with bulging pockets. His new haircut is so short that the scalp shows on the sides. He eyes the camera warily, as if he doesn't trust the photographer.

The boy is actually watching two cardboard suitcases just behind the photographer, for they contain all his family's belongings, including his mother's wedding scarf and the only photographs they have of her. Nearly as important to him is the canvas school satchel filled with notebooks from his lessons in the refugee camp. He hopes these will impress his American teachers with his academic skills.

I know what the boy was watching and thinking and what treasures filled his pockets because I was that child, nine years old, who set sail for America on March 3, 1949. My three sisters and I had passage on the *Marine Carp*, a converted American troop carrier pressed into service as a passenger liner after World War II. I was traveling with my oldest sister, Olga, twenty, my second sister, Kanta, sixteen, and my fourth sister, Fotini, ten. Our third sister, Glykeria, fifteen, was missing behind the Iron Curtain, perhaps dead. She had been left behind with our mother. After *Mana's* execution, our sister was driven at gunpoint into Albania with the rest of the villagers by the retreating Communist guerrillas. Now we had no idea where she was.

Although I had lost my mother, the only parent I had ever known, we weren't really orphans, because we had a father in America. That's how we had managed to get from the corrugated tin Quonset huts in Igoumenitsa, where a hanging sheet separated us from other families, to the docks of Piraeus. Now we would set sail for a country that had always seemed as remote and mythological to us as Atlantis.

Mana used to read us letters from this father who sold fruit and vegetables in Worcester, Massachusetts, and was considered an American millionaire by all the village. He had left Greece for America in 1910, a boy of seventeen with $20 in his pocket, and returned to take a bride in 1926. My absentee father's American citizenship and rumored fortune created envy among the villagers, who referred to my mother as the *Amerikana*. . . .

*

In the brief period of peace between the end of the European war and the outbreak of the Greek civil war in late 1946, *Mana* wrote, begging her husband to finish filing our papers so that we could emigrate at once, but he hesitated, worried about the risks of bringing adolescent daughters to a worldly place like America. "You have no idea how free the girls are here, running with strangers from an early age . . . ," he wrote. He ordered my mother to arrange a match for Olga, my oldest sister, with a man of good name, and then he would bring us.

But then it was too late. In the fall of 1947 Greek Communist guerrillas occupied the northern Greek villages where we lived. All the men, including my grandfather, Kitso Haidis, fled the mountains to avoid being conscripted, leaving the women and children behind. *Mana* wrote to her husband for advice, and he counseled her to stay and guard the house and property. . . .

My mother was an obedient peasant woman who never spoke to a man outside her family until she was betrothed at the age of eighteen to a visiting American fourteen years her senior. She had been brought up to follow men's orders. When the guerrillas came, she gave them our food without complaint and went on daily work details to help build fortifications and carry the wounded. . . . Although the guerrillas and her neighbors made her the object of special indignities because she was the rich *Amerikana*, she remained obedient and uncomplaining.

It was when the guerrillas demanded that she hand over her children that Eleni Gatzoyiannis finally chose to defy them.

In the spring of 1948 the guerrillas held a compulsory meeting in our village to announce that all children from three to fourteen would be taken to camps in Eastern Europe, where they would be reared and educated as Communists. They set out a table of food before the starving villagers, saying that any children whose parents volunteered them would immediately be fed. But despite the cries of their famished children, most of the mothers refused.

Then one day, hiding in my grandmother's bean field, I overheard two guerrilla officers say that all the children, volunteered or not, would be taken by force. When I ran to tell my mother, she chose defiance for the first time in her life and began to plan the escape that ended with her imprisonment, torture, and execution.

As I stood on the dock in Piraeus, I blamed my father for contributing to her death; if only he had moved faster, he could have brought us out during the brief peacetime in 1946 and we would be whole, living in America as a family. Now we were torn apart. My mother's bullet-riddled body had been tossed into a shallow mass grave with other victims and found months later by my grandfather, who interred her remains in the churchyard near the ruins of our house. My fifteen-year-old sister Glykeria was lost to us behind the Iron Curtain. My other three sisters and I were still together, thanks to my mother's courage and love, but we were penniless, owning no more than a change of clothes, and we were about to leave our homeland, cross an ocean to a strange country where no one spoke our language, and live with a father whom I had never seen but had always thought of with a mixture of love, longing, and anger.

If he really loved us, I thought, he would have taken us with him to America at the beginning, instead of leaving his young bride in Greece and returning every few years to visit. . . .

Now I imagined my father's face and tried to suppress my anger at the man who failed to save us in time. . . . I held my school satchel filled with my notebooks like a talisman, hoping that when he saw how good I was at arithmetic he would be impressed.

Even when he learned that his wife had been murdered and his children were living in a refugee camp, Father still had vacillated about sending for us. He wrote asking whether we would prefer to make our home in the village with our grandparents, go to Athens to live with our cousins, or join him in America. But our answer was quick and unanimous, because we remembered so clearly what our mother said on the day she told us goodbye, as the Communist guerrillas took her away to thresh wheat. She promised she would try to escape on her own with Glykeria and find us, but, she told Olga fiercely, "If we don't, I want you to telegraph your father and tell him to get you out to America as soon as possible. Your grandfather will try to talk you into staying behind. My parents only want someone to stay in Greece and care for them in their old age. But whether I'm living or dead, I won't rest until you're all in America and safe."

Then came the moment when she said goodbye to me and was led away down the mountain by the guerrillas until she disappeared into the distance, turning once to raise her hand in farewell. Nearly the last thing she told me and my sister Kanta was, "Remember this: anyone who stays in Greece, who doesn't go to America, will have my curse. When you leave the house tonight, I want you to throw a black stone behind you so you'll never come back." . . .

*

When our cousins heaved the two suitcases onto the launch and I firmly refused help with my school satchel, I noticed my grandfather's lip begin to tremble beneath his white mustache. "Take a good look at that sky," he growled for the last time. "You'll never see it again!"

I looked, seeing the unclouded blue sky that had hung over me all my life, and wondered what it would be like never to see it again. But I didn't hesitate as I followed my sisters onto the launch. . . .

As the ship began to pull away, I watched the figure of my grandfather shrinking. Suddenly he began to wave the walking stick he always carried, carved from the branch of a cornel tree and polished to a dark sheen by his hands. Finally it was only the frantic waving of his stick that distinguished him from the other dots on the harborside.

I put my hands in my pockets to take stock of the treasures I had with me—amulets to protect me against the uncertain future. There was the cross-shaped box on a chain that my mother had hung around my neck in the last moment we were together. It was her most magical possession, because it held a splinter of a bone from a saint, and it was the only thing she could give to protect me from being shot or stepping on a land mine during our escape. I had promised her I would be brave, and the cold hardness of the cross made me feel braver now.

I inventoried my other treasures. First, a white handkerchief my godmother had given me on the day between the wars when she left the village with her son to join her husband, Nassio, in America. . . .

I fingered the reed whistle that my Uncle Andreas had whittled for me when he taught me to make birdcalls. Andreas had always been the kindest man in my life, not like my stern, irascible grandfather. . . .

Then my fingers touched something cold and smooth, and I pulled it out of my pocket. It was the small black stone that I had picked up outside my house on the night of our escape, because my mother had ordered me to throw one behind me so that I would never return to the place that gave us so much suffering. I had kept that stone in my pocket for eight months, and now it was time to toss it into the sea.

My mother had often told us the story of how my father, an itinerant tinker of seventeen, when he boarded the ship for America, triumphantly tossed over the rail the fez that the Turkish occupiers of northern Greece forced men to wear in those days as a symbol of their subjugation. When the fez disappeared into the waves, she said, my father felt like a free man for the first time in his life.

Now it was my turn to throw this stone from my village into the same sea, to insure that I would never be pulled back to this land of war and famine, bombs, torture and executions. . . . Throwing the stone was the way to turn my back irrevocably on Greece and my face toward America, where my father waited.

AFTER READING

1. Write in your reading log. What did you understand this story to be about? How did you feel about it?

   Share what you wrote with your group.
2. Choose one activity.

   Activity A: With a partner, if possible, mark the places in the story where the author expressed positive feelings with a plus (+) and negative feelings with a minus (−). In the margin, write down the name of each feeling. What experiences, people, or objects did he feel both positively and negatively about?

   Activity B: With a partner, write a summary (five to seven sentences long) of the story. Then write your reaction to the story.

HOW I READ IT

1. Freewrite about *how* you read this passage the first time (about your process of reading). Was it easy or difficult to read? Why? Did you reread anything? What? Why? What did you do when you didn't understand something?

2. Share your writing with the class. Did you learn any new reading strategies from hearing what other people said? If so, what? Are your reading strategies similar to other people's? Different?

   In your reading log, write a response to these questions. (See Appendix C, p. 237, for more explanation and examples of **how we read**.)

HOW IT'S WRITTEN

Look back at the photograph and compare it with the story. Find the sentences in the story that refer to things in the picture. Do you see things in the photograph now that you didn't see before?

Do you think the author looked at the photo as he was writing the story? Why or why not? Discuss this with your group.

TOPICS FOR WRITING

Choose one activity.

Activity A: Find a photograph of you and your family (or some members of your family) taken before a major event or change occurred (such as a wedding, a first day of school, a trip, a graduation, a divorce or separation, or someone's leaving home).

   Write a piece about the picture including how the people look in the picture, their relationships to each other, and something of their history. Reread Gage's piece (especially through the eighth paragraph) and use it as a model. Include in your writing the kinds of details that he uses.

Activity B: In the story, the boy carries with him certain treasures in his pocket, which he calls "amulets to protect [him] against the uncertain future." These include a cross-shaped box on a chain from his mother, a white handkerchief from his grandmother, and a reed whistle from his uncle (see p. 15).

   Many of us hold onto or carry certain things we think are magical and will protect us or bring us luck. Write about something that you treasure and/or carry with you for luck or protection. Tell how and where you got it and what "magic" it has. In other words, tell its story.

Activity C: As a variation on Activity B, write a short story in which the main character has a magic amulet, something that protects him or her from danger and, possibly, death. The story must involve the character and the "magic" amulet. The story may be totally made up or it may have a basis in real life.

Activity D: The father in America delayed filling out the papers to bring his wife and children to America because he worried it was risky to bring adolescent daughters to this country. He wrote to his wife, "You have no idea how free the girls are here, running with strangers from an early age."

His attitude is shared by many parents, both immigrants and nonimmigrants, for their children, whether boys or girls. What about you and your experience? Do you think adolescents have too much freedom in this country? Write about this issue, telling your experience and expressing your opinion.

AFTER WRITING

1. Form a group with others who chose the same writing activity as you did. Read your story to the group. The listeners should write comments (feedback) on a slip of paper, based on the following questions:

   a. What did you understand the piece to be about?

   b. What did you like about the piece?

   c. What would you like to hear more about? (See Appendix F, p. 245, for more explanation of responding to classmates' writing.)

   Give your comments to the writer. (The writer may use the feedback later when revising the piece.)

2. Choose one piece from your group to read to the whole class.

3. Reread your listeners' comments. Revise your paper.

4. Write in your log about **how you wrote** this composition (your process of writing). For example, how did you choose your topic? What did you do first? Next? How many times did you revise it? What did you change? What was easy? What was difficult? (See Appendix D, pp. 238–239, for more explanation of how we write.)

BEFORE READING

1. Read the introductory information. Given this information, write down one question you expect the story to answer for you. Read your question to your group. Make a list of the questions and share them with the class.

2. With the class, locate Antigua and England on the map following p. xvii.

3. Listen to your instructor read the first paragraph of the story. Write down quickly what facts you know about the story so far. Share these with the class.

4. Read the rest of the story silently.

A Walk to the Jetty
Jamaica Kincaid

The novel Annie John *by Jamaica Kincaid tells of one girl's growing into adolescence on the Caribbean island of Antigua. At the end of the novel, we see Annie at age seventeen leaving her parents and her home to study nursing in England. "A Walk to the Jetty" is the title of the last chapter of the novel.*

"My name is Annie John." These were the first words that came into my mind as I woke up on the morning of the last day I spent in Antigua, and they stayed there, lined up one behind the other, marching up and down, for I don't know how long. At noon on that day, a ship on which I was to be a passenger would sail to Barbados, and there I would board another ship, which would sail to England, where I would study to become a nurse. My name was the last thing I saw the night before, just as I was falling asleep; it was written in big, black letters all over my trunk, sometimes followed by my address in Antigua, sometimes followed by my address as it would be in England. I did not want to go to England, I did not want to be a nurse, but I would have chosen going off to live in a cavern and keeping house for seven unruly men rather than go on with my life as it stood. I never wanted to lie in this bed again, my legs hanging out way past the foot of it, tossing and turning on my mattress, with its cotton stuffing all lumped just where it wasn't a good place to be lumped. I never wanted to lie in my bed again and hear Mr. Ephraim driving his sheep to pasture—a signal to my mother that she should get up to prepare my father's and my bath and breakfast. I never wanted to lie in my bed and hear her get dressed, washing her face, brushing her teeth, and gargling. I especially never wanted to lie in my bed and hear my mother gargling again.

Lying there in the half-dark of my room, I could see my shelf, with my books—some of them prizes I had won in school, some of them gifts from my mother—and with photographs of people I was supposed to love forever no matter what, and with my old thermos, which was given to me for my eighth birthday, and some shells I had gathered at different times I spent at the sea. In one corner stood my washstand and its beautiful basin of white enamel with blooming red hibiscus painted at the bottom and an urn that matched. In another corner were my old school shoes and my Sunday shoes. In still another corner, a bureau held my old clothes. I knew everything in this room, inside out and outside in. I had lived in this room for thirteen of my seventeen years. I could see in my mind's eye even the day my father was adding it onto the rest of the house. Everywhere I looked stood something that had meant a lot to me, that had given me pleasure at some point, or could remind me of a time that was a happy time. But as I was lying there my heart could have burst open with joy at the thought of never having to see any of it again.

If someone had asked me for a little summing up of my life at that moment as I lay in bed, I would have said, "My name is Annie John. I was born on the fifteenth of September, seventeen years ago, at Holberton Hospital, at five o'clock in the morning. At the time I was born, the moon was going down at one end of the sky and the sun was coming up at the other. My mother's name is Annie also. My father's name is Alexander, and he is thirty-five years older than my mother. . . . The house we live in my father built with his own hands. The bed I am lying in my father built with his own hands. If I get up and sit on a chair, it is a chair my father built with his own hands. When my mother uses a large wooden spoon to stir the porridge we sometimes eat as part of our breakfast, it will be a spoon that my father has carved with his own hands. The sheets on my bed my mother made with her own hands. The curtains hanging at my window my mother made with her own hands. The nightie I am wearing, with scalloped neck and hem and sleeves, my mother made with her own hands. When I look at things in a certain way, I suppose I should say that the two of them made me with their own hands. For most of my life, when the three of us went anywhere together I stood between the two of them or sat between the two of them. But then I got too big, and there I was, shoulder to shoulder with them more or less, and it became not very comfortable to walk down the street together. And so now there they are together and here I am apart. I don't see them now the way I used to, and I don't love them now the way I used to. The bitter thing about it is that they are just the same and it is I who have changed, so all the things I used to be and all the things I used to feel are as false as the teeth in my father's head. . . .

Lying in my bed for the last time, I thought, This is what I add up to. At that, I felt as if someone had placed me in a hole and was forcing me first down and then up against the pressure of gravity. I shook myself and prepared to get up. I said to myself, "I am getting up out of this bed for the last time." Everything I would do that morning until I got on the ship that would take me to England I would be doing for the last time, for I had made up my mind that, come what may, the road for me now went only in one direction: away from my home, away from my mother, away from my father, away from the everlasting blue sky, away from the everlasting hot sun, away from people who said to me, "This happened during the time your mother was carrying you." If I had been asked to put into words why I felt this way, if I had been given years to reflect and come up with the words of why I felt this way, I would not have been able to come up with so much as the letter "A." I only knew that I felt the way I did, and that this feeling was the strongest thing in my life. . . .

Now . . . I had nothing to take my mind off what was happening to me. My mother and my father—I was leaving them forever. My home on an island—I was leaving it forever. What to make of everything? I felt a familiar hollow space inside. I felt I was being held down against my will. I felt I was burning up from head to toe. I felt that someone was tearing me up into little pieces and soon I would be able to see all the little pieces as they floated out into nothing in the deep blue sea. I didn't know whether to laugh or cry. I could see that it would be better not to think too clearly about any one thing. The launch was being made ready to take me, along with some other passengers, out to the ship that was anchored in the sea. My father paid our fares, and we joined a line of people waiting to board. My mother checked my bag to make sure that I had my passport, the money she had given me, and a sheet of paper placed between some pages in my Bible on which were written the names of the relatives—people I had not known existed—with whom I would live in England. Across from the jetty was a wharf, and some stevedores were loading and unloading barges. I don't know why seeing that struck me so, but suddenly a wave of strong feeling came over me, and my heart swelled with a great gladness as the words "I shall never see this again" spilled out inside me. But then, just as quickly, my heart shriveled up and the words "I shall never see this again" stabbed at me. I don't know what stopped me from falling in a heap at my parents' feet.

When we were all on board, the launch headed out to sea. Away from the jetty, the water became the customary blue, and the launch left a wide path in it that looked like a road. I passed by sounds and smells that were so familiar that I had long ago stopped paying any attention to them. But now here they were, and the ever-present "I shall never see this again" bobbed up and down inside me. There was the sound of the seagull diving down into the water and coming up with something silverish in its mouth. There was the smell of the sea and the sight of small pieces of rubbish floating around in it. There were boats filled with fishermen coming in early. There was the sound of their voices as they shouted greetings to each other. There was the hot sun, there was the blue sea, there was the blue sky. Not very far away, there was the white sand of the shore, with the run-down houses all crowded in next to each other, for in some places only poor people lived near the shore. I was seated in the launch between my parents, and when I realized that I was gripping their hands tightly I glanced quickly to see if they were looking at me with scorn, for I felt sure that they must have known of my never-see-this-again feelings. But instead my father kissed me on the forehead and my mother kissed me on the mouth, and they both gave over their hands to me, so that I could grip them as much as I wanted. I was on the verge of feeling that it had all been a mistake, but I remembered that I wasn't a child anymore, and that now when I made up my mind about something I had to see it through. At that moment, we came to the ship, and that was that.

The goodbyes had to be quick, the captain said. My mother introduced herself to him and then introduced me. She told him to keep an eye on me, for I had never gone this far away from home on my own. She gave him a letter to pass on to the captain of the next ship that I would board in Barbados. They walked me to my cabin, a small space that I would share with someone else—a woman I did not know. I had never before slept in a room with someone I did not know. My father kissed me goodbye and told me to be good and to write home often. After he said this, he looked at me, then looked at the floor and swung his left foot, then looked at me again. I could see that he wanted to say something else, something that he had never said to me before, but then he just turned and walked away. My mother said, "Well," and then she threw her arms around me. Big tears streamed down her face, and it must have been that—for I could not bear to see my mother cry—which started me crying, too. She then tightened her arms around me and held me to her close, so that I felt that I couldn't breathe. With that, my tears dried up and I was suddenly on my guard. "What does she want now?" I said to myself. Still holding me close to her, she said, in a voice that raked across my skin, "It doesn't matter what you do or where you go, I'll always be your mother and this will always be your home."

I dragged myself away from her and backed off a little, and then I shook myself, as if to wake myself out of a stupor. We looked at each other for a long time with smiles on our faces, but I know the opposite of that was in my heart. As if responding to some invisible cue, we both said, at the very same moment, "Well." Then my mother turned around and walked out the cabin door. I stood there for I don't know how long, and then I remembered that it was customary to stand on deck and wave to your relatives who were returning to shore. From the deck, I could not see my father, but I could see my mother facing the ship, her eyes searching to pick me out. I removed from my bag a red cotton handkerchief that she had earlier given me for this purpose, and I waved it wildly in the air. Recognizing me immediately, she waved back just as wildly, and we continued to do this until she became just a dot in the matchbox-size launch swallowed up in the big blue sea.

I went back to my cabin and lay down on my berth. Everything trembled as if it had a spring at its very center. I could hear the small waves lap-lapping around the ship. They made an unexpected sound, as if a vessel filled with liquid had been placed on its side and now was slowly emptying out.

AFTER READING

1. Write an answer in your reading log to one or two of the questions you or your classmates asked before reading the story. Share your answers with the class.

2. In your reading log, make a **double entry**. On the left page of your notebook, copy sentences, phrases, or ideas that interest you, or tell in your own words some of what you understood. On the right page of your notebook, write your reactions, feelings, thoughts, associations, and so on. (See Appendix B.2, pp. 230–232, for an explanation and examples of double entries.) Reread the story as necessary.

   Share your writing with your group.

3. Choose one activity.

   Activity A: On pages 20 and 21, Annie mentioned several times the words "I shall never see this again" and referred to her "never-see-this-again feelings." Reread these pages. Explain in writing how this thought made her feel. How do you know how she felt? Read your writing to your group.

   Activity B: Imagine that you are a reporter from the school newspaper interviewing Annie as to why she felt so strongly about getting away. First, reread the passage for ideas, especially pp. 19–20; then write the interview (both your questions and Annie's answers). Read your writing to your group.

HOW I READ IT

1. How did asking questions before reading affect how you read the story? What purpose do you see in asking questions *before* reading something? With the class, talk about the use of questions before reading.

2. Reread the text, and circle five words you don't understand. Share your words with your group. As a group, try to figure out the meaning of each person's circled words. Look at the *contexts* (the surrounding words or phrases) in which the words appear or consult with each other. When absolutely necessary, use a dictionary.

3. How can you get clues to the meanings of words from context? Talk about this with the class.

   Write a few sentences in your reading log about this reading strategy.

HOW IT'S WRITTEN

1. Work with another person. Choose one activity.

   Activity A: Reread the piece, looking for words and phrases Kincaid used to describe *colors* and *sounds*. Circle these.

   Activity B: Reread the piece, looking for figures of speech that show comparison, such as similes and metaphors, which Kincaid used to describe feelings and events. Underline these.

   Note: A *simile* is a comparison of two unlike things usually using the words *like* or *as*.

   EXAMPLES:

   (1) "The launch left a wide path in it that looked *like* a road."

   (2) "They made an unexpected sound, *as if* a vessel filled with liquid had been placed on its side and now was slowly emptying out."

   Note: In a *metaphor*, a term that ordinarily stands for one thing is used to stand for another; a metaphor thus implies that one thing *is* another.

   EXAMPLES:

   (1) "The words 'I shall never see this again' stabbed at me." (This implies that words are a knife, capable of stabbing.)

(2) "a voice that raked across my skin" (This implies that a voice is a rake.)

2. Share your findings with your group.

3. Talk about this with the class: How did Kincaid help the reader understand the story and Annie's feelings by using colors, sounds, and figures of speech?

4. Write in your log about what you learned about writing from these activities.

TOPICS FOR WRITING

Choose one activity.

Activity A: Annie John left her parents and her country behind. Make a list of the kinds of leaving you have experienced. Choose one experience, and write one or two paragraphs about what happened, how you felt, and why the event was significant. Think about the colors you saw and the sounds you heard (loud or soft, pleasant or unpleasant). Try to include details of sound and color or figures of speech that show comparison.

Activity B: Write about an experience this story reminds you of. Tell what happened, how you felt, and why the event was significant. Do you remember the color of people's clothes or the colors of any objects in the setting? What sounds do you remember hearing? Try to include details of sound and color or figures of speech that show comparison.

Activity C: Based on your reading and experience, make a list of reasons people leave one country for another. Put your list into categories and give each category a title (for example, "Political").

Then, interview some of your classmates to find out why they left their country (if they did). Put them, along with Annie John, Nicholas Gage, and other characters from stories, into the appropriate categories. Finally, write a composition about why people leave one country for another, using examples from your own experience and from the experiences of these people.

Note: You may want to try a technique called **cubing** to help you gather ideas. See Appendix A.4, p. 228, for an explanation of cubing.

AFTER WRITING

1. Read your writing to your group. Ask your listeners to explain what they understand your important point to be and to tell what details especially stand out for them.

2. Give your story a title, if you haven't already done so.

3. Write in your log about how you wrote this composition. For example, was it easy or difficult to think of sounds, colors, and figures of speech? Did you use any special technique to gather ideas?

BEFORE READING

1. Find Botswana on the map in the front of the book. Suppose you had the time and money to travel. From here (where you are) to Botswana, what countries would you choose to travel through? (You can go in any direction—north, south, east, or west.) What countries would you want to stop in and visit? What countries might you skip? Make an itinerary.

   After you make up your itinerary, share your plans with a partner.

2. Read the introductory information below. Then read the piece as many times as you like.

Ancestral Oranges
Michelle Dominique Leigh

This excerpt seems like an entry in a traveler's journal. The traveler-writer paints an impression of Botswana through description and reflection.

On a train in Botswana, on the map a place in middle Africa, a place residing deep in the unconscious, the unknown primal Africa of the imagination. Stopping slowly at a station, looking out the window: small boys sell oranges. At this moment, seeing these oranges held out to me like glowing round suns, seeing these smiling children so real and familiar, so strangely remembered from a time before history, there is something I know. This is the birth of my world, this is my ancestry, this is the beginning and the heart and what the rest of the world has lost. It is fearfully good here; I sink into it. This is the source of the blood in my veins. This is the land of my body, the home of my soul. How gentle you are, children with oranges, ancient land, source.

AFTER READING

Write about this excerpt for five minutes in your log. What did you notice? Is it similar to your own experience? Is it different? How? How does it make you feel?

Share your log entry with your group.

HOW IT'S WRITTEN

1. Choose one activity.

   Activity A: With your group, mark the groups of words that are fragments (f) and those that are complete sentences (c). (If you can't
   tell which are fragments and which are complete sentences, ask your
   teacher for help.)
       Talk with your group about your findings. Discuss why you think
   the author used fragments as well as complete sentences. What do
   the fragments convey? Do they seem appropriate? What about the
   complete sentences? Does this style make the writing colorful?

   Activity B: How do you know the writer had eyes, ears, feelings?
   Mark the text to show that the writer used her senses. Do you think
   this writer was observant? Is the writing colorful?

2. Discuss these activities with the whole class.

3. Write for a few minutes in your log about how you might apply the
   lessons from these activities to your own writing.

TOPICS FOR WRITING

Choose one activity.

Activity A: Go to a particular place in the area, around the school, at
work, or in your neighborhood. Pick a place where you've never been
before and just stop and watch. Find a spot from which you can observe
and take notes. Write up your observations, taking care to provide a
beginning, middle, and ending. See if you can make the writing reflect
the sights, sounds, smells, and atmosphere of the place.

Activity B: Robert Louis Stevenson wrote, "For my part, I travel not to
go anywhere, but to go. I travel for travel's sake. The great affair is to
move" (from *Travels with a Donkey*, 1878). Would you agree with Stevenson that it's good just to travel? That you learn something by getting
out of your chair, your neighborhood, your culture? What has been your
experience with traveling? Do you have a travel experience that illumi-
nates Stevenson's words? Tell about it.

Activity C: Pretend you just landed on this planet from outer space.
Pick a real place in your area to land, for example, on the corner of a

busy intersection, on the front steps of the school, on a grassy field in a park, or on the playground. Write an entry on your "spacenet" computer to send back to your galaxy newsletter about what you see around you and what these earthlings are doing.

Note: You may want to read Appendix E, pp. 240–244, for some suggestions on writing.

AFTER WRITING

1. Exchange papers with a classmate. Write a response to your classmate's writing:

   a. Tell what you like best about the piece.
   b. Give the writer one or two specific suggestions to make the writing more colorful.

   (See Appendix F, pp. 245–246, for more explanation of responding to classmates' writing.)

2. Read your partner's comments. Read your paper aloud to your group. Afterward, write a note to yourself about how you will revise this piece.

3. Taking your partner's comments into consideration, revise the piece.

BEFORE READING

1. Read the title and introductory information below. In your reading log, write down at least two questions you think the article will answer.

    Share your questions with your group.

2. Read the article.

The Education of Berenice Belizaire
Joe Klein

Berenice Belizaire arrived in New York from Haiti unable to speak any English. After a few difficult years in high school, she began to excel in her courses, became the valedictorian of her graduating class, and is now in a highly select college, MIT (Massachusetts Institute of Technology). Her success story is not unusual.

When Berenice Belizaire arrived in New York from Haiti with her mother and sister in 1987, she was not very happy. She spoke no English. The family had to live in a cramped Brooklyn apartment, a far cry from the comfortable house they'd had in Haiti. Her mother, a nurse, worked long hours. School was torture. Berenice had always been a good student, but now she was learning a new language while enduring constant taunts from the Americans (both black and white). They cursed her in the cafeteria and threw food at her. Someone hit her sister in the head with a book. "Why can't we go home?" Berenice asked her mother.

Because home was too dangerous. The schools weren't always open anymore, and education—her mother insisted—was the most important thing. Her mother had always pushed her: memorize everything, she ordered. "I have a pretty good memory," Berenice admitted last week. Indeed, the other kids at school began to notice that Berenice always, somehow, knew the answers. "They started coming to me for help," she says. "They never called me a nerd."

Within two years Berenice was speaking English, though not well enough to get into one of New York's elite public high schools. She had to settle for the neighborhood school, James Madison—which is one of the magical American places, the alma mater of Ruth Bader Ginsburg among others, a school with a history of unlikely success stories. "I didn't realize what we had in Berenice at first," says math teacher Judith Khan. "She was good at math, but she was quiet. And the things she didn't know! She applied for a summer program in Buffalo and asked me how to get there on the subway. But she always seemed to ask the right questions. She understood the big ideas. She could think on her feet. She could explain difficult problems so the other kids could understand them. Eventually, I realized: she wasn't just pushing for grades, she was hungry for *knowledge*. . . .

She moved from third in her class to first during senior year. She was selected as valedictorian, an honor she almost refused (still shy, she wouldn't allow her picture in the school's yearbook). She gave the speech, after some prodding—a modest address about the importance of hard work and how it's never too late to try hard: an immigrant's valedictory. Last week I caught up with Berenice at the Massachusetts Institute of Technology where she was jump-starting her college career. I asked her what she wanted to be doing in 10 years: "I want to build a famous computer, like IBM," she said. "I want my name to be part of it."

Berenice Belizaire's story is remarkable, but not unusual. The New York City schools are bulging with overachieving immigrants. The burdens they place on a creaky, corroded system are often cited as an argument against liberal immigration policies, but teachers like Judith Khan don't seem to mind. "They're why I love teaching in Brooklyn," she says. "They have a drive in them we no longer seem to have. You see these kids, who aren't prepared academically and can barely speak the language, struggling so hard. They just sop it up. They're like little sponges. You see Berenice, who had none of the usual, preconceived racial barriers in her mind—you see her becoming friendly with the Russian kids, and learning chess from Po Ching [from Taiwan]. It is *so* exciting."

Dreamy hothouse: Indeed, it is possible that immigrant energy reinvigorated not just some schools (and more than a few teachers)—but *the city itself* in the 1980s. "Without them, New York would have been a smaller place, a poorer place, a lot less vital and exciting," says Prof. Emanuel Tobier of New York University. They restored the retail life of the city, starting a raft of small businesses—and doing the sorts of entry-level, bedpan-emptying jobs that nonimmigrants spurn. They added far more to the local economy than they removed; more important, they reminded . . . New Yorkers that the city had always worked best as a vast, noisy, dreamy hothouse for the cultivation of new Americans.

The Haitians have followed the classic pattern. They have a significantly higher work-force participation rate than the average in New York. They have a lower rate of poverty. They have a higher rate of new-business formation and a lower rate of welfare dependency. Their median household income, at $28,853, is about $1,000 less than the citywide median (but about $1,000 higher than Chinese immigrants, often seen as a "model" minority). They've also developed a traditional network of fraternal societies, newspapers and neighborhoods with solid—extended, rather than nuclear—families. "A big issue now is whether women who graduate from school should be allowed to live by themselves before they marry," says Lola Poisson, who counsels Haitian immigrants. "There's a lot of tension over that."

. . . Immigrants become Americans very quickly. Some lose hope after years of menial labor; others lose discipline, inebriated by freedom. "There's an interesting phenomenon," says Philip Kasinitz of Williams College. "When immigrant kids criticize each other for getting lazy or loose, they say, 'You're becoming American.'" (Belizaire said she and the Russians would tease each other that way at Madison.) It's ironic, Kasinitz adds, "Those who work hardest to keep American culture at bay have the best chance of becoming American success stories." If so, we may be fixed on the wrong issue. The question shouldn't be whether immigrants are ruining America, but whether America is ruining the immigrants.

AFTER READING

1. Did you learn the answers to your questions? Write the answers in your log. If you didn't get answers to your questions, write about what you learned instead.

2. Look back through the piece. Mark the sentences that express ideas that you value with a plus (+); mark those that you don't value with a minus (−). Talk with your group about what you value in the article, what you don't value, and why.

HOW IT'S WRITTEN

1. Where does the story about Berenice end? Find that place. What tells you that the story has ended? Where does the next section end? What is it about? Is there a third section? What is it about?

   Does the whole piece have a beginning, a middle, and an end? Do you think the parts go together logically? Explain why or why not.

   Now, talk about these questions with your group. How many sections do you agree the article has? What are they? Report to the class.

2. What sentence in the whole piece do you think best expresses the main point? In what part of the essay does it appear (beginning,

middle, or end)? What effect does its position have? Talk with your group and come to a consensus. Report to the class.

TOPICS FOR WRITING

Choose one activity.

Activity A: Write a "success story." Pick a person you know or can find out about, but not a famous person. If possible, interview this person to find out about feelings and attitudes. Also try to discover what the person thinks were major influences, turning points, or important people along the road to becoming successful. Use the story about Berenice as a model. (After you write down your ideas, think about the beginning, middle, and end.)

Activity B: Choose a sentence from the story that you can use to start a piece of your own writing. It might be one of the things you marked with a plus (+) in After Reading, question 2. (After you write down your ideas, think about the beginning, middle, and end.)

Activity C: Write a piece entitled "The Education of _____." It can be your story or another person's. (After you get your ideas down on paper, think about the beginning, middle, and end.)

AFTER WRITING

1. Read your partner's paper silently. On a separate piece of paper, answer the following questions:

   a. What do you understand the main point to be?

   b. What do you like best about the piece?

2. On your partner's paper, mark *B* for the beginning, *M* where the middle begins, and *E* where the end begins.

3. When you get your paper back, see if you agree with your partner about the beginning, middle, and end. If not, think about what confused your partner. Write down a few notes to yourself about how you will revise this piece. (See Appendix E, pp. 240–241, for some suggestions on beginnings and endings.)

4. Revise this piece.

BEFORE READING

1. What words come to your mind when you see the word *bilingualism?* Write down those words. As a class, put all the words on the chalkboard.

2. Put the words into categories, and give a title to each category. Put some categories on the chalkboard.

3. After looking at the words and categories of words on the board, which ones do you think would be especially important in an article on parents and children? Why?

4. Read the article.

Misconceptions with Roots in the Old Days
Lawrence Kutner

This article about bilingualism appeared in Lawrence Kutner's regular column, called Parent & Child, *in the* New York Times.

Even though he was born in Boston, Ed Barsamian grew up speaking Armenian at home. His family, bilingual immigrants, only spoke English when non-Armenian friends visited.

"If someone asked me my nationality then, I would have said I was Armenian first and American second," said Mr. Barsamian, who owns a specialty food store in Cambridge, Mass. He has tried to raise his two teen-age sons to use both languages, but has had only mixed success.

"It isn't a priority for my children to be bilingual the way it was with me," Mr. Barsamian continued. "They think of themselves as Americans first and as people of Armenian heritage second. I don't expect my children to marry Armenians or to teach their children the language. But I think they're missing a special part of growing up."

Raising a child to speak two or more languages can be especially difficult in the United States. Children whose parents are native English speakers often see little benefit to learning another language. Unlike in many other countries, the dominant culture in the United States is monolingual, with a decreasing but still strong inclination to remain so.

While schools have shown a growing interest in bilingual education, many children who were raised speaking a different language often feel considerable pressure to speak only English at school and in public. Immigrant parents routinely describe how their young children appear embarrassed to speak their native language unless they live in a community where that language is commonly spoken.

Bilingualism is a topic abounding with misconceptions. "In the United States more than in other countries, people are concerned that being bilingual is bad for children," said Dr. Elissa Newport, a professor of psychology at the University of Rochester who studies language acquisition. "But that isn't supported at all by the research."

Some of these misconceptions spring from the writings of psychologists early in the 20th century, who concluded that bilingual children couldn't compete academically with children who spoke only one language. But those early studies were flawed, especially since most of the testing of bilingual children was done in their second language, which led to an underestimation of their abilities.

"One of the biggest misconceptions people have is that if children learn a second language, it will be at the expense of the first," said Dr. René Cisneros, who studies language and literacy development among elementary-school children at the Julian Samora Research Institute at Michigan State University in East Lansing. "But the research shows that what a child learns in one language carries over to the other."

Although it's generally easier for young children than for adults to learn more than one language, there are tremendous variations in how quickly children become bilingual. "Language learning has little to do with intelligence," said Dr. Jeffrey L. Derevensky, an associate professor of educational psychology at McGill University in Montreal, who is studying bilingual education in Canada.

Toddlers who are learning two languages simultaneously may sometimes lag behind those who are mastering only one language. They may also blend both languages within a single sentence. Dr. Newport, whose husband is deaf and whose 7- and 9-year-old children are fluent in both English and American Sign Language, recalled how her children used to combine oral language and sign language when they were very young, even though she never did. But studies have shown that bilingual children catch up in both languages and stop blending them within a few years.

•   •   •

Multilingual immigrant parents also worry that using their native language at home will interfere with their child's mastery of English, and put them at a disadvantage in school. But recent studies have shown that, in fact, the opposite may be true.

"Children who know more than one language are significantly better at thinking about problems from more than one perspective, compared with children who are monolingual," said Dr. Naomi S. Baron, a professor of linguistics at the American University in Washington who wrote "Growing Up With Language: How Children Learn to Talk" (1992, Addison-Wesley, $21.95).

"But if your child doesn't have the opportunity to grow up bilingually, you can reap many of the same benefits by playing with language together early on," Dr. Baron added. Play can include synonym and antonym games, counting games and other ways that children can enjoy the concepts underlying how we use language.

AFTER READING

1. This article points out the difference between what people think (misconceptions) and what researchers have found (findings). Look through the article and identify three misconceptions (m) and three research findings (f).

   Talk about these with your partner to make sure you understand them.

2. Work with your group. Using the article as support, what would you say to someone who said the following:

   - If you learn a second language, you'll lose your first one.
   - If you want to learn English fast, you shouldn't speak your native language at home.
   - Bilingual children have trouble thinking about problems.
   - You have to be smart to learn a language.
   - Children learn languages quickly and easily.

3. Freewrite for a few minutes about your discussion, writing down the points you want to remember. When you finish, write one sentence that summarizes the dominant idea of what you wrote (the **kernel** idea). (See Appendix A.1, p. 223, for an explanation of kernel ideas.)

TOPICS FOR WRITING

Choose one activity.

Activity A: Choose one of the misconceptions or research findings that relates to your experience, your observations of others, or your reading (especially, "The Education of Berenice Belizaire"). It may remind you of a family situation or a personal experience, your observations of others, or something you've read. Explain the misconception or research finding you chose, and use your observations, experience, or reading to support your point(s).

Activity B: Write a dialogue between two people about a conflict around the issue of bilingualism—for instance, between a mother or grandmother and child, two parents, or a teacher and a parent. (You may do this with a partner.)

Activity C: Prepare a survey to find out people's attitudes toward bilingualism or bilingual education. Write four or five questions you want to ask. Try these questions out with your group. Conduct the survey. Then, write up the results, using the article as background. You may wish to do further research in the library.

AFTER WRITING

1. In your small group, read each other's papers silently or aloud. On a separate sheet of paper, write feedback to each writer:

    a. I think your main point is . . .

    b. One thing I like about your paper is . . .

    c. The one suggestion I have for improving it is . . .

2. Talk with your group about how your pieces connect to each other. Do they all fit the title "Two Worlds"? Do your pieces have any similar themes or issues? Write down the similarities and share them with the class. (These may stimulate you to do further research or writing.)

BEFORE READING

1. The article, which appeared as an op-ed piece in the *New York Times*, had a heading that read, "Students need English more than bilingualism." Based on that heading and the title, freewrite in your reading log about what you think the article might include.

   What position do you predict the author will take? What support do you think the author might include? What questions do you think the article should answer?

   Share your thoughts with a partner. Do you and your partner have similar or different predictions?

2. Read the article.

No Comprendo
Barbara Mujica

Barbara Mujica is professor of Spanish at Georgetown University in Washington, D.C.

Last spring, my niece phoned me in tears. She was graduating from high school and had to make a decision. An outstanding soccer player, she was offered athletic scholarships by several colleges. So why was she crying?

My niece came to the United States from South America as a child. Although she had received good grades in her schools in Miami, she spoke English with a heavy accent and her comprehension and writing skills were deficient. She was afraid that once she left the Miami environment she would feel uncomfortable and, worse still, have difficulty keeping up with class work.

Programs that keep foreign-born children in Spanish-language classrooms for years are only part of the problem. During a visit to my niece's former school, I observed that all business, not just teaching, was conducted in Spanish. In the office, secretaries spoke to the administrators and the children in Spanish. Announcements over the public-address system were made in an English so fractured that it was almost incomprehensible.

I asked my niece's mother why, after years in public schools, her daughter had poor English skills. "It's the whole environment," she replied. "All kinds of services are available in Spanish or Spanglish. Sports and after-school activities are conducted in Spanglish. That's what the kids hear on the radio and in the street."

Until recently, immigrants made learning English a priority. But even when they didn't learn English themselves, their children grew up speaking it. Thousands of first-generation Americans still strive to learn English, but others face reduced educational and career opportunities because they have not mastered this basic skill they need to get ahead.

According to the 1990 census, 40 percent of the Hispanics born in the U.S. do not graduate from high school, and the Department of Education says that a lack of proficiency in English is an important factor in the drop-out rate.

People and agencies that favor providing services only in foreign languages want to help people who do not speak English, but they may be doing them a disservice by condemning them to a linguistic ghetto from which they can not easily escape.

And my niece? She turned down all of her scholarship opportunities, deciding instead to attend a small college in Miami, where she will never have to put her English to the test.

AFTER READING

1. Reread what you wrote before you read the piece. Make notes on your freewriting: Which of your predictions proved true? Which did not? Add to your freewriting: What did the article say that was different from what you expected?

2. What is the author's main point? Work by yourself to find the sentence that you think best states the main point. Then work with your small group to try to agree on one sentence.

   Discuss with your group whether the example of the niece supports this sentence. Can you connect that sentence to all aspects of the example?

3. Write for a few minutes in your reading log about your thoughts and feelings about this editorial.

HOW I READ IT

1. Write for a few minutes in your reading log about how your predictions affected your reading. Did they make it easier or harder? Did you read faster because of the predictions? Or more slowly? What else did you notice about how you read?

2. Talk with a partner about the value of making predictions before you read. Consider how you might apply this technique to a reading assignment in another course you are studying (such as biology, history, sociology, or math).

Discuss your ideas with the class.

HOW IT'S WRITTEN

1. This article is composed of eight paragraphs. Make a descriptive outline of the composition. Describe what each paragraph *says* (What information does it contain?) and what each paragraph *does* (What is its function?). Some things paragraphs do are introduce an idea, develop a reason, give an example, explain a point, elaborate, describe, analyze, synthesize, restate, and conclude. (See Appendix B.4, pp. 233 and 236, for more explanation and an example of descriptive outlining.)

2. This piece starts out with a story. Where does the author make the main point? Using your descriptive outline, work with a partner to analyze the composition for its structure. How would you describe the structure? What do you think about this way of composing an article? Do you think it's effective? Will you remember it?

TOPICS FOR WRITING

Choose one activity.

Activity A: Bilingualism itself is a way of living in two worlds. Do you know someone whom you consider to be a model bilingual? Prepare questions you could use to interview that person. Here are some possible questions.

- What is it like to be bilingual?
- What activities do you conduct in English? In your other language?
- Do you feel a part of two worlds? In what way?
- What situations are easy for you? What situations are difficult?
- What are the benefits of being bilingual? The pitfalls?

Then interview the person. Take notes and tape record the interview if possible.

Finally, write a profile of the person. Think about what point you can make in your piece of writing.

Activity B: Whether you agree or disagree with what Barbara Mujica wrote, write your own piece. Begin your piece with a summary of what she says in her article. Then, pick a point with which you strongly agree or disagree. Tell how you feel, what you think about that point, and why you agree or disagree. Finally, tell what associations follow from your thoughts and feelings. What do they make you think of? You might include suggestions or solutions.

Activity C: Do you have a "no comprendo" story of your own? Have you had a personal experience in which you didn't understand what was happening because of your language ability or a cross-cultural misunderstanding? Begin by telling the story. Think about what the story means and make a point at the end. Try to surprise yourself with your ending.

AFTER WRITING

1. Go over your paper carefully with a pen in your hand, reading each word aloud so that your ear can hear it and touching each word with your pen to find errors and parts that don't sound right. Don't stop until you find at least three things to change.

2. Exchange papers with another person. Analyze your partner's composition, using the following questions as a guide:

   a. What point is the writer making? (Find the sentence that best expresses the writer's point.)

   b. Do the other paragraphs relate to the main point? What does each paragraph *say* and *do*?
      Talk with your partner about your analysis.

3. Write a note to yourself (in your log or on the bottom of your draft) about what you plan to revise in your piece.

4. Revise your piece.

BEFORE READING

1. For everything its season, and for every activity under heaven its time:

   a time to be born and a time to die;
   a time to plant and a time to uproot. . . .

   Have you heard or read these words before? Write for a few minutes in your reading log about how these words make you feel.

   Share with a partner some part of what you wrote.
2. Read the poem.

Ecclesiastes 3:1–8

This poem is taken from the Old Testament of The New English Bible, *a translation that uses present-day English rather than traditional biblical language.*

For everything its season, and for every activity under heaven its time:

   a time to be born and a time to die;
   a time to plant and a time to uproot;
   a time to kill and a time to heal;
   a time to pull down and a time to build up;
   a time to weep and a time to laugh;
   a time for mourning and a time for dancing;
   a time to scatter stones and a time to gather them;
   a time to embrace and a time to refrain from embracing;
   a time to seek and a time to lose;
   a time to keep and a time to throw away;
   a time to tear and a time to mend;
   a time for silence and a time for speech;
   a time to love and a time to hate;
   a time for war and a time for peace.

AFTER READING

1. With a partner, read the poem aloud, slowly and thoughtfully. If you don't know some of the individual words, try to guess what they mean from the ideas around them (from their context).

2. Choose one activity.

> **Activity A:** Read the poem again by yourself, line by line. Stop after each line, and let an image develop in your mind to match the words. In your log, describe some of the images you created, either in words or by drawing a picture. Share what you wrote or drew with your group. See what others did.
>
> **Activity B:** Freewrite for a few minutes on what you think the essential meaning (or the main point) of this piece is. At the end of your freewriting, summarize the meaning in one kernel sentence. Share your thoughts with the members of your group. Talk about whether you all have similar interpretations of the meaning or different ones.

HOW I READ IT

Think about how the images formed in your mind as you read the poem. Try to describe that process to your group, and find out how other people in the group formed images.

Write a few things in your log that you learned about how you and others in your group read.

HOW IT'S WRITTEN

What makes this piece poetry? Talk about it with your partner, and come up with three or four characteristics of poetry. Then, with your partner, add a line to the piece, making your line poetic also.

TOPICS FOR WRITING

Choose one activity.

Activity A: Think of a time when a negative event turned out to have a positive ending. Write about what happened and the outcome. Use as many details as you need to make the event clear to the reader. (One of the techniques for **gathering ideas**, such as clustering, might help you get started. See Appendix A.2, pp. 224–225.)

Activity B: Pick a line from the poem that has special meaning for you, or add one of your own. Put it at the top of your paper. Write about it, explaining what it means to you.

Activity C: Choose a line from the poem that strikes you as true because of your experience or reading, for example, the line "a time to kill and a time to heal." Explain how words that are opposites (in this case, *kill* and *heal*) can be related, using examples from your experience, observation of others, or reading. The examples may be personal, social, historical, political, or some other type. In any case, describe the experience or event in as much detail as you can. (One of the techniques for gathering ideas might help you recall details. See Appendix A, p. 223.)

AFTER WRITING

1. Read your piece of writing to your group. Ask your group to tell you:

   a. What do they think your main point is?

   b. What part would they like to hear more about?

   c. What will they remember about your piece?

2. Write in your log about how you wrote this piece. For example, was it easy or hard? Did you write it in one sitting? How did you get your ideas? How did you decide on your main point? How did the poem affect your writing?

BEFORE READING

1. Read the title, subtitle, and introductory information. Freewrite for a
   few minutes on what you think are the burdens and privileges of being a multiracial child.
       Discuss what you wrote with your partner.

2. This story is broken into four sections, marked with a *. When you
   come to the end of each section, write down one thing you expect
   the next section to say.

The Colorings of Childhood
On the Burdens, and Privileges,
Facing My Multi-racial Son

David Updike

> *The author, who is white, married an African woman. In this memoir,
> he writes about questions of race and identity. He ponders what having
> parents of different complexions will mean for his child growing up in the
> United States.*

Five or six years ago, when my older sister revealed to the rest of our
family her intention of marrying her boyfriend, from Ghana, I remember
that my reaction, as a nervous and somewhat protective younger brother, was
something like "Well, that's fine for them—I just wonder about the children."
I'm not sure what I was wondering, exactly, but it no doubt had to do with the
thorny questions of race and identity, of having parents of different complexions, and a child, presumably, of some intermediate shade, and what that
would mean for a child growing up here, in the United States of America.

I had no idea, at the time, that I, too, would one day marry an African,
or that soon thereafter we would have a child, or that I would hear my own
apprehensions of several years before echoed in the words of one of my wife's
friends. She was a white American of a classic liberal mold—wearer of Guatemalan shawls, befriender of Africans, espouser of worthy causes—but she was
made uneasy by the thought of Njoki, her friend from Kenya, marrying me, a
white person. She first asked Njoki what my "politics" were and, having been
assured that they were okay, went on to say, "Well, I'm sure he's a very nice
person, but before you get married I just hope you'll think about the children."

I recognized in her remarks the shadow of my own, but when it is one's own marriage that is being worried about, one's children, not yet conceived, one tends to ponder such comments more closely. By this time, too, I was the uncle of two handsome, happy boys, Ghanian-American, who, as far as I could tell, were suffering no side effects for having parents of different colors. Njoki, too, was displeased.

"What is she trying to say, exactly—that *my* child will be disadvantaged because he looks like me?" my wife asked. "So what does she think about me? Does she think *I'm* disadvantaged because I'm African?"

I responded that our liberal friend was trying to get at the complicated question of identity, knowing, as she did, that the child, in a country that simplifies complicated, racial equations to either "black" or "white," wouldn't know to which group he "belonged."

"To both of them," Njoki answered, "or to neither. He will be Kenyan-American. The ridiculous part is that if I was marrying an African she wouldn't mind at all—she wouldn't say, 'Think of the children,' because the child would just be black, like me, and it wouldn't be her problem. She wouldn't have to worry about it. Honestly," she finally said, her head bowed into her hand in resignation, "this country is so complicated."

*

. . . As I slowly pondered the woman's remarks, it occurred to me that she was not saying, "He won't know who he is" but something closer to, "*I* won't know who he is—I won't know to which group this child belongs, the black people or the white." Added to this is the suppressed, looming understanding that, however the child sees himself, however we see the child, the country at large will perceive the child as "black," and, consequently, this son or daughter of a friend, this child to whom we might actually be an aunt or uncle, parent or grandparent, cousin or friend, this person whom we love and wish the best for in life, will grow up on the opposite side of the color line from us and, as such, will be privy to a whole new realm of the American Experience, which we, by virtue of our skin color, have previously avoided; and this—for the vast majority of white Americans—is a new and not altogether comforting experience. . . .

*

By some unexpected confluence of genes our son Wesley's hair is, to our surprise, relatively straight—long, looping curls that tighten slightly when it rains—and this, too, will mean something in America, means something already to the elderly neighborhood women who tell us, with a smile, that he has "good" hair, and to other people, friends and strangers both, who tell us he looks like he is from Central America, or India, or the Middle East, implicitly meaning *rather than black*. Children, however, are less circumspect in their observations, and I have no doubt my son will be called a few names while growing up, both by white children and by brown; he may be told that he is really "black," and he may be told that he thinks he's "white"; in Kenya, I have been assured, he will be considered "half-caste"—an unpleasant linguistic relic from colonial days. He may also be treated badly by teachers prone to impatience, or a lack of empathy, with students of lighter, or darker, complexions than their own. He may be embarrassed by the sound of his mother's language; he may be embarrassed by my whiteness. He may go through a time when he is, indeed, confused about his "identity," but in this respect I don't think he will be much different from other children, or teenagers, or adults. There is no way of my knowing, really, what his experience as a multi-racial child will be, or, for that matter, how helpful I or his mother will be to him along the way. We can only tell him what we think and know, and hope, as all parents do, that our words will be of some use. . . .

*

Wesley will visit Africa and live there for a time, and will know the Kenyan half of his family there and the American half here, and into the bargain will know his Ghanian uncle and his Ghanian-American cousins and a whole West African branch of his extended family. And it may just be that, contrary to the assumptions of concerned friends, this child of a "mixed" marriage will suffer no great disadvantages at all, but rather will enjoy advantages denied the rest of us; for as the child of two cultures he will "belong" to neither of them exclusively but both of them collectively, will be a part of my Americanness and Njoki's Africanness, and will be something neither she nor I ever will be—African-American—and as such will be a part of a rich and varied culture that will always hold me at arm's length. And in these layers of identity lies an opportunity for a kind of expansion of the world, a dissolution of the boundaries and obstacles that hold us all in a kind of skittish, social obeisance, and he thus may be spared the suspicions and apprehensions that plague those of us who have grown up with an exclusive, clearly defined sense of belonging. In the end, my son will be, simply, an American child, an American adult. His will be a wider, more complicated world than mine was, and to him will fall the privilege and burden, as it falls to us all, of making of it what he will.

AFTER READING

1. Reread the article and annotate it. (See Appendix B.3, pp. 233 and 235, for an explanation of **annotating** and an example.) As you annotate, look for the following things:

   what you expected

   what you didn't expect

points about race and identity

the burdens of being a multiracial child

the privileges of being multiracial

a sentence that best expresses the main point

Talk about what you found with your partner.

2. Write a summary of the article. Include in your summary a statement about the main point.

HOW IT'S WRITTEN

1. With a partner, choose one activity.

Activity A: This article contains a number of different points of view, according to different people. Reread the text and mark the different views: *N* for Njoki, *A* for author, *P* for parents, *AA* for African Americans, *WA* for white Americans, and *AF* for Africans. What are the different views?
   What is the effect of all these different viewpoints on the topic? What is the effect on you, the reader? Is it useful? Does it help the writer make his point?

Activity B: Read the last paragraph again. What does the author say in this paragraph? What does the paragraph *do* for the piece as a whole? (For ideas on what paragraphs *do*, see Descriptive Outlining, Appendix B.4, pp. 233 and 236.)
   What do you think about the ending of the piece? Is it effective? Would you suggest any changes, or is it just right?

2. Report your answers and discuss them with the class.

TOPICS FOR WRITING

Choose one activity.

Activity A: Do you know something about the burdens and privileges of growing up in a multiracial family, from your own experience or from your observations of others? Write about what you know, telling some major incident(s) that happened. If appropriate, try to show various viewpoints. Write several endings and choose the best one.

Activity B: Do you think that a common culture transcends ethnic differences? For example, do children who grow up in the United States have more in common with the children from different ethnic groups who grow up with them? Or would children growing up in the U.S. have more in common with children from the country of their ethnic background? Tell about your experience and draw your own conclusions.

Activity C: Choose a sentence from the article that you find meaningful or powerful. Use it as a beginning to your own piece of writing (a story or memoir, an essay, or a letter).

AFTER WRITING

1. Write for a few minutes about how you wrote this piece. Respond to some of these questions:

   What part was easy to write? What was difficult?

   How do you feel about the whole piece?

   Did your ideas change and develop as you wrote? Where? Why?

   Did you surprise yourself? What surprised you?

   Were you able to say what you wanted?

   How much time did you spend on the piece?

   Compare writing this to writing another piece. What was different? The same?

   Reflect on your progress in your writing.

2. Attach a blank sheet of paper to your writing and give it to two different people. Ask one reader to underline two or three key phrases and write why these phrases seem important. Ask the other reader to write two or three sentences that explain the meaning of your piece.

3. Read your readers' responses. Consider them. Make a note to yourself about how you might revise this piece.

4. Revise your piece.

BEFORE READING

1. The first sentence of this article says, "I had thought that I would live my mother's life." As a child, the author thought her life would be like her mother's. Freewrite for five minutes, expressing your thoughts on this.

   Reread your freewriting and underline the important ideas. Then, unless it is private, read your freewriting to a partner. When you finish, decide whether you and your partner consider yourselves similar to or different from your mothers (or parents).

2. Read the article.

On Turning Fifty
Judy Scales-Trent

In her midforties, Judy Scales-Trent changed her name, changed her profession from lawyer to teacher and writer, and moved from Washington, D.C., to Buffalo, N.Y. She thought a great deal about what she gained and what she lost. The week before she turned fifty, she wrote this piece, first as a journal entry. She said: "My thoughts were so powerful that I had to write them down in order to move them outside my body, in order to manage them, in order to transform painful feelings into marks on paper. And as I wrote and rewrote, as I polished and smoothed out the phrases of the essay, I also polished and smoothed out the feelings in my heart."

I had thought that I would live my mother's life. I suppose all girls do. Like my mother, I would have a dignified and successful husband, one who would take care of me and our children, who would provide a life of status and comfort. I would be involved in my church. I would take classes and volunteer in my community. I would passionately enjoy my garden and my sewing.

This has not been my life. It has been more the life of my sisters. Like my mother, they are married, each with three children. My eldest sister now has four grandchildren: there will be more. In my eyes, they live a life of comfort—trips to far-off places, a summer house in the country.

This has not been my life. I live alone, with one small dog. A university professor, I do much of my work alone. I am no longer married. My teenage son lives in another state, long miles away. If I am to have any security or status or physical comfort, I must give it to myself.

It is at times like this, reckoning times, that I wonder where I went wrong. For I long for family—a husband, children, grandchildren. And this is not a mild longing. At times like this when I allow myself to feel it, the longing is so fierce that I close my eyes to hold back its power. I started down the path of my mother's life, but somewhere along the way I walked away from it. Where did I go wrong? Or did I go right? For it is at times like these, reckoning times, that I also remind myself that the life I now lead is the right one.

There was a moment, one morning, when I understood its rightness. It took place during the frenzy of my move from Washington, D.C., when I flew to Buffalo to sign closing papers for my new house. Isabel, a new colleague at the law school, picked me up at the airport and made me welcome as an overnight guest in her home. And it was the next morning, as I came downstairs, on my way to go to the attorney's office, that I was struck by something, something not yet clear in my mind. I remember the moment. I can see it clearly. I walked into the living room. The sun was streaming in through a stained-glass piece hung against the window. High ceilings, richly colored rugs on wooden floors, plants spilling over in profusion on a low, wooden bench; mugs and coffee and bread and jam on a coffee table in front of the sofa; stacks of books everywhere. And Isabel, sitting on the sofa, drinking her morning cup of coffee, reading a book. The sun made a golden picture. I stopped and stared, overwhelmed by the beauty and the quiet. "Is this what my life will be like?" I asked. She smiled. "Yes."

I must have longed, without knowing, for this—the sun and books, a quiet room, the generosity of friends. And that is my life now. For the very first time, my life is a seamless piece of fabric. There is no sense of working or not working. For the very first time, I do what I am. There is profound joy in this wholeness.

But there is no denying that this wholeness has come late. I will soon be fifty. The number feels important. Life does not go on forever. A friend and I once talked about this getting older. I told her that sometimes I felt as if I could see the end. Did she feel the same? "No," she answered, "but sometimes I can *feel* the end." The end. Feeling the end. This is a powerful thought. I see the signs: the eyes that do not work so well during the day, and even less well at night; the bones that complain when I push myself up out of bed in the morning; the skin that softens and sags. Fades.

My father has just turned eighty, my mother seventy-eight. They have been in good health all their lives. Now age makes them vulnerable and frail. My father is impatient. "Why should I no longer be able to drive," he rails, angry at life's betrayal. He has always been active—tennis, swimming, long daily walks. Now that he can no longer go for his walks around the neighborhood, now that he can no longer swim, he does not give up. He goes to the Y six days a week, and walks back and forth across the pool, buoyed and strengthened by the water. He counts the steps—precious steps, and calls me in Buffalo to tell me how many miles he has walked. My mother still gardens and sews and goes to her classes. And she, who never exercised before, now takes daily exercise classes at the church. They have a morning routine. She drives my father to the pool and waits while he walks. Then she drives them both to the church, where he waits for her.

I am moved by my parents' courage and their devotion to each other. Soon they will lose each other. Soon I will lose them. And still they teach me. Still, I learn from them. Just as they once taught me how to tie my shoes and to count, just as they once taught me to write thank-you notes, now they teach me how to suffer loss after loss with dignity and grace.

I am more interested in death now. It seems more familiar. I see and read things in a different way. Sometimes I remember a phrase from a spiritual, and hope that someone will sing it at my funeral:

> Steal away,
> steal away,
> steal away to Jesus.
> Steal away
> steal away home.
> I ain't got long to stay here.

Sometimes I come across words which I read with new meaning, like this Indian death song:

> From the middle
> of the great water
> I am called by the spirits.

Through the words I feel a broad and generous grace. There is calm, peacefulness, rightness. Homecoming.

There is a special poignancy to this fall. I do not want it to come. More than usual, I hold on to summer. This fall feels different. It feels like the announcement of the fall of my life. I accept and deny at the same time. For the first time, I want to plant bulbs. I want to store away the promise of spring, to make sure that its sweetness will return. This fall I will dig in the ground and plant daffodils and jonquils of all different kinds—daffodils and jonquils, and crocuses to announce their coming.

And as I plan this latest addition to my garden, I think that in many ways I am indeed living my mother's life. She is an independent woman who can work alone, contented, joyously, for days and weeks at a time. And she is passionate about her work. She creates her own projects in her garden and in her sewing room. She plans, she designs, she works and reworks until it suits her. She takes classes to refine her art. I used to consider myself a failure because in my family the women sew, and because I do not have the patience to sew—to pin and baste and stitch and then take it out and start all over again if the shoulder is off-line, if the dress doesn't drape just so. But in reality that is also how I work. For I too am passionate about my work. And I can work alone—joyously, contented, for days and weeks at a time. And when I write, I too pin and baste and stitch, and then I take it apart and do it over again if a phrase is off-line, if a sentence doesn't fall just so.

It pleases me to find this similarity between my mother's life and mine. I rejoice in my work. It is a good life.

It is not enough.

That day, my fiftieth birthday, is coming soon now. I am getting ready. Friends in Washington and Buffalo are giving me parties. I am having a dress made—short and red and silky. I am looking for dancing shoes. My parents will fly from Greensboro to the Washington party. I will go to these celebrations, as I go into my fiftieth year, embraced by family and friends. And I will look at these days the way life teaches me to look—with one eye laughing, one eye weeping.

AFTER READING

1. Make a **triple entry** (three columns) in your reading log. On the left page of your notebook, copy three or four sections (sentences, paragraphs, etc.) from the text that confused, surprised, or interested you. In the middle column, write your questions, feelings, thoughts, opinions, and associations for each entry. (See Appendix B, pp. 233–234, for an explanation and example of a triple-entry notebook.)

   Exchange your log with another person in your group. Write a response to your partner's entries in the third column.

   Discuss your entries with your partner. What did you learn about the text from reading your partner's entries?

2. Reread "On Turning Fifty." When you finish, mark the places where the author shows emotions. Write in the margin the name of each emotion.

   Compare what you wrote with your partner or group. How many different emotions did you name?

HOW IT'S WRITTEN

This piece contains some lessons on revision. Reread the introductory note about the author. She tells something about how and why she wrote and revised this piece.

How does she define revision? Write her definition in your notebook. Compare what you wrote with a partner.

Do you see any places in her piece where she might have had painful memories? Are there any places where you think she "polished and smoothed" her feelings? Of course, we cannot be sure our impressions are correct; we would have to ask the writer. Discuss these questions with your partner.

TOPICS FOR WRITING

Choose one activity.

Activity A: Did you ever make a major decision not to stay on the path you were on but to take a completely different one? What happened? Tell about your experience and whether you think it was the best thing for you. At the end or beginning of your piece, compare your experience to this writer's.

Activity B: Was one of your birthdays, or some other event, momentous? What was happening in your life? How long ago did it occur? Write a composition (or a poem or song) entitled "On Turning _____."

Like this writer, you might start your piece as a journal entry. Revise it to smooth and polish the phrases.

Activity C: Pick one experience or event the writer described that speaks to you, that reminds you of something in your own life. Restate the writer's experience briefly. Then tell about your own experience.

Activity D: Write down three or four sentences using these words: Once I _____. Now I _____.

EXAMPLES:

(1) Once I lived in a small quiet town. Now I live in the heart of Manhattan.

(2) Once I was a pack-a-day smoker. Now I am a fitness and health food nut.

(3) Once I wanted to travel to faraway lands. Now I find it exciting to stay home.

Choose the sentence that you think will be the most interesting to explore. Write a first paragraph about your "Once" statement.

Then, write a second paragraph about your "Now" statement. When you have finished, write a beginning paragraph that ties the two parts together.

AFTER WRITING

1. Read your piece (or a portion of it) aloud to yourself. After you have finished reading, write down the emotions you felt as you wrote the piece and the emotions you wanted to express.

   Exchange your paper with one person. Ask that person to read it and mark in the margins the emotions he or she thinks are being expressed. Compare what the person wrote with what you intended.

2. Revise one section of the piece to see if you can more effectively express the emotions you wanted to come through.

BEFORE READING

1. What are *the Americas*? Look on the map in the front and see all the different countries that are included in the Americas. Do this with a partner.

2. If you were *a child of the Americas*, what different varieties of Americans could you be? For instance, could you be a Guatemalan child of a Colombian mother and a New York father? Think of several possibilities. Explain one possibility to your group.

3. Read the poem silently while the teacher reads it aloud. Then read it aloud to yourself and take turns reading it to your group.

Child of the Americas
Aurora Levins Morales

In this poem, the author describes herself as a unique, integrated, wonderful mix of cultures and backgrounds. The personality that emerges counteracts the melting pot myth—that the melting pot causes everyone to look and act alike and takes the spice out of diverse cultures.

I am a child of the Americas,
a light-skinned mestiza of the Caribbean,
a child of many diaspora, born into this continent at a crossroads.
I am a U.S. Puerto Rican Jew,
a product of the ghettos of New York I have never known.
An immigrant and the daughter and granddaughter of immigrants.
I speak English with passion: it's the tongue of my consciousness,
a flashing knife blade of crystal, my tool, my craft.

I am Caribeña, island grown. Spanish is in my flesh,
ripples from my tongue, lodges in my hips:
the language of garlic and mangoes,
the singing in my poetry, the flying gestures of my hands.
I am of Latinoamerica, rooted in the history of my continent:
I speak from that body.

I am not african. Africa is in me, but I cannot return.
I am not taína. Taíno is in me, but there is no way back.
I am not european. Europe lives in me, but I have no home there.

I am new. History made me. My first language was spanglish.
I was born at the crossroads
and I am whole.

AFTER READING

1. Make a list of three or four questions you have about the poem's vocabulary and meaning. In your group, try to answer each other's questions. If you get stuck, save the question(s) for the whole class.

2. After some discussion with your group, write, by yourself, a four- or five-sentence summary of the poem.
   Share your summaries. Choose one to read aloud or write on the chalkboard for the whole class.

3. Pick a line or phrase that strikes you and write about it in your reading log.

HOW IT'S WRITTEN

Choose one activity.

Activity A: With a partner, find a line that you think best expresses the main point of the poem.
   Then, discuss with your group the lines that you chose. As a group, write a statement (one to three sentences) that you think expresses the main point of the poem. Put the group's statement on the board. Read all the statements and pick the one that you would present to the outside world as your class's best effort.

Activity B: As a group, study one of the metaphors in the poem. Try to explain its meaning. Choose one person from your group to explain the metaphor to the class.

TOPICS FOR WRITING

Choose one activity.

Activity A: Following the pattern of this poem, write a poem about yourself.

Activity B: Choose a line from the poem that strikes you. Use it to begin a piece of your own. (It may be another poem, a story, or a biographical piece.)

Activity C: Tell a story (either report a true story or make it up) about a child born of two parents from different parts of the world. How did the couple meet? What different backgrounds did they come from? How did their parents feel about the couple getting married? What does the child have (qualities, likes and dislikes, talents, etc.) from its parents and sets of grandparents?

Activity D: Write about the idea of the *melting pot*. Start with how this poem and author seem to define the melting pot. Then tell what you think of it. What examples do you see around you that support or refute the notion of a melting pot?

AFTER WRITING

1. Form a group of people who wrote on the same topic. Read each other's papers and give feedback to one another. Tell what you like, what you think the main point is, and what you suggest to make each piece clearer.

2. Form a second group of people who wrote on different topics. Read each other's papers. Write in your log about what you learned from reading the different papers.

3. Revise your writing if you wish.

About All the Readings in This Unit

PREPARE FOR WRITING

1. Reread all of the entries in your reading log for this unit.

2. With the class, list some *issues* that arise from the concept of two worlds. *Note:* An *issue* is a concern shared by many people. An issue can be stated in a few words (leaving home) or by questions (How do people feel when they leave home? Can people do anything to make leaving home easier?).

3. Choose one or two issues from your class list and make some *generalizations* about them. *Note:* A *generalization* is a judgment or observation that can apply to many similar people, things, or experiences. A generalization should be expressed in a complete sentence.

   EXAMPLES:

   (1) People who leave home have to cope with feelings of sadness.

   (2) Some people, when leaving home, experience conflicting feelings, such as both relief and sadness.

WRITING

Write down one generalization you can make about the way people experience two worlds. Write a composition in which you support your generalization through examples from the readings in this unit or from your own experience. You may want to include some of the writing you did for this unit.

AFTER WRITING

1. Before you exchange your paper with someone, go over it carefully with your pen in hand, reading each word aloud so that your ear can hear it and touching each word with your pen. This proofreading technique should help you find errors. Don't stop until you find at least three things you want to change.

2. Give your writing to two different people to read. They should write their reactions or responses to your writing in their reading log, just as they would for the readings in this book.

3. Read your readers' responses. Reread your piece, asking yourself these questions:

   a. What point does this writing make? Is it clear?

   b. What do I like about the piece?

   c. How could it be improved?

4. Write about how you wrote this piece. For example, did you do anything different from the way you wrote the other pieces in this unit? What changes could you make? (See Appendix D, pp. 238–239, for more explanation of how we write.)

My Way or Theirs?
Liu Zongren

During his two years in the United States as a visiting journalist, Liu Zongren found many customs and attitudes different from those of his native Chinese culture. Some of these strange customs he rejected; others he accepted, at least in part. In his book Two Years in the Melting Pot, *he tells how he was personally affected and often changed by his experience in a foreign land. Here he writes about table manners, clothes, raising children, and going home.*

TABLE MANNERS

There were many American customs which puzzled me. I was very impatient with table formality. Why do people have to remember to change plates, forks, knives, and spoons so many times in one meal? I was especially bothered by that piece of cloth called a napkin. English gentlemen tuck a white napkin under their chins during a meal and Americans put one on their laps. I had trouble remembering to do this even a year and a half after I had arrived and had been to a number of fancy restaurants. Even if I did place it on my lap, it always slipped onto the floor. I often remembered to use my napkin only when I saw someone wipe his mouth with one; I then hastily picked mine up and spread it across my lap, stealing a look to see if others had noticed my lack of etiquette.

CLOTHES

The concept of [the Mao] jacket conforms with the Chinese teaching of modesty, taught very early to children. They are told not to differ from others in appearance, not to be conspicuous, or they will provoke gossip. "She is frivolous," people might say if a woman did her hair in a fancy way; or, if she wore western clothing, they might comment, "Her blouse is too open at the neck!"

Of course, this is not the way Americans judge each other. Everyone tries to be different—and sometimes this goes to an extreme. One morning I glanced out of a classroom window to see a bright-colored figure walking across the lawn in front of University Hall. The sun glistened on her scarlet dress and bright red boots; her huge gold earrings sparkled, yet the part that caught the sunshine most was her hair. It was dyed half-red and half-yellow. In China, even a crazy woman would not dare walk out in the open looking like that.

In America, the overriding need to be recognized as an individual is so often expressed in the way one dresses. The exceptions are the teenagers who choose to dress alike and happily submit to the styles dictated by their peers. Parents and schools may not approve of certain fads in clothing yet they find it virtually impossible to control the dress codes. Other than the teenagers, I discovered no restrictions on how people should dress. I never saw two persons dressed identically, except by choice; the businessmen and bank workers on LaSalle Street dressed in three-piece suits and ties, all wearing their wing-tipped shoes. Still, they had enough variety in their outfits to appear different from one another. A young professor at Circle [the Chicago campus of the University of Illinois] wore a different tie and shirt every day, even if he wore the same suit. With all the clothing changes they made every day, there was little chance that two professors would show up looking alike. . . .

I bought few clothes in the United States, not wanting to spend two hundred dollars for a suit I would never wear back in China. Most of my western Chicago clothes would go into a storage trunk, as my father's had— mere reminders of his ten-year period of service abroad. I wore the same jacket and two pairs of pants all through the seasons, just as I had in Beijing. I thought little of this until two Chinese colleagues from Illinois State University told me they felt embarrassed when they wore the same clothes two days in a row. "Everyone in America changes every day," they said. "We don't have many clothes but we don't want to look shabby. We learned a trick—don't laugh at us. We take off the clothes we wear today and hang them in the closet. Tomorrow we put on another set. The day after tomorrow, we will wear the first set again; then next day, we mix the two sets up and we thus have a new set of clothes."

I laughed, not at my two colleagues, but at people who spend time worrying about what clothes they should wear. It is a waste of time for people to fuss over clothes, and it is also a waste for Chinese to try to find ways to restrict others' manner of dress. I hope that Chinese society will become more open, as America is, about the matter of clothing. A few western suits and blue jeans can hardly change centuries of Chinese teaching—history has already proved that. A billion people are like an immense ocean which can easily accommodate a few drops of foreign pigment without changing color. Western life is very appealing to many young Chinese today, who think that a better life can be achieved by adopting western life-styles. Let them try—they will soon learn.

RAISING CHILDREN

[A Chinese woman who sold stamps at the World's Fair in Knoxville] suggested that I watch how [American] parents reacted when children chose stamps. "The adults never interfere," she said. "If they agree to buy stamps, they just let the children choose on their own. They don't even give opinions. They only pay for them." At the bookstand I later observed that children had just as much freedom in selecting books. The parents interfered with their children's choices only when a parent didn't want to pay for the selected volume.

Most Chinese parents help their children select purchases. They love their children as much as any parent does, and they like to buy things for them. After a Chinese mother has agreed to pay for an item, she lets her child make a choice. Then she says, "This one is no good," or "That one is better than this one." If the child insists on the one he or she has chosen and it is not to the liking of the mother, more often than not the mother will refuse to buy the thing at all. Those mothers who give too much independence to their children are not considered good mothers by Chinese standards. "She spoils her son too much," her neighbor or colleagues will say.

I like the way American parents treat their children. The young ones are treated as small adults—that's why, I think, Americans are so much more independent than Chinese. In Chicago, I had noticed that parents often left their young children with baby-sitters while they went to a party or to the theater. Chinese parents seldom do that. I made a mental note that, after I got back to China, I would give my son more freedom in deciding his own affairs. My wife is too dominating in this respect. I would persuade her to follow American parental practices.

GOING HOME

Home now meant much more than just my wife and our son. It also meant the life I was born into, the surroundings and environment that looked Chinese, the people with whom I shared a culture, and the job at my office which I had, in the past, sometimes resented. I longed for them all. As one Chinese saying goes, all water returns to the sea; all leaves go back to their roots. My roots were in China, in Beijing, in my family. It was time I went home. . . .

I reflected on the fact that most of the successful Chinese I had met in Chicago—doctors and professors—never thought of themselves as Americans. "China is my country. Someday I will go back," one professor told me. These Chinese have a deeper sense of homeland than members of other ethnic groups I met in the United States. They have preserved more ancient Chinese customs and traditions than have the Chinese on either the mainland or Taiwan. It appears easier for a European immigrant to adjust to American society; a Chinese always thinks of his homeland. It is not merely a difference of skin color; it is cultural. I was glad to have become more aware of the importance of upholding my cultural values. . . .

After twenty months of observing American life, I had become more satisfied with the idea of my simple life in China, and I hoped that our country would never be one in which money is of first importance. I would never in my lifetime have the many possessions my middle-class American friends have. Yet, it seemed to me as if they were really only living the same cycle of life that I do in China, except on a higher economic rung of the ladder. We shared the same fundamental needs: family, friends, a familiar culture.

The Sacred Seed of the Medicine Tree
Can Indian Identity Survive?

Linda Hogan

Linda Hogan is a Native American (Chickasaw) poet and novelist. She currently teaches creative writing at the University of Colorado.

Near Minnesota's Grand Portage Indian Reservation, along the Canadian border, is a 300-year-old cedar. It grows from a stone, overhanging Lake Superior, and has been twisted in a spiral by the wind. Some Anishnabe and Cree people still call it "The Medicine Tree." . . .

It is a beautiful tree. There are places in the side of the trunk and on the branches where small offerings are made, mostly by the Indians in the region who visit the tree to pray. There are sometimes coins and photographs left at the tree, but more often offerings of tobacco in red, yellow, and black cotton from those who still feel the powerful being of the land and observe the Indian traditions of medicine.

The reason the tree was considered nameworthy at all amid the surrounding forest of nameless cedars is that it appears to be the oldest tree, and it also appears to be rootless. There is a mystery as to how it holds and is held by the rocks. It is an oracle of survival, having lived with no visible sustenance and apparently without anchor through the strong winds, stone-cracking ice, and shifting earth. Because of its tenacity, it has earned the right to a name.

In many ways Indian people are like that tree. Rootless, it seems sometimes, the trunk of our traditions growing twisted and gnarled by the strong winds and ice storms of history—invasions, and the constant threat of extinction. We have seen our most sacred ways of knowing, the special medicines, diminished to witchery and changed into someone else's systems of beliefs.

One day my daughter came home from school and said that in geography they were learning about the Indians and a man named Crazy Horse, and wasn't it terrible what we did to the Indians.

I was quiet. I looked at her. Black hair. Brown skin. She is one of the descendants of the Crazy Horse band. She is an Indian young woman.

"We?" I said. I felt my heart beating in something like fear, a physical reaction, something else like anger. Can all this be lost again—the necessity of history, survival, the lessons our generation fought hard to know, to remember, to pass on?

The truth is, she cannot identify herself with what she has learned of Indians at school, with the words, usually in the past tense, that have been used to describe us. Even with Indian family and friends, even with my hope that her ways will reflect the larger values of our cultures, she does not see herself. And there is also the paradox that the dominating culture imbues the Indian past with great meaning and significance. . . . And it is the romantic past, not the present, that holds meaning and spiritual significance for so many members of the dominating culture. . . .

One of the only things I know for sure is that life is tenacious, and it grows in the most unlikely places. Lichens without water for years can suddenly resurrect after a rain. As we do. At the spring powwow this year in Denver, . . . I saw the young couples, proud and beautiful, holding up their new children to be seen by all of us who have grown through the cracks of history, part of the medicine tree, and for us, with all this new life, every moment is a ceremony.

Stowaway

Armando Socarras Ramírez (as told to Denis Fodor and John Reddy)

Fidel Castro became prime minister of Cuba in 1959. At first he was admired by most Cubans as a dedicated revolutionary. Gradually, however, more and more people became disturbed by his close ties to the Soviet Union and began to leave the country. Many left legally; others found ways to escape. One teenager decided to try a unique method of escape. In "Stowaway," Armando Socarras Ramírez tells the story of his incredible flight from Cuba.

The jet engines of the Iberia Airlines DC-8 thundered in ear-splitting crescendo as the big plane taxied toward where we huddled in the tall grass just off the end of the runway at Havana's José Martí Airport. For months, my friend Jorge Pérez Blanco and I had been planning to stow away in a wheel well on this flight, No. 904—Iberia's once-weekly, nonstop run from Havana to Madrid. Now, in the late afternoon of June 3, 1970, our moment had come.

We realized that we were pretty young to be taking such a big gamble; I was seventeen, Jorge sixteen. But we were both determined to escape from Cuba, and our plans had been carefully made. We knew that departing airliners taxied to the end of the 11,500-foot runway, stopped momentarily after turning around, then roared at full throttle down the runway to take off. We wore rubber-soled shoes to aid us in crawling up the wheels and carried ropes to secure ourselves inside the wheel well. We had also stuffed cotton in our ears as protection against the shriek of the four jet engines. Now we lay sweating with fear as the massive craft swung into its about-face, the jet blast flattening the grass all around us. "Let's run!" I shouted to Jorge.

We dashed onto the runway and sprinted toward the left-hand wheels of the momentarily stationary plane. As Jorge began to scramble up the 42-inch-high tires, I saw there was not room for us both in the single well. "I'll try the other side!" I shouted. Quickly I climbed onto the right wheels, grabbed a strut, and, twisting and wriggling, pulled myself into the semi-dark well. The plane began rolling immediately, and I grabbed some machinery to keep from falling out. The roar of the engines nearly deafened me.

As we became airborne, the huge double wheels, scorching hot from takeoff, began folding into the compartment. I tried to flatten myself against the overhead as they came closer and closer; then, in desperation, I pushed at them with my feet. But they pressed powerfully upward, squeezing me terrifyingly against the roof of the well. Just when I felt that I would be crushed, the wheels locked in place and the bay doors beneath them closed, plunging me into darkness. So there I was, my five-foot-four-inch 140-pound frame literally wedged in amid a spaghettilike maze of conduits and machinery. I could not move enough to tie myself to anything, so I stuck my rope behind a pipe.

Then, before I had time to catch my breath, the bay doors suddenly dropped open again and the wheels stretched out into their landing position. I held on for dear life, swinging over the abyss, wondering if I had been spotted, if even now the plane was turning back to hand me over to Castro's police.

By the time the wheels began retracting again, I had seen a bit of extra space among all the machinery where I could safely squeeze. Now I knew there *was* room for me, even though I could scarcely breathe. After a few minutes, I touched one of the tires and found that it had cooled off. I swallowed some aspirin tablets against the head-splitting noise and began to wish that I had worn something warmer than my light sport shirt and green fatigues.

Up in the cockpit of Flight 904, Captain Valentín Vara del Rey, forty-four, had settled into the routine of the overnight flight, which would last eight hours and twenty minutes. Takeoff had been normal, with the aircraft and its 147 passengers, plus a crew of 10, lifting off at 170 m.p.h. But right after lift-off, something unusual had happened. One of three red lights on the instrument panel had remained lighted, indicating improper retraction of the landing gear.

"Are you having difficulty?" the control tower asked.

"Yes," replied Vara del Rey. "There is an indication that the right wheel hasn't closed properly. I'll repeat the procedure."

The captain relowered the landing gear, then raised it again. This time the red light blinked out.

Dismissing the incident as a minor malfunction, the captain turned his attention to climbing to assigned cruising altitude. On leveling out, he observed that the temperature outside was 41 degrees F. Inside, the pretty stewardesses began serving dinner to the passengers.

Shivering uncontrollably from the bitter cold, I wondered if Jorge had made it into the other wheel well and began thinking about what had brought me to this desperate situation. I thought about my parents and my girl, María Esther, and wondered what they would think when they learned what I had done.

My father is a plumber, and I have four brothers and a sister. We are poor, like most Cubans. Our house in Havana has just one large room; eleven people live in it—or did. Food was scarce and strictly rationed. About the only fun I had was playing baseball and walking with María Esther along the seawall. When I turned sixteen, the government shipped me off to vocational school in Betancourt, a sugarcane village in Matanzas Province. There I was supposed to learn welding, but classes were often interrupted to send us off to plant cane.

Young as I was, I was tired of living in a state that controlled *everyone's* life. I dreamed of freedom. I wanted to become an artist and live in the United States, where I had an uncle. I knew that thousands of Cubans had got to America and done well there. As the time approached when I would be drafted, I thought more and more of trying to get away. But how? I knew that two planeloads of people are allowed to leave Havana for Miami each day, but there is a waiting list of eight hundred thousand for these flights. Also, if you sign up to leave, the government looks on you as a *gusano*—a worm—and life becomes even less bearable.

My hopes seemed futile. Then I met Jorge at a Havana baseball game. After the game we got to talking. I found out that Jorge, like myself, was disillusioned with Cuba. "The system takes away your freedom—forever," he complained.

Jorge told me about the weekly flight to Madrid. Twice we went to the airport to reconnoiter. Once a DC-8 took off and flew directly over us; the wheels were still down, and we could see into the well compartments. "There's enough room in there for me," I remember saying.

These were my thoughts as I lay in the freezing darkness more than five miles above the Atlantic Ocean. By now we had been in the air about an hour, and I was getting lightheaded from the lack of oxygen. Was it really only a few hours earlier that I had bicycled through the rain with Jorge and hidden in the grass? Was Jorge safe? My parents? María Esther? I drifted into unconsciousness.

The sun rose over the Atlantic like a great golden globe, its rays glinting off the silver-and-red fuselage of Iberia's DC-8 as it crossed the European coast high over Portugal. With the end of the 5,563-mile flight in sight, Captain Vara del Rey began his descent toward Madrid's Barajas Airport. Arrival would be at 8 A.M. local time, the captain told his passengers over the intercom, and the weather in Madrid was sunny and pleasant.

Shortly after passing over Toledo, Vara del Rey let down his landing gear. As always, the maneuver was accompanied by a buffeting as the wheels hit the slipstream and a 200-m.p.h. turbulence swirled through the wheel wells. Now the plane went into its final approach; now, a spurt of flame and smoke from the tires as the DC-8 touched down at about 140 m.p.h.

It was a perfect landing—no bumps. After a brief post-flight check, Vara del Rey walked down the ramp steps and stood by the nose of the plane waiting for a car to pick him up, along with his crew.

Nearby, there was a sudden, soft plop as the frozen body of Armando Socarras fell to the concrete apron beneath the plan. José Rocha Lorenzana, a security guard, was the first to reach the crumpled figure. "When I touched his clothes, they were frozen as stiff as wood," Rocha said. "All he did was make a strange sound, a kind of moan."

"I couldn't believe it at first," Vara del Rey said when told of Armando. "But then I went over to see him. He had ice over his nose and mouth. And his color . . ." As he watched the unconscious boy being bundled into a truck, the captain kept exclaiming to himself, "Impossible! Impossible!"

The first thing I remember after losing consciousness was hitting the ground at the Madrid airport. Then I blacked out again and woke up later at the Gran Hospital de la Beneficencia in downtown Madrid, more dead than alive. When they took my temperature, it was so low that it did not even register on the thermometer. "Am I in Spain?" was my first question. And then, "Where's Jorge?" (Jorge is believed to have been knocked down by the jet blast while trying to climb into the other wheel well, and to be in prison in Cuba.)

Doctors said later that my condition was comparable to that of a patient undergoing "deep freeze" surgery—a delicate process performed only under carefully controlled conditions. Dr. José María Pajares, who cared for me, called my survival a "medical miracle," and, in truth, I feel lucky to be alive.

A few days after my escape, I was up and around the hospital, playing cards with my police guard and reading stacks of letters from all over the world. I especially liked one from a girl in California. "You are a hero," she wrote, "but not very wise." My uncle, Elo Fernández, who lives in New Jersey, telephoned and invited me to come to the United States to live with him. The International Rescue Committee arranged my passage and has continued to help me.

I am fine now. I live with my uncle and go to school to learn English. I still hope to study to be an artist. I want to be a good citizen and contribute something to this country, for I love it here. You can smell freedom in the air.

I often think of my friend Jorge. We both knew the risk we were taking, and that we might be killed in our attempt to escape Cuba. But it seemed worth the chance. Even knowing the risks, I would try to escape again if I had to.

Snow
Julia Alvarez

Julia Alvarez left the Dominican Republic for the United States when she was ten years old. She now writes fiction and poetry and teaches writing.

Yolanda: Our first year in New York we rented a small apartment with a Catholic school nearby, taught by the Sisters of Charity, hefty women in long black gowns and bonnets that made them look peculiar, like dolls in mourning. I liked them a lot, especially my grandmotherly fourth grade teacher, Sister Zoe. I had a lovely name, she said, and she had me teach the whole class how to pronounce it. *Yo-lan-da.* As the only immigrant in my class, I was put in a special seat in the first row by the window, apart from the other children so that Sister Zoe could tutor me without disturbing them. Slowly, she enunciated the new words I was to repeat: *laundromat, corn flakes, subway, snow.*

Soon I picked up enough English to understand holocaust was in the air. Sister Zoe explained to a wide-eyed classroom what was happening in Cuba. Russian missiles were being assembled, trained supposedly on New York City. President Kennedy, looking worried too, was on the television at home, explaining we might have to go to war against the Communists. At school, we had air-raid drills: an ominous bell would go off and we'd file into the hall, fall to the floor, cover our heads with our coats, and imagine our hair falling out, the bones in our arms going soft. At home, Mami and my sisters and I said a rosary for world peace. I heard new vocabulary: *nuclear bomb, radioactive fallout, bomb shelter.* Sister Zoe explained how it would happen. She drew a picture of a mushroom on the blackboard and dotted a flurry of chalkmarks for the dusty fallout that would kill us all.

The months grew cold, November, December. It was dark when I got up in the morning, frosty when I followed my breath to school. One morning as I sat at my desk daydreaming out the window, I saw dots in the air like the ones Sister Zoe had drawn—random at first, then lots and lots. I shrieked, "Bomb! Bomb!" Sister Zoe jerked around, her full black skirt ballooning as she hurried to my side. A few girls began to cry.

But then Sister Zoe's shocked look faded. "Why, Yolanda dear, that's snow!" She laughed. "Snow."

"Snow," I repeated. I looked out the window warily. All my life I had heard about the white crystals that fell out of American skies in the winter. From my desk I watched the fine powder dust the sidewalk and parked cars below. Each flake was different, Sister Zoe had said, like a person, irreplaceable and beautiful.

A Story of Conflicts
Yeghia Aslanian

Yeghia Aslanian came to the United States in 1979 and received a doctorate in TESOL (Teaching English to Speakers of Other Languages) from Teachers College, Columbia University, in New York City. He now teaches at the Borough of Manhattan Community College of the City University of New York.

Mine is a story of conflicts. I was born into an Armenian (consequently Christian) family in Isfahan, Iran, a town with a predominantly Islamic culture. I had to cope with the stigma of being a "bad" Armenian or a "dirty" Armenian (depending on who was doing the cursing). Although by the 1960s and '70s you could see Armenians in socially prominent positions, when I was a child we were often looked upon as an alien ethnic group who were not supposed to mingle with Muslims. There was a separate Armenian section of Isfahan, but because the language of instruction at elementary school was Persian (or Farsi), I had two languages and two cultures to grapple with. Having to struggle to catch up with classmates whose mother tongue was Persian, I felt Armenian to be a hindrance to my social progress and social image. As soon as I'd open my mouth to say something, they'd know I was not one of them, so the conversation would end right there and then.

Childhood humiliation can make or break a person; it made me. When I realized that my social image was at stake, at school or in the street, I plotted against myself. I began to devote myself to Persian—reading, copying and memorizing long stretches of Persian texts. I studied my school subjects day in and day out and managed in this way to get a head start over my classmates, rehashing what I had learned for those of them not in the mood to apply themselves. Little by little, I gained acceptance at school—at the expense of my Armenian.

During my first six years of school, I had lessons in Armenian only a few hours a week. In high school the situation was worse, for it was a government school and I was taught no Armenian at all. My Armenian identity was increasingly subjugated. The only place I had a slight possibility of using Armenian was at home—if there was anything parents and children could talk about in a cultural milieu in which children were supposed to be seen and not heard.

My parents were functionally illiterate in Persian, and so if I read a doctor's prescription (which was always in Persian) for them, they considered me worthy of all the money they'd spent on me and all the troubles they'd endured for me. I always suspect that my desire for learning was a response to my parents' being illiterate. That I graduated from school with honors heightened their confidence in me, and it also made it clear to me that I could maintain my self-esteem in my little world without Armenian. And yet, because I had not achieved the proficiency in my parents' language that other Armenian students normally acquired by high school, if I ran into a friend who "knew" Armenian, I'd feel inferior to him. The two languages and the two cultures were tearing me apart.

When it was time to go to the university, I stayed awake many a night pondering my future. What to do? Wishing to preserve both my self and my image, I could not choose between my two equally powerful cultural heritages, in both of which I thought I had somehow failed. An answer presented itself in English, which I had studied as a foreign language in high school, with enough success so that from the very beginning I thought, or at least my teachers thought, that I had a special ability for languages. In fact, the pull of English had been so irresistible that I enrolled in a night school to study it further. Now, thinking it would resolve my dilemma, I made English language and literature my undergraduate major. I devoted myself completely to this third route, shutting off the other two, except for the occasional required course in Persian and answering some friends' letters in Armenian. I felt great relief and was finally at peace with myself. Or was I?

I received a BA in English language and literature from Tehran University, an MA in Teaching English as a Second Language from the American University in Beirut, and a doctorate from Columbia's Teachers College in Teaching English to Speakers of Other Languages. But when I finished this last degree, I realized that I wasn't at peace with my English identity either, that abandoning the two worlds that had formed me had cost [caused] me excruciating pain, and that to be truly happy with myself I had to recapture the Armenian and Persian languages. I made up my mind to regain my origins. I began to read, write, and translate from English to Persian and vice versa. I opened my long-forgotten Armenian books—I have very few of them!—reading them very slowly. And as I've grown a bit more comfortable, I've started reading Armenian classic and modern literature. I feel I'm coming alive again.

If all goes well, my daughter will have to learn four languages: English, Armenian, Italian (my wife is Italian), and Persian. I think the idea of using only English in this country ignores the cultural wealth and linguistic variety that immigrants have always brought with them. A society like this one should be able to tolerate differences and make the best of them. I'm aware of how our ESL students are enriched by their struggle to learn a new language and adapt to a new culture at the same time they work to preserve their own heritage. I myself rarely miss the two weekly one-hour radio programs in Armenian and Persian on WEVD, "the station that speaks your language." And as I try hard to grow in my three languages and cultures, I find my inner conflicts gradually subsiding. Or at least I think so, and thinking is a reality.

Chocolate Tears and Dreams
Summer 1953

Evelyn C. Rosser

> *Evelyn Rosser grew up as the only girl in a family of five in rural Georgia. She learned to entertain herself by reading, and she began to write stories, like the ones she had read in books. As a teenager, though, she began to write for a different reason: She used her journal to express her secrets, fears, and dreams. She says, "I could not have survived without it."*

Summer 1953   Today my brothers and I went to the movies. Last week Dick Tracy was trapped in a well. I had to know whether he got out alive. On the way to the movies, we noticed a new ice cream parlor. My brother Sonny said we had enough money to buy a five-cent cone each. Edward wanted strawberry. Sonny wanted vanilla. I wanted chocolate.

A teenage white girl was standing behind the counter. When we reached the counter, she walked away. She busied herself cleaning a table. We stood at the counter and waited for her to finish cleaning the table. She turned her head to look at us and started wiping the table again. By that time my brother Sonny was mad. He knocked hard on the counter several times. The girl didn't turn around. Sonny knocked again, this time louder. The girl ran from the room. A mean-looking man came out, drying his hands on a stained apron. "What do you want?" he yelled at us. "We want some ice cream," my brother answered. The man just stared at him. "I mean we want to buy some ice cream," added my brother. The man continued to stare. Then he said, "We don't serve niggers here!" He walked away, leaving us alone at the counter.

My brother Sonny wanted to jump across the counter and smash his face in. I begged him not to. I could do without the ice cream. We went to the movies, but I had a hard time keeping my mind on Dick Tracy. Today was the first time someone has ever called me a nigger to my face. Mama was right, I'm getting too old to play with dolls. There are more important things to think about.

I Stop Writing the Poem
Tess Gallagher

Tess Gallagher is a writer of poetry, essays, and fiction. She lives in Port Angeles, Washington, where she is completing a book of short stories to be published by Scribner in 1997. This poem appears in Moon Crossing Bridge, *her tribute to her late husband, Raymond Carver.*

I Stop Writing the Poem

to fold the clothes. No matter who lives
or who dies, I'm still a woman.
I'll always have plenty to do.
I bring the arms of his shirt
together. Nothing can stop
our tenderness. I'll get back
to the poem. I'll get back to being
a woman. But for now
there's a shirt, a giant shirt
in my hands, and somewhere a small girl
standing next to her mother
watching to see how it's done.

Becoming/The True Self

What lies behind us and what lies before us are small matters compared to what lies within us.

RALPH WALDO EMERSON

1. Read the title of this unit. What does it mean to you? In your reading log, write for a few minutes about the title.

2. Read the quote. What connection do you see between Emerson's words and the title? Freewrite for five more minutes about the title and the quotation.

3. Reread what you wrote and underline two ideas you like. Summarize these ideas for a partner. Read your partner's summary. Then write down one connection between your ideas and your partner's. Share your ideas with your group.

BEFORE READING

1. Read the introductory information. What does the term *self-esteem* mean to you? Write for five minutes in your log about your personal definition of self-esteem.

2. Make a list of the characteristics of your true self in your log.

3. Read "Believing in the True Self."

Believing in the True Self
Gloria Steinem

Gloria Steinem has been an articulate campaigner for women's rights since the 1960s. In 1972, she founded Ms., *a magazine on women's issues edited by women. In her book,* Revolution from Within: A Book of Self-Esteem, *she discusses how and why we develop, or don't develop, self-esteem.*

If you bring forth what is within you, what you bring forth will save you. If you do not bring forth what is within you, what you do not bring forth will destroy you.

JESUS, *The Gnostic Gospels**

Why does one baby reach for certain toys, while another doesn't? Why does one respond more to touch and another to sound? Or one thrive on company and another on calm? No one knows—but we do know that frequent frustration of these preferences will make an infant irritable and angry, then uncertain, passive, and finally unlikely to initiate anything at all.

Why does one child choose to color with paints while another builds with blocks? Why does one create adventures in the imagination while another seeks them in the outside world? No one knows—but we do know that children who are encouraged to follow their own interests actually learn more, internalize and retain that learning better, become more creative, and

*The Gnostic Gospels—written about two centuries after the death of Jesus, rediscovered only in 1945, and not fully translated until the 1970s—are the record of a Jesus who presented himself as a teacher, not the son of God, and taught that God is within each of us. For background and major quotations, see Elaine Pagels, *The Gnostic Gospels*, New York: Random House, 1979; Vintage, 1981.

have healthier and more durable self-esteem than those who are motivated by reward, punishment, or competition with other children.

Why do some adults absorb information better by hearing it than seeing it? Why does one sibling remember stories and ideas while another remembers names and numbers? Why are some people gifted at languages, and still others drawn to anything mechanical? Why do some have perfect pitch and others have "green thumbs"? Why are some of us alert in the morning and others hopeless until noon; some gregarious and others shy; some sexually attracted to the same gender, some to the opposite gender, and some to the individual regardless of gender? No one knows. But we do know that, like children, adults whose innermost feelings and preferences are ignored, ridiculed, punished, or repressed come to believe that there is something profoundly, innately "wrong" with them. And conversely, those who are able to honor these inner promptings know what it is to feel at home with themselves.

AFTER READING

1. Look at the passage and number the "why" questions. Choose one question and freewrite about it in your log.

2. With your partner, talk about what you wrote. Then look at how Steinem answered the question. Is her answer similar to or different from yours?

HOW IT'S WRITTEN

1. Reread the whole piece again. Notice that the sentences are arranged the same way in each paragraph. This is called *parallel structure*. Describe the structure to your group.

2. Talk with the class about the effect of using parallel structure.

TOPICS FOR WRITING

Choose one activity.

Activity A: Think of a family member or close friend who is different from you in one or several of the ways mentioned in this passage. Write about the difference(s) and include an incident that showed the difference(s) clearly.

Activity B: Interview an older person who has known you all your life. Find out what you were like as a child. Write up the interview.

Activity C: Reread the quotation from the Gnostic Gospels at the beginning of this piece. Write an essay explaining what the quotation means to you. Use personal examples to illustrate its meaning.

AFTER WRITING

1. Exchange your paper with two other people in your group. Read each of their papers several times. Think about what the person is saying or trying to say. If you wish, mark some of the key sentences. Then write a three- or four-sentence summary of what you think each person is saying.

2. Read your readers' summaries of your own paper. Think about how you could make your ideas clearer. Write your thoughts or insights in your log.

3. Revise your piece.

BEFORE READING

1. Read the title and introductory information. Freewrite for five minutes about what might make someone decide to become a writer.

2. Read the essay.

Becoming a Writer
Russell Baker

Growing Up, *Russell Baker's autobiographical account of his youth, includes this story of his early decision to become a writer.*

The notion of becoming a writer had flickered off and on in my head . . . but it wasn't until my third year in high school that the possibility took hold. Until then I'd been bored by everything associated with English courses. I found English grammar dull and baffling. I hated the assignments to turn out "compositions," and went at them like heavy labor, turning out laden, lackluster paragraphs that were agonies for teachers to read and for me to write. The classics thrust on me to read seemed as deadening as chloroform.

When our class was assigned to Mr. Fleagle for third-year English I anticipated another grim year in that dreariest of subjects. Mr. Fleagle was notorious among City students for dullness and inability to inspire. He was said to be stuffy, dull, and hopelessly out of date. To me he looked to be sixty or seventy and prim to a fault. He wore primly severe eyeglasses, his wavy hair was primly cut and primly combed. He wore prim vested suits with neckties blocked primly against the collar buttons of his primly starched white shirts. He had a primly pointed jaw, a primly straight nose, and prim manner of speaking that was so correct, so gentlemanly, that he seemed a comic antique.

I anticipated a listless, unfruitful year with Mr. Fleagle and for a long time was not disappointed. We read *Macbeth*. Mr. Fleagle loved *Macbeth* and wanted us to love it too, but he lacked the gift of infecting others with his own passion. He tried to convey the murderous ferocity of Lady Macbeth one day by reading aloud the passage that concludes

> . . . I have given suck, and know
> How tender 'tis to love the babe that milks me.
> I would, while it was smiling in my face,
> Have plucked my nipple from his boneless gums. . . .

The idea of prim Mr. Fleagle plucking his nipple from boneless gums was too much for the class. We burst into gasps of irrepressible snickering. Mr. Fleagle stopped.

"There is nothing funny, boys, about giving suck to a babe. It is the—the very essence of motherhood, don't you see."

He constantly sprinkled his sentences with "don't you see." It wasn't a question but an exclamation of mild surprise at our ignorance. "Your pronoun needs an antecedent, don't you see," he would say, very primly. "The purpose of the Porter's scene, boys, is to provide comic relief from the horror, don't you see."

Late in the year we tackled the informal essay. "The essay, don't you see, is the . . ." My mind went numb. Of all forms of writing, none seemed so boring as the essay. Naturally we would have to write informal essays. Mr. Fleagle distributed a homework sheet offering us a choice of topics. None was quite so simpleminded as "What I Did on My Summer Vacation," but most seemed to be almost as dull. I took the list home and dawdled until the night before the essay was due. Sprawled on the sofa, I finally faced up to the grim task, took the list out of my notebook, and scanned it. The topic on which my eye stopped was "The Art of Eating Spaghetti."

This title produced an extraordinary sequence of mental images. Surging up to the depths of memory came a vivid recollection of a night in Belleville when all of us were seated around the supper table—Uncle Allen, my mother, Uncle Charlie, Doris, Uncle Hal—and Aunt Pat served spaghetti for supper. Spaghetti was an exotic treat in those days. Neither Doris nor I had ever eaten spaghetti, and none of the adults had enough experience to be good at it. All the good humor of Uncle Allen's house reawoke in my mind as I recalled the laughing arguments we had that night about the socially respectable method for moving spaghetti from plate to mouth.

Suddenly I wanted to write about that, about the warmth and good feeling of it, but I wanted to put it down simply for my own joy, not for Mr. Fleagle. It was a moment I wanted to recapture and hold for myself. I wanted to relive the pleasure of an evening at New Street. To write it as I wanted, however, would violate all the rules of formal composition I'd learned in school, and Mr. Fleagle would surely give it a failing grade. Never mind. I would write something else for Mr. Fleagle after I had written this thing for myself.

When I finished it the night was half gone and there was no time left to compose a proper, respectable essay for Mr. Fleagle. There was no choice next morning but to turn in my private reminiscence of Belleville. Two days passed before Mr. Fleagle returned the graded papers, and he returned everyone's but mine. I was bracing myself for a command to report to Mr. Fleagle immediately after school for discipline when I saw him lift my paper from his desk and rap for the class's attention.

"Now, boys," he said, "I want to read you an essay. This is titled 'The Art of Eating Spaghetti.'"

And he started to read. My words! He was reading *my words*, out loud to the entire class. What's more, the entire class was listening. Listening attentively. Then somebody laughed, then the entire class was laughing, and not in contempt and ridicule, but with openhearted enjoyment. Even Mr. Fleagle stopped two or three times to repress a small prim smile.

I did my best to avoid showing pleasure, but what I was feeling was pure ecstasy at this startling demonstration that my words had the power to make people laugh. In the eleventh grade, at the eleventh hour as it were, I had discovered a calling. It was the happiest moment of my entire school career. When Mr. Fleagle finished he put the final seal on my happiness by saying, "Now that, boys, is an essay, don't you see. It's—don't you see—it's of the very essence of the essay, don't you see. Congratulations, Mr. Baker."

For the first time, light shone on a possibility. It wasn't a very heartening possibility, to be sure. Writing couldn't lead to a job after high school, and it was hardly honest work, but Mr. Fleagle had opened a door for me. After that I ranked Mr. Fleagle among the finest teachers in the school.

AFTER READING

In your reading log, make a double entry. On the left page of your notebook, copy sentences, phrases, or ideas that interest you, or tell in your own words some of what you understood about the essay. On the right page of your notebook, write your reactions, feelings, thoughts, associations, and so on. (See Appendix B.2, pp. 230–232, for an explanation and examples of double entries.) Reread the essay as necessary.

HOW IT'S WRITTEN

1. Reread the second paragraph. Notice all the ways Baker gives a detailed description of Mr. Fleagle. Make a list of the details Baker uses to help us "see" Mr. Fleagle.

2. Reread the second paragraph. Underline *prim* or *primly* each time Baker uses these words. Why do you think he repeats these words so many times? Discuss this with your group.

TOPICS FOR WRITING

Choose one activity.

Activity A: Write a description of someone you know well. Use Russell Baker's writing as a model. That is, write a sentence that tells this person's age. Then write a sentence that describes one distinguishing feature of the person's face and hair. Next, write a sentence that describes this person's clothing. Return to the face and write a sentence that describes two features of the face, and end this sentence with a description of the way this person speaks.

   Read over what you have written. Is there one word that goes with this person the way *primly* goes with Mr. Fleagle? If so, include the word in your description at least ten times.

Activity B: Russell Baker describes the moment when Mr. Fleagle read his essay aloud in class as "the happiest moment of my entire school career." Write a short essay about the happiest moment in your school career. Tell the story step-by-step the way Russell Baker did.

Activity C: We have all had people in our lives who influenced us in some way to make a choice about our future. Write an essay in which you describe a person who influenced you. Include in your essay a description of this person that helps readers to visualize him or her.

AFTER WRITING

1. Read your writing aloud to your group. Ask group members to tell you what they understood and what details stood out for them.

2. Choose one person from the group to report to the class, giving a one- or two-sentence summary of what each person in the group wrote about.

3. In your log, write about how you wrote this piece. Was it easy or hard? What part was the most difficult? The easiest? Explain. Did the reading affect the way you wrote? If so, how?

BEFORE READING

1. Think about the name of the main character of the story, "Johnnie-ruth." Is it a boy's name or a girl's? How do you know? Discuss this name with your group. Are there names in your native language that are a combination of a man's and a woman's?

2. Look through the passage. Note the small breaks (marked by *). While reading, when you get to each break, stop and write in your reading log one thing that is in your mind (for example, a question, a reaction, confusion, an association, an image, or a prediction). Now read "Johnnieruth."

Johnnieruth
Becky Birtha

Becky Birtha is an African-American lesbian writer. She has published two books of short stories. "Johnnieruth," the story included here, won a Pushcart Prize, a national award for short fiction published by small presses.

Summertime. Nighttime. Talk about steam heat. This whole city get like the bathroom when somebody in there taking a shower with the door shut. Nights like that, can't nobody sleep. Everybody be outside, sitting on they steps or else dragging half they furniture out on the sidewalk—kitchen chairs, card tables—even bringing TVs outside.

Womenfolks, mostly. All the grown women around my way look just the same. They all big—stout. They got big bosoms and big hips and fat legs, and they always wearing runover houseshoes, and them shapeless, flowered numbers with the buttons down the front. Cept on Sunday. Sunday morning they all turn into glamour girls, in them big hats and long gloves, with they skinny high heels and they skinny selves in them tight girdles—wouldn't nobody ever know what they look like the rest of the time.

When I was a little kid I didn't wanna grow up, cause I never wanted to look like them ladies. I heard Miz Jenkins down the street one time say she don't mind being fat cause that way her husband don't get so jealous. She say it's more than one way to keep a man. Me, I don't have me no intentions of keeping no man. I never understood why they was in so much demand anyway, when it seem like all a woman can depend on em for is making sure she keep on having babies.

*

We got enough children in my neighborhood. In the summertime, even the little kids allowed to stay up till eleven or twelve o'clock at night—playing in the street and hollering and carrying on—don't never seem to get tired. Don't nobody care, long as they don't fight.

Me—I don't hang around no front steps no more. Hot nights like that, I get out my ten speed and I be gone.

That's what I like to do more than anything else in the whole world. Feel that wind in my face keeping me cool as a air conditioner, shooting along like a snowball. My bike light as a kite. I can really get up some speed.

All the guys around my way got ten speed bikes. Some of the girls got em too, but they don't ride em at night. They pedal around during the day, but at nighttime they just hang around out front, watching babies and running they mouth. I didn't get my Peugeot to be no conversation piece.

My mama don't like me to ride at night. I tried to point out to her that she ain't never said nothing to my brothers, and Vincent a year younger than me. (And Langston two years older, in case "old" is the problem.) She say, "That's different, Johnnieruth. You're a girl." Now I wanna know how is anybody gonna know that. I'm skinny as a knifeblade turned sideways, and all I ever wear is blue jeans and a Wrangler jacket. But if I bring that up, she liable to get started in on how come I can't be more of a young lady, and fourteen is old enough to start taking more pride in my appearance, and she gonna be ashamed to admit I'm her daughter.

I just tell her that my bike be moving so fast can't nobody hardly see me, and couldn't catch me if they did. Mama complain to her friends how I'm wild and she can't do nothing with me. She know I'm gonna do what I want no matter what she say. But she know I ain't getting in no trouble, neither.

Like some of the boys I know stole they bikes, but I didn't do nothing like that. I'd been saving my money ever since I can remember, every time I could get a nickel or a dime outta anybody.

*

When I was a little kid, it was hard to get money. Seem like the only time they ever give you any was on Sunday morning, and then you had to put it in the offering. I used to hate to do that. In fact, I used to hate everything about Sunday morning. I had to wear all them ruffly dresses—that shiny slippery stuff in the wintertime that got to make a noise every time you move your ass a inch on them hard old benches. And that scratchy starchy stuff in the summertime with all them scratchy crinolines. Had to carry a pocketbook and wear them shiny shoes. And the church we went to was all the way over on Summit Avenue, so the whole damn neighborhood could get a good look. At least all the other kids'd be dressed the same way. The boys think they slick cause they get to wear pants, but they still got to wear a white shirt and a tie; and them dumb hats they wear can't hide them baldheaded haircuts, cause they got to take the hats off in church.

There was one Sunday when I musta been around eight. I remember it was before my sister Corletta was born, cause right around then was when I put my foot down about the whole sanctimonious routine. Anyway, I was dragging my feet along Twenty-fifth Street in back of Mama and Vincent and them, when I spied this lady. I only seen her that one time, but I still remember just how she look. She don't look like nobody I ever seen before. I *know* she don't live around here. She real skinny. But she ain't no real young woman, either. She could be old as my mama. She ain't nobody's mama—I'm sure. And she ain't wearing Sunday clothes. She got on blue jeans and a man's blue working shirt, with the tail hanging out. She got patches on her blue jeans, and she still got her chin stuck out like she some kinda African royalty. She ain't carrying no shiny pocketbook. It don't look like she care if she got any money or not, or who know it, if she don't. She ain't wearing no house-shoes, or stockings or high heels neither.

Mama always speak to everybody, but when she pass by this lady she make like she ain't even seen her. But I get me a real good look, and the lady stare right back at me. She got a funny look on her face, almost like she think she know me from some place. After she pass on by, I had to turn around to get another look, even though Mama say that ain't polite. And you know what? She was turning around, too, looking back at me. And she give me a great big smile.

I didn't know too much in them days, but that's when I first got to thinking about how it's got to be different ways to be, from the way people be around my way. It's got to be places where it don't matter to nobody if you all dressed up on Sunday morning or you ain't. That's how come I started saving money. So, when I got enough, I could go away to some place like that.

*

Afterwhile I begun to see there wasn't no point in waiting around for handouts, and I started thinking of ways to earn my own money. I used to be running errands all the time—mailing letters for old Grandma Whittaker and picking up cigarettes and newspapers up the corner for everybody. After I got bigger, I started washing cars in the summer, and shoveling people sidewalk in the wintertime. Now I got me a newspaper route. Ain't never been no girl around here with no paper route, but I guess everybody got it figured out by now that I ain't gonna be like nobody else.

The reason I got me my Peugeot was so I could start to explore. I figured I better start looking around right now, so when I'm grown, I'll know exactly where I wanna go. So I ride around every chance I get.

Last summer, I used to ride with the boys a lot. Sometimes eight or ten of us'd just go cruising around the streets together. All of a sudden my mama decide she don't want me to do that no more. She say I'm too old to be spending so much time with boys. (That's what they tell you half the time, and the other half the time they worried cause you ain't interested in spending more time with boys. Don't make much sense.) She want me to have some girl friends, but I never seem to fit in with none of the things the girls doing. I used to think I fit in more with the boys.

But I seen how Mama might be right, for once. I didn't like the way the boys was starting to talk about girls sometimes. Talking about what some girl be like from the neck on down, and talking all up underneath somebody clothes and all. Even though I wasn't really friends with none of the girls, I still didn't like it. So now I mostly just ride around by myself. And Mama don't like that neither—you just can't please her.

*

This boy that live around the corner on North Street, Kenny Henderson, started asking me one time if I don't ever be lonely, cause he always see me by myself. He say don't I ever think I'd like to have me somebody special to go places with and stuff. Like I'd pick him if I did! Made me wanna laugh in his face. I do be lonely, a lotta times, but I don't tell nobody. And I ain't met nobody yet that I'd really rather be with than be by myself. But I will someday. When I find that special place where everybody different, I'm gonna find somebody there I can be friends with. And it ain't gonna be no dumb boy.

I found me one place already, that I like to go to a whole lot. It ain't even really that far away—by bike—but it's on the other side of the Avenue. So I don't tell Mama and them I go there, cause they like to think I'm right around the neighborhood someplace. But this neighborhood too dull for me. All the houses look just the same—no porches, no yards, no trees—not even no parks around here. Every block look so much like every other block it hurt your eyes to look at, afterwhile. So I ride across Summit Avenue and go down that big steep hill there, and then make a sharp right at the bottom and cross the bridge over the train tracks. Then I head on out the boulevard—that's the nicest part, with all them big trees making a tunnel over the top, and lightning bugs shining in the bushes. At the end of the boulevard you get to this place call the Plaza.

It's something like a little park—the sidewalks is all bricks and they got flowers planted all over the place. The same kind my mama grow in that painted-up tire she got out from masquerading like a garden decoration—only seem like they smell sweeter here. It's a big high fountain right in the middle, and all the streetlights is the real old-fashion kind. That Plaza is about the prettiest place I ever been.

Sometimes something going on there. Like a orchestra playing music or some man or lady singing. One time they had a show with some girls doing some kinda foreign dances. They look like they were around my age. They all had on these fancy costumes, with different color ribbons all down they back. I wouldn't wear nothing like that, but it looked real pretty when they was dancing.

I got me a special bench in one corner where I like to sit, cause I can see just about everything, but wouldn't nobody know I was there. I like to sit still and think, and I like to watch people. A lotta people be coming there at night—to look at the shows and stuff, or just to hang out and cool off. All different kinda people.

*

This one night when I was sitting over in that corner where I always be at, there was this lady standing right near my bench. She mostly had her back turned to me and she didn't know I was there, but I could see her real good. She had on this shiny purple shirt and about a million silver bracelets. I kinda liked the way she look. Sorta exotic, like she maybe come from California or one of the islands. I mean she had class—standing there posing with her arms folded. She walk away a little bit. Then turn around and walk back again. Like she waiting for somebody.

Then I spotted this dude coming over. I spied him all the way cross the Plaza. Looking real fine. Got on a three piece suit. One of them little caps sitting on a angle. Look like leather. He coming straight over to this lady I'm watching and then she seen him too and she start to smile, but she don't move till he get right up next to her. And then I'm gonna look away, cause I can't stand to watch nobody hugging and kissing on each other, but all of a sudden I see it ain't no dude at all. It's another lady.

Now I can't stop looking. They smiling at each other like they ain't seen one another in ten years. Then the one in the purple shirt look around real quick—but she don't look just behind her—and sorta pull the other one right back into the corner where I'm sitting at, and then they put they arms around each other and kiss—for a whole long time. Now I really know I oughtta turn away, but I can't. And I know they gonna see me when they finally open they eyes. And they do.

They both kinda gasp and back up, like I'm the monster that just rose up outta the deep. And then I guess they can see I'm only a girl, and they look at one another—and start to laugh! Then they just turn around and start to walk away like it wasn't nothing at all. But right before they gone, they both look around again, and see I still ain't got my eye muscles and my jaw muscles working right again yet. And the one lady wink at me. And the other one say, "Catch you later."

I can't stop staring at they backs, all the way across the Plaza. And then, all of a sudden, I feel like I got to be doing something, got to be moving.

I wheel on outta the Plaza and I'm just concentrating on getting up my speed. Cause I can't figure out what to think. Them two women kissing and then, when they get caught, just laughing about it. And here I'm laughing too, for no reason at all. I'm sailing down the boulevard laughing like a lunatic, and then I'm singing at the top of my lungs. And climbing that big old hill up to Summit Avenue is just as easy as being on a escalator.

AFTER READING

1. Share with your group one question, reaction, confusion, or association from your log. Talk about these.

2. As a group, summarize your discussions for the class.

HOW IT'S WRITTEN

1. "Johnnieruth" is a story told in the voice of a working-class African-American teenager who speaks African-American or Black English, one of the many varieties of English spoken in the world today. This variety of English has its own set of grammatical rules, just like Standard American English. With a partner, find examples that show the following rules being applied in Johnnieruth's speech. (The rules are excerpted from Smitherman, *Talkin and Testifyin*.)

   a. Rule: *BE* is not used to describe things that don't happen again and again. That is, if it's unusual, omit forms of the verb *be*.

   EXAMPLE:

   African-American English: The coffee cold.
   Standard American English: The coffee is cold.

   b. Rule: *BE* is used only if something happens every day.

   EXAMPLE:

   African-American English: He be tired.
   Standard American English: He is tired everyday.

   c. Rule: *BE* is not used before adjectives when they describe something that does not change.

   EXAMPLE:

   African-American English: He tall.
   Standard American English: He is tall.

   d. Rule: Most verbs do not change for person. That is, the same form of the verb is used for I, you, he, she, it, etc.

EXAMPLE:

African-American English: He do the same.
Standard American English: He does the same.

2. With a partner, look through the story and see if you can identify another grammatical rule of African-American English that is not listed above. Discuss what you found with the whole class.

3. Write for five minutes in your log about when it would be appropriate to speak a different variety of English and when it would be appropriate to speak Standard American English. Discuss what you wrote with your group and with the whole class.

TOPICS FOR WRITING

Choose one activity.

Activity A: On her way to church, when Johnnieruth sees the woman who is dressed differently, she says to herself, "I didn't know too much in them days, but that's when I first got to thinking about how it's got to be different ways to be, from the way people be around my way." Write a composition about the first time you realized there were other ways to be besides the way the people around you were. Be sure to describe the place, the time in your life, the situation, the people around you, your feelings toward them, and exactly what made you realize things could be different.

Activity B: As Johnnieruth rides her bicycle back up the hill at the end of the story, she thinks about "Them two women kissing and then, when they get caught, just laughing about it." Describe a time when you expected people to act ashamed and they acted proud instead. What was the situation? How did you react as the witness?

Activity C: Should parents make different rules for boys and girls? Explain your point of view in an essay. Use personal examples or your observations of others to support what you say.

AFTER WRITING

1. Before reading your piece of writing to your group, decide what kind of feedback you'd like to get. For example, you could ask, "Do you like

it?" "Is everything clear?" "How could I make the images stronger?" or "Do you like the ending?" Dictate your questions to your group.

2. Read your writing aloud to your group. Then ask everyone to write a response to your questions. If there's time, the others can share their responses aloud before giving them to you. Notice if the responses are similar or different.

3. In your log, write one or two things you learned about your writing and yourself today.

1. Read the title and introductory information. How are you different from what American culture (or your native culture) says you should be? Write in your log for five minutes.
   Talk about what you wrote with your group.
2. Write down what you understand by the word *homage*. Talk about this with your group.
3. Read "homage to my hips."

homage to my hips
Lucille Clifton

Lucille Clifton is an African-American poet who often writes poems about the parts of her body. She enjoys telling audiences at her readings that she writes poems to celebrate that she is not what American culture tells her she should be: She is not young, not thin, not white.

these hips are big hips
they need space to
move around in.
they don't fit into little
petty places. these hips
are free hips.
they don't like to be held back.
these hips have never been enslaved.
they go where they want to go
they do what they want to do.
these hips are mighty hips.
these hips are magic hips.
i have known them
to put a spell on a man and
spin him like a top!

AFTER READING

1. Write a sentence in your reading log that summarizes the meaning of the poem as you understand it. Compare it with what another person wrote.

2. With a partner, choose one activity.

   Activity A: What would Gloria Steinem think of Lucille Clifton's poem? Support your opinion with a quotation from Steinem's piece.

   Activity B: Make a list, in your own words, of all the things Clifton's hips can and cannot (or will not) do.

   Activity C: Although it claims to be about hips, this poem is also about some social issues. Write down one line of Clifton's poem and then explain the social issue it is about.

3. Share your findings with the class.

TOPICS FOR WRITING

Choose one activity.

Activity A: Choose a sentence from the poem that you find especially meaningful. Copy it down exactly as it's written. Be sure to use quotation marks and tell where you took the sentence from. Then use it as the beginning of something you write: a short essay, a story, a memory, a poem, a letter.

Activity B: Think of a part of your own body that you are especially proud or fond of. Write a poem about it, using Clifton's poem as a model.

Activity C: In the United States, 95 percent of the people enrolled in weight-loss programs are women. What does this tell you about U.S. culture? Do you think women in other countries are also very concerned about losing weight—or being thin? Is this a concern in your native country? Explain this phenomenon. Do you think it is good or bad? Explain your point of view.

AFTER WRITING

1. Give your paper to another person in your group for feedback. If possible, find someone from a different culture and/or a different gender to read it. Ask the person to respond to what you wrote from the perspective of that other culture and/or gender.

2. Write in your log about what you learned from your reader's feedback. Think about the changes you might want to make in your writing to take different kinds of audiences into account.

3. Revise your writing.

BEFORE READING
---

1. With the class, make a cluster around the word *gangs*. (See Appendix A.2, pp. 224–225, if you need to refresh your memory on how to do clustering.)

2. Read the title and the subtitle at the beginning of the article. What do you think this article is going to be about? As a class, predict one thing you think the article might say.

3. Read "Rekindling the Warrior."

Rekindling the Warrior
Gangs Are Part of the Solution, Not Part of the Problem

Luis J. Rodriguez

Luis J. Rodriguez is an award-winning poet, journalist, and critic. He is currently working with a photographer on a book about Salvadoran gang members in Los Angeles and their impact on El Salvador.

Over the past year and a half, I have spoken to thousands of young people at schools, jails, bookstores, colleges, and community centers about the experiences addressed in my book *Always Running: La Vida Loca, Gang Days in L.A.*

What stays with me is the vitality and clarity of the young people I met, many of them labeled "at risk." They saw in my experiences and my book both a reflection of their lives and the possibility of transcendence, of change, which otherwise appears elusive. In those faces I saw the most viable social energy for rebuilding the country and realigning its resources. They are the future, but this society has no clear pathway to take them there.

For one thing, today's youth are under intense scrutiny and attack. Schools, for the most part, fail to engage their creativity and intellect. As a result, young people find their own means of expression—music being the most obvious example, but also the formation of gangs.

Despite conventional thinking, gangs are not anarchies. They can be highly structured, with codes of honor and discipline. For many members, the gang serves as family, as the only place where they can find fellowship, respect, a place to belong. You often hear the word *love* among gang members. Sometimes the gang is the only place where they can find it.

Gabriel Rivera, director of the Transitional Intervention Experience of Bend, Oregon, and a former East Los Angeles gang member, came up with a concept he calls "character in motion" to describe the essence, not the form, of gang participation.

"[Character in motion] is marked by the advertent or inadvertent beginnings of physical, psychological, and spiritual struggle that happens for every young person." writes Rivera. "[It] is what happens when a young person responds to the inevitable inner call to embrace 'the journey,' and chooses to honor that journey above all else with a courage that relies upon connecting with one's 'warrior energy.'"

The warrior needs to be nurtured, directed, and guided—not smothered, crushed, or corralled. This energy needs to be taken to its next highest level of development, where one matures into self-control, self-study, and self-actualization. Most anti-gang measures have nothing to do with any of this. A serious effort would address the burning issue of adolescent rage. It would address a basic need for food, shelter, and clothing, but also needs for expressive creativity and community.

Sociopathic behavior exists within the framework of a sociopathic society. Under these circumstances, gangs are not a problem; they are a solution, particularly for communities lacking economic, social, and political options.

Two examples: Two years ago, I did a poetry reading in a part of eastern Ohio that was once alive with coal mines and industry but now has 50 to 70 percent unemployment in some areas. Many of the young people are selling drugs to survive. In this sense, they could be from the South Bronx or the Pine Ridge Reservation. They are, however, "white." They are listening to their own music ("Wherever kids find obstacles, I find music," an independent record producer recently told *Rolling Stone* magazine), and establishing ganglike structures to survive.

Soon after the 1992 Los Angeles rebellion, members of the Crips and the Bloods, two of the city's most notorious gangs, circulated a plan. They included proposals to repair the schools and streets and get rid of drugs and violence. At the end of the plan, they wrote: "Give us the hammers and the nails, and we will rebuild the city."

It was a demand to take responsibility, which rose from the inner purpose of Crip and Blood warrior consciousness, and a demand for the authority to carry out the plan. Unfortunately, no one took them up on it.

These young people face great barriers to educational advancement, economic stability, and social mobility—but little or none to criminal activity or violence (as everyone knows, prison is no deterrence; for some youth it is a rite of passage).

Power is the issue here. Without autonomy to make decisions that affect their lives, these young people can only attempt to approximate it, too often with disastrous results.

You want to stop the body count? Empower the youth.

AFTER READING

1. Reread the piece, annotating it. Mark the places that you feel you understand very well. Write questions next to the parts you don't understand or are confused by. (See Appendix B.3, pp. 233 and 235, for an explanation of annotating and an example.)

   Using your annotations, discuss the reading with your group.

2. Explain to your group why Rodriguez thinks gangs are a positive, not a negative, phenomenon. Use examples from the text.

3. Write for five minutes in your log about your understanding of the concept of "character in motion." Use your own words. Then explain your ideas to a partner.

HOW I READ IT

Freewrite about *how* you read this piece. For example, how did making predictions (Before Reading, question 2) affect how you read? How accurate were your predictions? What did you do when you came to words you didn't know? (See Appendix C, p. 237, for an explanation and examples of how we read.)

TOPICS FOR WRITING

Choose one activity.

Activity A: Imagine you are inviting Luis Rodriguez and Gloria Steinem to be guest speakers at a meeting of the Los Angeles city government. At the meeting, the city's leaders will decide whether the Crips and the Bloods should be allowed to help rebuild Los Angeles. Write a letter to each of them, explaining why you think it is important for them to be there and what you would like them to emphasize.

Activity B: Write a true story of a situation in which you were a member of a group that adults thought was bad but you knew was really good. Describe the experience. Explain how the adults misjudged the group. Then describe what was really happening in the group. What did you learn from this experience?

Activity C: Imagine that you had the opportunity to interview the leader of one of the major gangs in Los Angeles. Prepare a list of questions you would like to ask the gangleader.

Find two other people who did this activity. Role-play the interview of the gang leader. Have one person play the role of the gang leader and the others play the interviewers. Write down the gang leader's answers. Prepare to present your role-play to the whole class. Ask class members to tell you, based on the article, if they think your role-play is realistic.

AFTER WRITING

If you did Activity A or B, write about how you wrote your piece. If you did Activity C, write about what you learned.

BEFORE READING
---

1. This passage was taken from a short story entitled "Safe." Freewrite in your reading log for five minutes about what the word *safe* means to you.
2. Make a list of situations in which you feel unsafe. What do you do to protect yourself in these situations? Talk about your list with a part-ner. Are there similarities or differences on your lists, or both?
3. Read the passage.

Safe
Cherylene Lee

Cherylene Lee is a prize-winning fiction writer, playwright, and poet. The story "Safe" appeared in an anthology of contemporary Asian-American fiction. This is an excerpt from it.

Safe. That is the most important consideration for our family. Perhaps there is a Chinese gene encoded with a protein for caution. Or perhaps it's because my father's tailor shop is not doing so well or because of my mother's blindness. Perhaps it's because my mother and father married late in life and weren't sure how to protect their children.

We try to take precautions. My mother won't go out at night for fear of what the darkness holds. She doesn't like me to take a shower after dinner for fear I might get a cramp and somehow drown in the shower's spray. She doesn't like me to walk home from school alone, nor does she like me to walk home with boys. She'd rather I walked home with girls, at least three for maximum protection so one can always run for help. I've tried to explain to her, I like walking alone, it's not always possible to walk in female threes, I don't even have that many girlfriends. "You have to watch out at your age, you can't be too safe," she warns, "but don't hang around with the fast ones."

My father is just as bad. He's so afraid someone will dent his car, he won't park in a lot that doesn't have two spaces side by side for his ten-year-old station wagon. He refuses to go into a grocery store if he could be the first or last customer—"That's when robbers are most likely to come." He won't eat in restaurants without first wiping the chopsticks, rice bowl, tea cup, or plate, silverware, and glass—"So many germs everywhere." He has more locks and alarms on his tailor shop door than the bank that's two doors down. It takes him ten minutes to open them up each day, turn off the alarms, before call-ing my mother to let her know that he has arrived safely.

We live in San Francisco—a city with its share of dangers though my parents have done their best to shield my brother and me from having to face most of them. More than from just physical harm, they've tried to protect us from loss—loss of face, loss of happiness, loss of innocence. So far we have been protected by their constant vigilance. Not that I have been sheltered so much I can't go places on my own or do things without my parents' consent, but their warnings, cautions, and dire predictions have had an effect.

AFTER READING

1. Cherylene Lee lists several ways her character's mother and father try to protect themselves and their children from harm. Reread the story and mark with a plus (+) the ways that you have experienced. Mark with a minus (−) the ones you have not experienced. Then freewrite for a few minutes about this.

2. Talk with a partner about what you wrote.

HOW IT'S WRITTEN

1. Choose one activity.

   Activity A: Reread the passage. Underline every word that relates in some way to the idea of safety or protection. Why do you think the author uses so many of these words? What effect does it have on the reader?

   Activity B: The author has a paragraph about the mother and a paragraph about the father. Make a list of the things the mother fears and a list of the things the father fears. What are the similarities and differences between the two parents' fears?

   Activity C: Reread the passage. Look for places where the author tells us how her character feels about her parents' efforts to protect her. Are there places where she agrees or disagrees with her parents? How do you know what her feelings are? Underline any sentences or phrases that help you know her opinion.

2. Share your findings with other people who worked on the same activity. Discuss your findings with the class.

TOPICS FOR WRITING

Choose one activity.

Activity A: Tell the true story of a time you did something your parents warned you not to do. What happened? Did your parents find out? Did you or your parents learn a lesson from this experience?

Activity B: The writer says about the parents in the story, "More than from just physical harm, they've tried to protect us from loss." Tell the true story of some kind of harm your parents tried to protect you from. Tell what happened and draw some conclusions. You may want to discuss these questions: In what ways did your parents try to help you take precautions? In what ways were they influenced by their own upbringing or the countries in which they were raised? Were their efforts to protect you successful? Why or why not?

Activity C: Nowadays, there is a lot of crime in our cities and even in our small towns. What precautions do you think people should take to protect themselves from becoming the victims of crime? Write an essay in which you tell at least three things people can do for protection. Be sure to give examples and explain why you think such precautions are necessary.

AFTER WRITING

1. Read what you wrote to your group. Ask your listeners to restate what they think your important points are and to tell what details especially stand out for them.

2. Give your piece a title, if you haven't already done so.

3. Write in your log about how you wrote this composition. For example, was it easy or difficult to think of examples to support your ideas? Did you use any special techniques to gather ideas?

<hr />

BEFORE READING

1. Read the introductory information. With a partner, make a list of the skills you think a good waitress or waiter should have.

2. Read the story.

I'm Working on My Charm
Dorothy Allison

This is an excerpt from a short story called "I'm Working on my Charm." In this story, a teenage girl works as a waitress in a diner in order to save money to go to college. The girl's mother, who also works in the diner, gives her daughter some tips on how to be a good waitress.

When I was sixteen I worked counter with my mama back of a Moses Drugstore planted in the middle of a Highway 50 shopping mall. I was trying to save money to go to college, and ritually, every night, I'd pour my tips into a can on the back of my dresser. Sometimes my mama'd throw in a share of hers to encourage me, but mostly hers was spent even before we got home—at the Winn Dixie at the far end of the mall or the Maryland Fried Chicken right next to it.

Mama taught me the real skills of being a waitress—how to get an order right, get the drinks there first and the food as fast as possible so it would still be hot, and to do it all with an expression of relaxed good humor. "You don't have to smile," she explained, "but it does help." "Of course," she had to add, "don't go 'round like a grinning fool. Just smile like you know what you're doing, and never *look* like you're in a hurry." I found it difficult to keep from looking like I was in a hurry, especially when I got out of breath running from steam table to counter. Worse, moving at the speed I did, I tended to sway a little and occasionally lost control of a plate.

"Never," my mama told me, "serve food someone has seen fall to the floor. It's not only bad manners, it'll get us all in trouble. Take it in the back, clean it off, and return it to the steam table." After awhile I decided I could just run to the back, count to ten, and take it back out to the customer with an apology. Since I usually just dropped biscuits, cornbread, and baked potatoes—the kind of stuff that would roll on a plate—I figured brushing it off was sufficient. But once, in a real rush to an impatient customer, I watched a ten-ounce T-bone slip right off the plate, flip in the air, and smack the rubber floor mat. The customer's mouth flew open, and I saw my mama's eyes shoot fire. Hurriedly I picked it up by the bone and ran to the back with it. I was running water on it when Mama came in the back room.

"All right," she snapped, "you are not to run, you are not even to walk fast. And," she added, taking the meat out of my fingers and dropping it into the open waste can, "you are not, not ever to drop anything as expensive as that again." I watched smoky frost from the leaky cooler float up toward her blonde curls, and I promised her tearfully that I wouldn't.

AFTER READING

1. Read the story again and underline the skills the mother teaches her daughter. Compare what you underlined with the list you and a partner made before you read the story.

2. The mother tells the daughter to never *look* like she is in a hurry. With your partner, talk about these questions: Why is this an important skill? Does the daughter succeed? Why or why not?

HOW IT'S WRITTEN

The writer never directly says how her mother feels when she drops the steak, but there are several places in the text where we know she is angry. The writer is using language and description to show emotion, not tell it. (See Appendix E, pp. 243–244, for some ideas on showing instead of telling.) Reread the last two paragraphs. Make a list of the words or descriptions the writer uses to show the mother's emotion. Talk to a partner about your list.

TOPICS FOR WRITING

Choose one activity.

Activity A: People often give us advice about how to be a better worker, better student, better son or daughter, or better friend. Sometimes the *way* the advice is given can either help us or make us stay the same.

Tell about a time when you were given some advice. Who gave the advice and why? How was the advice given? Was it given angrily, in a friendly way, critically? How did you feel when you were given this advice? Was the advice useful? Why or why not? Did the way in which you were given the advice affect your response to it? Why or why not?

Activity B: In the story, the mother advises the daughter to take any food she drops into the back, brush it off, and return it to the steam table so it can be served again. There may be times at work when we are asked to cut corners or cheat a little in the interest of getting the job done quickly. Has this ever happened to you? Do you think it is a good idea to cut corners, or should the job always be done properly? Why? Use the example from the story or one from your experience to illustrate your point.

Activity C: Ask someone you know—a friend, family member, or neighbor—to tell you a story about when he or she started working at a new job. Listen and take notes. Write down the story and try to capture the person's voice and the emotions (such as humor, fear, or anger) the person expressed that are part of the story.

AFTER WRITING

1. Attach a blank page to your paper. Pass the paper around so that two or three of your group members can write comments.

2. Read your readers' comments. Then read your writing to someone from another group.

3. Write in your log about what you learned from your three different readers.

BEFORE READING

1. Read the introductory information and title. Make a list of the typical first jobs teenagers have. Which ones have you had? Share your list with your group.

2. Read the essay.

My First Job
Leticia Fuentes

Leticia Fuentes was a student at the Borough of Manhattan Community College, City University of New York, when she wrote this essay. She grew up in Mexico.

I was in high school. I was seventeen years old. I used to go to school, do my homework, and watch TV every single day. One day, I told my mother that I wanted a part time job like other girls had. For example, I wanted to work at a supermarket or clothing store. She encouraged me to do it.

I filled out several applications for jobs in my neighborhood. After two weeks, someone finally called me from McDonald's. A manager told me that my application was accepted and I had to go for an interview. He gave me the date.

During my first interview, I was so nervous. Then I went to an orientation. There were four new workers and each of us was happy. You could see it in our eyes. The orientation lasted about forty-five minutes. The manager, Kevin, explained a little bit about the McDonald's Corporation and its policy. He told us about the staff. We also saw a videotape in which we learned how to punch in and punch out when we arrived and left or took our breaks. After we saw the videotape, we answered some questions. He gave us a chance to ask some questions too. Then each of us received a uniform: a hat, a skirt, a shirt, and a name tag. A few minutes later, the manager introduced us to the crew. On my first day of work, I was one hour early and very nervous. I put on my uniform. I felt odd wearing it, but the worst thing was I had to wear a hat. That hat was my headache the whole time I worked at McDonald's. I didn't like it, but I had to wear it.

The first thing I learned was how to make french fries. It was so easy. First, fill the basket and put it in the hot oil or "computerized french fries machine" as the managers call it. Just press a button and when they are done, the machine tells you. A big red sign goes on when the french fries are done.

Then put a little bit of salt and make up the sizes of french fries by scooping them into the three different containers: small, medium, and large. I worked at the french fries station for two weeks.

On my third week, I learned how to work the cash register. This part was hard. First of all, my English was terrible. I could understand people, but I couldn't speak very well. Sometimes this problem made me feel terrible. But I started to work on it. When I was at home, I used to practice repeating what I had to say. I worked especially on this phrase: "Hi, may I help you?" I also had to learn the names of all the food and the prices of everything. Little by little, I lost my fear to speak out. I made many mistakes, but I learned how to be a good listener and to be very careful with every word I said.

I think I will never forget my first job because it was my first experience like that. I had fun there and met many friends. I learned to work as a team. And you know what? Sometimes I miss my cheeseburgers and french fries.

AFTER READING

Make a list of all the tasks Leticia Fuentes performed in her job at McDonald's. Even though her job may seem repetitive and limited, Fuentes did not seem bored. What made the job challenging for her? Discuss this with your group. Make a list of the valuable skills Fuentes learned on her first job.

HOW IT'S WRITTEN

1. People who write for newspapers try to answer several questions to give their readers the information they need. This is called the *Reporter's Formula*. The questions are: who, what, when, where, why, and how? Make an outline of Fuentes's essay by writing down these questions and listing her answers. Which question(s) does she use to develop her writing in detail?

2. Look back at the first paragraph of the essay. It has several short sentences. Working with a partner, see if you can rewrite the introduction and turn it into three sentences instead of six. Share your revision with your group. Choose the revision you like best to share with the class.

3. Compare the revised introduction with the original. Which one do you prefer? Why?

TOPICS FOR WRITING

Choose one activity.

Activity A: Interviewing people who work

1. Every day we come in contact with people who work. Make a list of questions you could ask people to discover what their work is, how they came to do the work, and how they feel about their work. Include the questions in the Reporter's Formula (who, what, where, when, why, how).

2. Share your questions with someone else who is doing the same activity. Add any questions you didn't think of to your list.

3. Make a list of people you could interview. You can include family, friends, or strangers. Think about the people with whom you come into contact every day.

4. Find someone to interview about his or her job. Write a short essay in which you describe the person, the type of work, how this individual came to do this work, and how this person feels about the work.

Activity B: Exploring your career goals
Read the following questions and freewrite responses to each one.

1. What are your career goals?

2. Imagine you are looking back at your life from your old age. Have you achieved your goals? Are you pleased by what you have done? Why or why not?

3. How did you determine your career goals? In what ways were you influenced by your parents? Your peers? Your likes and dislikes? The current job market?

4. What traits and skills do you already have that will help you succeed in your career goals? What traits and skills do you need to develop?

5. What are the advantages and disadvantages of your particular career goals?

6. Is your goal merely to make a living? Do you hope for wealth or fame? Can you picture yourself really loving what you plan to do?

Write an essay about your career goals. Explain why you have these particular goals, what you think will make you good at this kind of work, what you still need to learn to be good at this work, what the advantages and disadvantages of this work are, and what you hope to accomplish by doing this kind of work.

Activity C: Learning from others/Finding role models

Many people discover they are more likely to succeed in their career goals if they find someone who can serve as a mentor or as a role model for success.

1. Make a list of questions you could ask if you were interviewing someone who has already achieved your career goal. Through your questions, try to discover what difficulties had to be overcome, what advice this person can give you, if this person loves the work, and what the advantages and disadvantages of this career are.

2. Share your questions with someone else who is doing the same activity. Add any questions you didn't think of to your list.

3. Make a list of people you could interview.

4. Interview one of the people on your list. Then write an essay in which you describe the person you interviewed and his or her successes. Include in your essay what you learned from this person.

AFTER WRITING

1. Find other people who chose the same activity to write about. Share your writing with them. Report back to the class what was similar or different about each person's writing, both in *what* they wrote and *how* they wrote it.

2. After hearing the pieces of writing, make a list of the kinds of careers people in your group are pursuing. Share your list with the class. Working together as a class, make a list of the reasons people chose these particular careers. What do people hope to gain by pursuing these careers?

BEFORE READING
---

1. Read the introductory information. Talk to your group about the definitions of *blue-collar* and *white-collar*. How do you make such distinctions in your native culture? Do you have special terms to describe different kinds of work? If so, translate them into English for your group.
2. Read "New-Collar Work"

New-Collar Work
Telephone Sales Reps Do Unrewarding Jobs

Dana Milbank

In this article from The Wall Street Journal, *Dana Milbank describes the stressful working conditions of the three to four million telephone sales representatives in the United States who do "blue-collar jobs in a white-collar world." Milbank uses extensive examples from the lives of individuals to illustrate the difficult lives of these workers.*

Bev DeMille is having a bad night.

The 51-year old telemarketer is on her 14th phone call of the shift, but so far she has sold just one magazine renewal . . . Ms. DeMille glares at her video screen. [She] knows that pressure goes with the job. Working for nine other employers in her 10 years in telemarketing, she has seen co-workers take tranquilizers to relieve stress. She has seen people fired for missing sales targets. When confronted once on a previous job for leaving her desk to go to the ladies room without permission, she retorted: "My bladder couldn't see you. . . ."

That strain is felt by many of the nations estimated three million to four million telephone sales representatives, 70% of whom, according to Telemarketing Magazine, are women. One worker is likely to talk with hundreds of indifferent or outright hostile customers daily, while being monitored by supervisors who insist that sales reps remain cheerful and stick to their scripted patters. Under the circumstances, workers burn out quickly and feel unappreciated. . . .

Tough work, but this sort of job is among the largest segments of the American work force. Ralph Whitehead, a professor at the University of Massachusetts at Amherst who writes about workplace trends, calls them the "new-collar workers." He says they now make up nearly 40% of workers born after 1945. Some are salespeople or data processors, some work in finance or government. What they have in common is computers and telephones. They do blue-collar jobs in a white-collar world.

The new-collar workers spend their days not in factories but in air-conditioned offices. But unlike professionals and executives, who enjoy some variety in their work, they are stuck doing limited and repetitive tasks. They have little time for camaraderie and no chance for advancement.

As it happens, tens of thousands of telemarketers do their thing in Omaha, the industry's hub. Restless in their careers, telemarketers here, as elsewhere, feel capable of more than their work allows them to do. . . .

Each rep will make at least 100 calls in a typical shift. . . . A rep will speak to the person he or she is trying to reach about half the time and will "convert" about 15% of those who hear the "presentation."

A chart on the wall provides a constant measure of performance. It lists everybody's guaranteed pay for the previous week—currently $7.50 per hour—and the actual pay from commissions. The best anybody is doing is to make $13 an hour. . . .

Three weeks into her job . . . Annette Peterson broke down in the middle of a call and began sobbing. An Arkansas man had called her a string of epithets. Before that, a woman advised her, "Why don't you get a real job and a real life?" Others just hung up.

The supervisor took Ms. Peterson aside and reminded her of the first lesson of telemarketing: Don't take the rejection personally. But she does anyway. "Some people talk to you as if you're scum," she says. "That's why most people quit."

Of course, telemarketing work has its attractions for some people: students, retirees, homemakers and others who aren't suited for or inclined to do blue-collar jobs and don't want the responsibility of a professional job. Others see this work as something to do when they are between jobs and looking for other employment. . . .

Bev DeMille agrees: "This job is nobody's first choice—it becomes a way of life when you can't do anything else."

But like many other new-collar workers, Ms. DeMille sees no good alternative. "Who's going to hire someone 51 years old with a bum back?" she asks. "It's all I've got left to do. I'm going to retire in another 14 years, if I can just hang on that long."

AFTER READING

1. Choose one activity. Make sure each activity is done by at least one person in your group.

Activity A: Read the article again and write down the answers to the basic questions in the Reporter's Formula: who, what, when, where, why, and how.

Activity B: Read the article again. Make a list of all the main ideas in the article. Under each main idea, list the facts and examples the writer uses to support that idea.

Activity C: Newspaper articles are often a mixture of facts, opinions, and examples. Go through the article again, labeling each fact (f), opinion (o), or example (e) you find.

2. Talk to your group about what you did in the activity you chose.

HOW IT'S WRITTEN

Dana Milbank, the author of this article, interviewed new-collar workers and toured one of their workplaces. Find the places where she integrated this material into the article. Discuss with your group how the author did this.

TOPICS FOR WRITING

Choose one activity.

Activity A: With a partner, interview and observe people who work at your school whose jobs seem especially limited, repetitive, or stressful. If possible, write down the workers' exact words and carefully observe their relationship to their work environment. Write an article for your school newspaper about these workers.

Activity B: With a partner, interview and observe people who work at your school whose jobs seem particularly challenging, rewarding, stimulating, or relaxing. If possible, write down their exact words and carefully observe their relationship to their work environment. Write a composition comparing the jobs of the workers you interviewed and observed with those of the new-collar workers described in the article.

Activity C: Write a summary of this article, using the following steps.

Preparation

1. What are the answers to the questions: who, what, when, where, why, and how? (See Activity A in the After Reading section for this article.)

2. Write down the main ideas in the article and the facts and examples used to support those ideas. (See Activity B in the After Reading section.)

Writing

3. Write a one-paragraph summary of the article in your own words. Be sure to summarize all of the information you wrote down in the preparation section.

AFTER WRITING

Talk with your group about which activity you did, how it went, and how you wrote.

BEFORE READING

1. In your group, define the following terms: *cooperative, small business, big business*, and *nonprofit corporation*. (You may use a dictionary.) Discuss these various kinds of structures: who has the top job, who makes the decisions, how is the work done, and how are earnings divided.

2. This piece is about a bakery cooperative, a nonprofit corporation. Tell your group one thing you think it will say.

3. Read "The Bread Shop."

The Bread Shop
(interview with Kay Stepkin, Director of the Bakery Cooperative)

Studs Terkel

> *A native of Chicago, Studs Terkel has traveled all over the world doing interviews with people about many topics, including work, the Great Depression, and American dreams. Many of these interviews appear in Terkel's books. The interview below is an excerpt from his book,* Working: People Talk About What They Do All Day and How They Feel About What They Do. *The first five paragraphs of the reading are Terkel's introduction to the interview.*

We're in The Bread Shop. "We've taught all sorts of people how to make bread. The Clay People are across the street. They teach people ceramics. The Weaving Workshop is a block down. They give lessons in weaving and teach people how to make their own looms. . . . It's an incredible neighborhood. . . ."

There are posters in the window and stickers on the door: "Peace and Good Will Toward People"; "Children of the New Testament"; "Needed: Breadmakers, Hard Work, Low Pay"; "We have bread crumbs and scraps for your birds."

There are barrels of whole wheat flour. There are huge cartons and tins of nuts, vanilla, honey, peanut butter. Varieties of herb tea are visible. On the counter are loaves—whole wheat, cinnamon raisin, oatmeal, rye, soy, sunflower, corn meal. . . . "We average 200 to 250 loaves a day. We use any ingredient that's in its natural state. We don't use white flour."

Among her customers, as well as health food stores, are conventional groceries, *including a huge supermarket. "The stores pick it up. We don't have a car. It's about half-wholesale and half-retail. The retail part is the most enjoyable, because we meet people and talk to 'em and they ask questions." . . .*

There is an easy wandering in and out of customers and passersby, among whom are small boys, inhaling deeply, longingly, in comic style. It is late afternoon and a few of her colleagues are relaxing. She is twenty-nine years old.

I'm the director. It has no owner. Originally I owned it. We're a nonprofit corporation 'cause we give our leftover bread away, give it to anyone who would be hungry. Poor people buy, too, 'cause we accept food stamps. We sell bread at half-price to people over sixty-five. We never turn anybody away. A man came in a few minutes ago and we gave him a loaf of bread. We give bread lessons and talks. Sometimes school children come in here. We show 'em around and explain what we're doing. . . .

Everything we do is completely open. We do the baking right out here. People in the neighborhood, waiting for the bus in the morning, come in and watch us make bread. We don't like to waste anything. That's real important. We use such good ingredients, we hate to see it go into a garbage can. . . .

We have men and women, we all do the same kind of work. Everyone does everything. It's not as chaotic as it sounds. Right now there's eight of us. Different people take responsibility for different jobs. We just started selling tea last week. Tom's interested in herbs. He bought the tea.

We hire only neighborhood people. We will hire anyone who can do the work. There's been all ages. Once we had a twelve-year-old boy working here. A woman of forty used to work here. There isn't any machinery here. We do everything by hand. We get to know who each other is, rapping with each other. It's more valuable to hear your neighbor, what he has to say, than the noise of the machine. A lot of people are out of work. Machines are taking over. So we're having people work instead of machines. . . .

". . . You work in one place, get to know the people, you go home at night and you're lonely because you don't know anyone in your neighborhood. I see this as a means of bringing all that together. I like the idea of people living together and working together."

We start about five thirty in the morning and close about seven at night. We're open six days a week. Sundays we sell what's left over from Saturday and give bread lessons. We charge a dollar a lesson to anyone who wants to come. . . .

We try people out. We take them as a substitute first. You can't tell by words how someone's gonna do. We ask people to come as a sub when someone is absent. Out of those we choose who we'll take. We watch 'em real close. We teach 'em: "This is the way your hands should move." "This is how you tell when your bread's done, if it feels this way." . . .

We try to discourage people from the start, 'cause it's hard having a high turnover. If someone applies for a job, I tell 'em all the bad points. Some of 'em think it's something new or groovy. I let 'em know quickly it's not that way at all. It's *work*. Each person's here for a different reason. Tom's interested in ecological things, Jo enjoys being here and she likes working a half-day. . . .

We each make seven dollars a day. At first we didn't make any salaries at all. After two weeks, we each took out five dollars. It sounds unscientific, but most of us could get by. Everyone was living with someone. We all get help from one another. . . . We get our food real cheap. We can each take a loaf a day out of the store. The store pays all our taxes.

Our prices are real reasonable. I went into a grocery store and saw what they were selling bread for. Machine-made whole wheat was selling at forty-five cents. So we made it at fifty cents a loaf. It would cost fifty cents to make that bread at home using the same ingredients. We priced it that way on purpose. . . .

I believe people will survive if we depend on ourselves and each other. If we're working with our hands instead of with machines, we're dealing with concrete things, personal, rather than abstract things, impersonal. Unless we do something like this, I don't see this world lasting. So I really have no future to save money for. (Laughs.) . . . I'd say times are worse for this planet than they've ever been, so each tries to be the best he can, she can. I am doing exactly what I want to do.

Work is an essential part of being alive. Your work is your identity. It tells you who you are. It's gotten so abstract. People don't work for the sake of working. They're working for a car, a new house, or a vacation. It's not the work itself that's important to them. There's such a joy in doing work well.

When people ask what you do, what do you say?

I make bread. (Laughs.)

AFTER READING

1. Look back through the piece. Mark the things you feel positively about with a plus (+) and those you feel negatively about with a minus (−).

Then, freewrite about what you understand from reading this piece and how it makes you feel.

Share some of what you wrote and marked with your group.

2. With your group, reread the text and mark the points that describe a cooperative. Add these to your earlier definition as examples of how a cooperative might work.

HOW I READ IT

Did you and your group predict accurately some of the things the article said? Did that help you read? How? What surprised you? Did particular sentences connect with your experience? Did that help your reading or not? Write a few notes to yourself about what helped you read and what got in the way.

Tell your partner about how you read. Did your partner read differently from you? How?

TOPICS FOR WRITING

Choose one activity.

Activity A: Places of work have various management structures, management styles, and leaders (or bosses). All of these factors affect the atmosphere in the workplace and how workers feel. Think about the jobs you've had and the atmosphere at those workplaces. Compare one of your jobs with the cooperative bakery. Consider points like the treatment of workers, hiring, training, pay, attitudes, and atmosphere. Draw your own conclusions at the end.

Activity B: In the piece, cooperative director Kay Stepkin says, "We do everything by hand. . . . A lot of people are out of work. Machines are taking over. So we're having people work instead of machines."

Some people fear that machines are taking over, and many have lost jobs due to changing technology. What do you think of this situation? Have you or someone you know ever been replaced by a machine? What are the benefits, or disadvantages, of making things by hand instead of turning on a machine? In a composition, tell what you think based on your experience or that of others.

Activity C: Go to a workplace in your neighborhood—a small business, a cooperative, or another type of business. Observe and take notes so you can describe the place, the atmosphere, what the business is, what work is done, how it's done, and other characteristics of the business. If possible, talk to some of the employees about how they feel about working there. Write your piece as a feature article for a local newspaper.

Activity D: Reread the last two paragraphs of this piece. What do you think of these sentiments? Do you agree or disagree or have a different opinion? To get more ideas, look back at any other pieces on work you have read in this unit (those by Fuentes, Allison, and Milbank). Begin with a quote from one of these pieces and write your thoughts and opinions.

AFTER WRITING

1. Form a group of people who wrote on the same topic. Read each other's pieces. Talk about the differences in content and form among your papers.

2. Write in your log about what you learned from reading and talking about each other's writing. Also, like a professional writer, make a list of two or three new ideas or topics you could write about another time.

BEFORE READING

1. What words come to your mind when you see the word *stress?* Write down those words. As a class, put all the words on the chalkboard.

2. How would you fill in the blank in this sentence?

   I had a _____ stressful year last year.

   Share what you wrote with your partner. Talk about why you wrote the answer you did.

3. Read the passage about the stress test. Then read the stress scale and figure out your stress score.

A Scale of Stresses
Susan Ovelette Kobasa

The scale of stresses can tell you approximately how much stress you have had in the past year. However, it won't tell you how you handled it. The scale, which was developed by medical researchers Thomas Holmes and Richard Rahe, is used in many studies on stress.

In the 1960s, medical researchers Thomas Holmes and Richard Rahe developed a popular scale, which you may have seen, that was a checklist of stressful events. They appreciated the tricky point that *any* major change can be stressful. Negative events like "serious illness of a family member" and "trouble with boss" were high on the list, but so were some positive life-changing events, like marriage. You might want to take the Holmes-Rahe test to find out how much pressure you're under. But remember that the score does not reflect how you deal with stress—it only shows how much you have to deal with. And we now know that the way you handle these events dramatically affects your chances of staying healthy.

By the early 1970s, hundreds of similar studies had followed Holmes and Rahe. And millions of Americans who work and live under stress worried over the reports. Somehow, the research got boiled down to a memorable message. Women's magazines ran headlines like "Stress causes illness!" If you want to stay physically and mentally healthy, the articles said, avoid stressful events.

But such simplistic advice is impossible to follow. Even if stressful events are dangerous, many—like the death of a loved one—are impossible to avoid. Moreover, any warning to avoid *all* stressful events is a prescription for staying away from opportunities as well as trouble. Since any change can be stressful, a person who wanted to be completely free of stress would never marry, have a child, take a new job or move.

The notion that all stress makes you sick also ignores a lot of what we know about people. It assumes we're all vulnerable and passive in the face of adversity. But what about human resilience, initiative and creativity? Many come through periods of stress with more physical and mental vigor than they had before. We also know that a long time without change or challenge can lead to boredom, and physical and mental strain.

A SCALE OF STRESSES

This is a list of events that occur commonly in people's lives. The numbers in the column headed "Mean Value" indicate how stressful each event is. More specifically, a high number means the event is intensely stressful and will take a long time to adjust to.

Thinking about the last year, note the events that happened to you. By each event, indicate the number of times that it occurred in the past twelve months. Multiply this number, or frequency, by the number in the "Mean Value" column. Adding all of these products (event frequency × value) will give you your total stress score for the year. A total score of **150–199** indicates mild life crisis. **200–299:** moderate life crisis. **300+:** major life crisis.

LIFE EVENT	MEAN VALUE			STRESS INDEX
Death of spouse	____	×	100 =	____
Divorce	____	×	73 =	____
Marital separation	____	×	65 =	____
Jail term	____	×	63 =	____
Death of close family member	____	×	63 =	____
Personal injury or illness	____	×	53 =	____
Marriage	____	×	50 =	____
Fired at work	____	×	47 =	____
Marital reconciliation	____	×	45 =	____
Retirement	____	×	45 =	____
Change in health of family member	____	×	44 =	____
Pregnancy	____	×	40 =	____
Sex difficulties	____	×	39 =	____
Gain of new family member	____	×	39 =	____
Business readjustment	____	×	39 =	____
Change in financial state	____	×	38 =	____

Death of close friend	____ ×	37 =	____
Change to different line of work	____ ×	36 =	____
Change in number of arguments with spouse	____ ×	35 =	____
Mortgage over $10,000	____ ×	31 =	____
Foreclosure of mortgage or loan	____ ×	30 =	____
Change in responsibilities at work	____ ×	29 =	____
Son or daughter leaving home	____ ×	29 =	____
Trouble with in-laws	____ ×	29 =	____
Outstanding personal achievement	____ ×	28 =	____
Wife beginning or stopping work	____ ×	26 =	____
Begin or end school	____ ×	26 =	____
Change in living conditions	____ ×	25 =	____
Revision of personal habits	____ ×	24 =	____
Trouble with boss	____ ×	23 =	____
Change in work hours or conditions	____ ×	20 =	____
Change in residence	____ ×	20 =	____
Change in schools	____ ×	20 =	____
Change in recreation	____ ×	19 =	____
Change in church activities	____ ×	19 =	____
Change in social activities	____ ×	18 =	____
Mortgage or loan less than $10,000	____ ×	17 =	____
Change in sleeping habits	____ ×	16 =	____
Change in number of family get-togethers	____ ×	15 =	____
Change in eating habits	____ ×	15 =	____
Vacation	____ ×	13 =	____
Christmas	____ ×	12 =	____
Minor violations of the law	____ ×	11 =	____
	TOTAL	=	

AFTER READING

1. Write in your journal for a few minutes about what you just read and did. What stresses did you have, and how did you score? How do you feel about it? Were you surprised?

2. Read through Kobasa's passage about the stress scale again. Underline some sentences that you think are important to remember, especially after finding out your score. Share the sentences you underlined with your partner.

3. If you wish, share your score with your group, and report to your group the stresses you had. Compile a group list of stresses, noting the number of people in the group who had the same stress. Which stresses were the most common?

   Report your group's list to the class.

4. Choose one activity.

   Activity A: Are there any stresses that you or your group did not name or don't understand? Find out if anyone in the class can explain them. If not, try to find explanations before the next class. Then report to the whole class.

   Activity B: With your partner, pick a character from one of the earlier readings in this book, and see how he or she would rate on the scale. Does the rating help to explain the character's behavior?

   Activity C: Read "Hope Emerges As Key to Success in Life" in Extra Readings, p. 141. The author, Daniel Goleman, talks about the role that hope plays in relieving stress. Write about these two pieces, "A Scale of Stresses" and "Hope Emerges As Key to Success in Life." Compare what the pieces say and how they differ. How do you feel about what they each say? What associations follow, or how do the articles connect to your experience?

HOW I READ IT

In your reading log, write about how you read the scale. Was it easy or hard? How long did it take you to figure out what to do? What helped you? Were you a slow or fast reader of the scale?

Share what you wrote with your group.

HOW IT'S WRITTEN

1. With your group, talk about how the stresses are arranged. What is the order? Why? Do you agree with the order? If not, which stresses do you think are out of order? Why? Which items on the list surprised you? Which items didn't surprise you? Why?

2. Where on the scale would you put "moving to a new culture" or "starting college"? What other items are missing that you might like to add?

3. What does looking at the order of stresses tell you about writing? Write about this for a few minutes in your log.

TOPICS FOR WRITING

Choose one activity.

Activity A: Choose one of the stressful events you underwent this past year, and write the story of what happened. Tell it from beginning to end, giving as many details as you need to make it clear.

Activity B: All of the events on the list are common in people's lives. A person might wonder how such a common occurrence as starting a new school year, trouble with the boss, or getting married could be stressful. Choose an event on the list that you are familiar with. Write about the situation, describing what happens to a person that makes it stressful. Use details that *show* us the stress.

Activity C: Choose one or two of the sentences you underlined in After Reading, question 2. Write a composition or a letter starting with the sentences you chose. You can explain them, agree or disagree with them based on your experience, or use them as advice to someone under stress.

AFTER WRITING

1. Read your piece aloud to your group. Ask group members to tell you what they understood and one thing that was not clear to them.

2. Choose the piece from your group that you think the class would like to hear, and ask a volunteer to read it aloud.

BEFORE READING

1. In your group, make a list of situations in which you or someone you know cried. Share your list with the class.

2. Freewrite for ten minutes about how people react to crying in your native culture. Is it acceptable to cry? Are there some situations in which it is more acceptable to cry than others? Share your writing with your group.

It's O.K. to Cry
Tears Are Not Just a Bid for Attention

Jane Brody

Jane Brody has been the "Personal Health" columnist for the New York Times *since 1965. She has written many books on nutrition, good food, and health, as well as several cookbooks. The article below appeared in the* New York Times.

Crying is hardly an activity encouraged by society. Tears, be they of sorrow, anger or joy, typically make Americans feel uncomfortable and embarrassed. Edmund S. Muskie may well have lost his bid for the 1972 Presidential candidacy when he wept while denouncing a newspaper publisher for printing a letter that insulted his wife.

The shedder of tears is likely to apologize, even when a devastating tragedy was the provocation. The observer of tears is likely to do everything possible to put an end to the emotional outpouring. But judging from recent studies of crying behavior, links between illness and crying and the chemical composition of tears, both those responses to tears are often inappropriate and may even be counterproductive.

People are the only animals definitely known to shed emotional tears. Since evolution has given rise to few if any purposeless physiological responses, it is logical to assume that crying has one or more functions that enhance survival.

Although some observers have suggested that crying is a way to elicit assistance from others (as a crying baby might from its mother), the shedding of tears is hardly necessary to get help. Vocal cries, whines or whimpers such as animals use would have been quite enough, more likely than tears to gain attention. So, it appears, there must be something special about tears themselves.

Indeed, the new studies suggest that emotional tears may play a direct role in alleviating stress. University of Minnesota researchers who are studying the chemical composition of tears have recently isolated two important chemicals, leucine-enkephalin and prolactin, from emotional tears. The first of these may be an endorphin, one of the body's natural pain-relieving substances.

Both chemicals are found only in tears that are shed in response to emotion. Tears shed because of exposure to a cut onion would contain no such substance.

. . . researchers at several other institutions are investigating the usefulness of tears as a means of diagnosing human ills and monitoring drugs.

At Tulane University's tear analysis laboratory Dr. Peter Kastl . . . and his colleagues report that they can use tears to detect drug abuse and exposure to medication, to determine whether a contact lens fits properly or why it may be uncomfortable, to study the causes of "dry eye" syndrome and the effects of eye surgery, and perhaps even to measure exposure to environmental pollutants.

At Columbia University Dr. Linsy Farris and colleagues are studying tears for clues to the diagnosis of diseases away from the eyes. Tears can be obtained painlessly without invading the body and only tiny amounts are needed to perform highly refined analyses.

Tears are produced continuously by the tiny lacrimal glands in the upper, outer corners of the eyes, under the lids. Every time you blink (on average 13 times a minute) your eyelids carry a film of tears across the corneas. . . . The windshield-wiper effect of the blink also helps to cleanse the eyes of debris and irritating chemicals and perhaps even to fight infection, since tears contain antibacterial enzymes.

Tears that do not evaporate leave through the lacrimal canal and sac at the inner corner of the eye. From there they drain through the nose, which is why you usually have to blow your nose when you cry. Tears shed down the face represent an overflow of the lacrimal ducts, as might happen to gutters during a downpour.

Crying behavior and sounds may also be useful in diagnosing abnormalities in infants. Two California researchers found that ailing babies typically have high-pitched, shrill cries.

Crying also seems to serve as a means of communication for babies before they learn to talk; Mothers soon learn to distinguish between cries of pain, fear and hunger, and those of crankiness. . . .

As for adults, Dr. Frey's studies of more than 200 men and women who kept "crying diaries" for a month found that 85 percent of the women and 73 percent of the men said they felt better after crying. On average, the participants reported a 40 percent reduction in stress after crying.

Despite this reported relief, men do not cry often—only one-fifth as often as women. Forty-five percent of the men, but only 6 percent of the women, shed no emotional tears during the monthlong study. Furthermore, when men do cry they often fail to shed tears; the tears well up in their eyes but do not spill over.

Dr. Frey suggests that the holding back of tears may be a reason why men develop more stress-related diseases than women do. Dr. Margaret Crepeau of the Marquette University College of Nursing found that people with stress-related disorders—for example, ulcers and colitis—were more likely than healthy people to view crying as a sign of weakness or loss of control. The ill people also reported that they cried less often. . . .

If the theory that tears relieve stress is correct, how does one account for tears of joy? Traditional explanations are that crying at graduations, weddings and happy endings really reflects unhappy feelings, such as the "loss" of a child to a new spouse or anxiety about the child's future. However, a more likely reason is simply that tears of joy are a response to intense emotion, which is stressful whether the feeling is sad or happy.

In any event Dr. Frey believes the evidence gathered is sufficiently convincing to warrant a change in attitude toward crying. It's time, he says, for adults to stop telling children things like "Now, now, don't cry" and "Big boys don't cry." Crying is a natural phenomenon and the withholding of tears appears to be a danger to health.

AFTER READING

1. Working with your group, reread the article and underline the benefits of crying.

2. Which things did you underline that you did not know before you read this article? Did learning this new information change your opinion about crying?

3. Write two or three sentences about what you thought and felt before and after you read the article.

HOW IT'S WRITTEN

1. With a partner, choose one activity.

   Activity A: Reread the first two paragraphs. In this introduction, Jane Brody describes the assumptions many people share about crying. At the end of her introduction, she tells why they are wrong.

Why do you think she chose to start her essay this way? Is the introduction effective? Why or why not?

Activity B: The author uses recent scientific research to support her argument. Examine the way Jane Brody does this by working on the following:

a. Reread the article and make a list of the experts Brody cites. What does each one tell us? Write a brief summary next to each expert's name. Explain why you think the author uses so many experts' opinions.

b. Writers often incorporate information from other sources into their own articles. Look at the places where Jane Brody does this. What words and expressions does she use to let us know the ideas are not her own but are those of scientific experts? Make a list of these words and expressions.

2. Share your findings with the class.

TOPICS FOR WRITING

Choose one activity.

Activity A: Despite the fact that there are benefits to crying, many people never cry. Write a paper in which you argue the benefits of crying. Try to convince your reader that it's OK to cry. Use examples from your own experience to show why you feel this way. Use at least two experts' opinions to support your argument.

Activity B: Think of a time when someone you know was crying for an emotional release. Describe the situation. Write a letter to this person now. Explain what you used to think about crying. Tell how your opinion has changed from reading the article about crying. Quote a sentence or part of a sentence from the article that you think will be particularly helpful to this person.

Activity C: Pick a sentence or two from the article that connect to something in your experience. Use the sentence(s) to begin a piece of your own—an essay, a story, or a letter.

AFTER WRITING

1. Go over your paper carefully with a pen in your hand, reading each word aloud so that your ear can hear it and touching each word with your pen to find errors and parts that don't sound right. Continue going over your paper until you find at least three things to change.

2. Form a group with two or three people in the class who wrote about the same topic. Read your papers aloud to one another. Notice the different ways in which you approached the same topic. Make a list of the similarities and differences in your papers.

3. Report to the whole class on what your group wrote about, giving a one- or two-sentence summary of each person's ideas about crying. Explain what the members of your group agree and disagree on.

BEFORE READING

1. Read the title and introductory material. Choose one of the following activities.

   Activity A: Freewrite for five minutes about a time when you broke up with someone you cared about.

   Activity B: Freewrite for five minutes about a time when someone you cared about broke up with you.

   Activity C: Freewrite for five minutes about a time when a friend of yours or someone you were close to went through the breakup of a relationship.

2. Read "Going Through the House."

Going Through the House
Claire Braz-Valentine

A poet and playwright, Claire Braz-Valentine lives in California and teaches creative writing at Soledad Prison. The poem that follows was taken from a collection of writing called Breaking Up Is Hard to Do, Stories by Women.

I don't care
really I don't.
I can remove you from my life
throw you out
like last year's calendar.

So you want another woman.
So fine.
I'll start with the refrigerator,
remove your peanut butter,
your hot sauce,
that stupid stuff you put on your steaks,
and the last piece of the cake I made for your birthday
I'll put them,
no I'll throw them,
I will smash them to smithereens in the garbage can.

I'll go through the closet,
grab that shirt of yours
that I used to wear in the garden
the sock you forgot in the corner
wad them up
tear them up
shred them
take them into the street and
drive my car over them
get them out of my sight.

I'll yank that smart ass teddy bear
you bought me for Christmas
right off of my bed pillow
rip its seedy little eyes out
wipe that wise ass grin off its face
hang its skin from a nail
on the tree you planted
Then I'll kill the tree.

I'll take every card you ever gave me
not read those dumb sappy lies anymore
about how you'll love me forever,
burn them up,
pulverize them into cat litter.
I can do it with my eyes closed.

I'll get that picture from the living room
that you bought at the flea market
and rip it up
flush it down the toilet.
You always had rotten taste anyway.

I'll yank clothes that you liked me to wear
off of their hangers,
go to Goodwill.
Go to hell.
Give them to her, the new woman,
but as you say
she's so much smaller than I.
Who gives a shit?
I sure don't.

I'll get all my cleaning supplies
scrub the whole house
get your prints off.
Take a hot bath,
not a scalding one,
get your prints off me,
cut my hair,
paint my fingernails.
You always hated that,
wear the big earrings you said are flashy,
and lots of the perfume that made you sneeze,
get your smug scumsucking voice off my answering machine,
not forward your mail,
return it to sender,
tell them you died.

I'll do these things
I really will.
I don't care
really I don't.

AFTER READING

1. A good way to respond to a poem is to explain how it makes you feel and what it reminds you of in your own life. Freewrite in your log about this for five minutes.

    Share what you wrote with a partner.

2. The author says "I don't care really I don't." Is she telling the truth? How do you know? Underline two or three places in the poem to support your opinion. Share your findings with your group.

HOW I READ IT

Freewrite for a few minutes about how you read this poem. For example, did you read it differently from the way you would read a newspaper article or a short story? Explain.

HOW IT'S WRITTEN

1. With a partner, choose one activity.

   Activity A: The poet is very specific about what her lover has left behind. Reread the poem and underline the items that were left behind. What do these items tell us about the person who left? Which items make the poet the angriest? How do you know?
   Look at the items you have underlined. Which ones appeal to the senses of the reader? With a partner, make a list of the senses (hearing, seeing, smelling, etc.) and put the items in the appropriate categories. Some items may appeal to more than one sense.

   Activity B: The poet uses strong active verbs to tell what she will do to the things her lover left behind. Look at these stanzas again and underline the verbs she uses. If you are unsure of the meanings of some of the words, look them up in the dictionary.
   Make a list of the verbs you underlined. Some of the verbs are stronger than others. Put a plus (+) beside the ones you think are strongest.
   Beside each verb on your list, make notes about the senses to which the verb appeals. For example, "burn them up" can help us think of the temperature of the hot fire, see the flames, hear the fire burning, and smell the smoke.

2. Share your findings with your group.

TOPICS FOR WRITING

Choose one activity.

Activity A: Remember a time when you got really angry. What did you do to express your anger? What images/colors/sensations come to mind when you remember this experience? Write a poem that tells about this time when you were angry. Use as many sensory details as you can to express how you felt.

Activity B: Think about a time when you were angry at someone. Write a letter to this person starting with "I don't care I really don't." Tell what you would like to do to show your anger. Be as specific as possible.

Activity C: Write about an incident that made you angry or upset or happy or sad. Tell the whole story from beginning to end. Use language that is appropriate for the story and your feelings.

Activity D: Tell the true story of an experience of breaking up. It could be a story about you breaking up with someone you cared for, about someone you cared for breaking up with you, or about someone you know who went through this experience. Show the emotions in the situation by using specific details and active verbs.

AFTER WRITING

The following techniques will help you rewrite your piece.

1. Using verbs effectively:

   a. Underline the verbs in your piece of writing. Could any of them be stronger? Using a thesaurus, look up one of your verbs. What other verbs could be used to describe this action? Look up two more verbs. Use three new verbs to expand the meaning in your writing.

   b. Share your writing with your group. Ask your group members to listen for the verbs. Which ones do they remember?

2. Using images effectively:

   a. Read your piece to the people in your group. What colors or specific images do they remember? Which ones show anger best? Make a list of the effective images from the pieces your group read. Share them with the class.

   b. Look back at your writing. Make a list of the sensory details you have used already. Which ones have you left out? Try to include at least two images for each of the senses. That is, use two images for sound, two for taste, two for touch, two for sight, and two for smell.

   c. Reread your piece of writing to the members of your group. Ask them to tell you which images are the most effective.

A PRIVATE WRITING ACTIVITY

1. We are often asked to do writing in school that we then rewrite, change, and correct. But sometimes writing can be a very private activity that we share with no one. Writing about what upsets us can actually be therapeutic.

   Since anger is such a difficult emotion to deal with, some people have found it helpful to write a letter to the person they are angry at and then destroy the letter without ever showing it to anyone.

   Write a letter to someone who has made you angry. It doesn't matter how long ago the situation happened, as long as you still feel angry when you remember it. Tell this person exactly how angry you feel and why. When you have finished, destroy your letter.

2. Report back to your class about this writing experience. Was it helpful to write the letter? Why or why not? How did it feel to write something and then destroy it?

3. With your group, make a list of the ways writing could be considered therapeutic.

BEFORE READING

1. Read the introductory information and look at the title. What do you think the author means by the expression *falling away?* Write for five minutes in your reading log about what you think this means. Share your writing with a partner. If your partner wrote something that helps you to better understand what this phrase means, add your partner's ideas to your reading log.

2. Look up *fall away* in the dictionary. Which meaning do you think Aldrich intends in her essay? Why? Copy the definition in your reading log. Read "Falling Away, Here at Home."

Falling Away, Here at Home
Julia Aldrich

In the essay that follows, Julia Aldrich, a poet, talks about her young daughter, who has an incurable disease. The author describes the experience of taking her daughter home, so that she can live the last days of her life in a familiar place rather than in a hospital.

"What's next?" my daughter asks. Her soft, expressive face has that wooden look I have seen once or twice in the last few months when she has spoken of her own death, so I know that she is asking me: Is this the place we have come to now?

It is.

She is 23. She has adrenal cancer. Adrenocortical carcinoma is rare, with only about 150 cases a year. It is, as yet, incurable.

Nonetheless, all along the way, there have been choices to make: experimental chemotherapies, drug programs. Even at this point, when her disease has moved too quickly to justify further treatment, there is an option to go into the hospital in an attempt to "relieve symptoms." But we have come home. . . .

. . . the public health nurse, a young woman, my daughter's age, . . . has come to the house. . . .

She is a noticing woman. I see her glance move from the photograph, on the bookcase, of the deep-dimpled laughing girl with her college friends, to my daughter's starved face and matchstick arms. I feel that she also notices the depth of my anguish, beneath my calm.

We speak together of the hospice concept: that it is a good thing for a dying person to be at home, cared for by the family, with a home-care team providing management of pain and other symptoms as well as help for the family. Although the hospice concept is still new in the United States . . . it is the idea itself that has given me courage to bring my daughter home.

The social worker assigned by the county is a trusted co-worker of the public health nurse. . . . Together [they help me] find a [local] doctor whose practice is house calls only. She is kind, sensible and accustomed to home care. Unbelievably, we have a team. . . .

. . . [Our friends] . . . are extraordinarily tender, and sensitive to our needs. Two friends who visit with babies bring radiant smiles to my daughter's face. A few old friends and family members come to visit; others dissolve in grief, and let go. . . .

It is the second week of being home, and the week of my daughter's dying. Since the cancer was diagnosed six months ago, each month has been different; then, each week. It is only in the last six weeks that the disease has begun to visibly lay waste to her body. And it is only in the last week that it has taken on, in her life, an omnipresence.

Now each day is different, as her body systems break down. . . .

"She is falling," I tell the social worker. That is how it seems to me: a falling away.

Since the weekend, she has not wanted company for her own sake. She has not wanted to speak on the phone, nor have her letters read to her. She wants her music. She wants her back rubbed. She wants to be held.

Wednesday night, she showers, as usual, with my help, but says it is very tiring for her. By Thursday evening she cannot rise from her bed. She is restless and uncomfortable. I bring my quilt and pillows to sleep in her room. It is the first night she has not slept straight through.

Friday morning the doctor and the public nurse and the social worker coordinate their visits. . . .

The doctor thinks there will be no medical emergency; if I panic, not to call the hospital, but her. The nurse, too, says I may call at any time.

In the afternoon an old friend visits . . . bringing fruit, bread, supper. I have never been so glad to see her face at my back door. Yet when she leaves, I feel neither abandoned nor alone. Friends and neighbors are at the ready. And I am totally engrossed, with my daughter, in a ritual of holding on, and letting go.

She is falling away. Her breathing pattern has changed. Each time she asks me to help her up, to a sitting position, she is heavier, with less strength in her arms.

When she takes her evening medication, she has difficulty in holding up her head and swallowing. I grind her nighttime pills in pear juice. She makes a concentrated effort and gets it down. We are both inordinately pleased.

It is likely she didn't need this last medication. Yet it has been the small daily rituals that have held us up in these months, and now, because it is "bedtime" by the clock, I turn off her recorder cassette and bring in my quilt and pillows.

But this is not a night like any other night, and I sit at her bedside and sing to her; not her songs, but mine, old ones, from the 40's, astonished that I remember the words. Again, we are both somehow pleased.

The next time she reaches out to be pulled up, she is almost dead weight; yet she leans forward and flings her arms around me, in a strange, heavy embrace. When I lower her back to her pillows, she lies still.

There is a click in her throat, like a telephone receiver put back on the hook, on the other end of the line. A second click. And a third. I pray with all my heart that this is how it will end. And it is.

AFTER READING

1. Freewrite for five minutes about what the essay says, how it makes you feel, or what it reminds you of or makes you think about.

2. Look back at your definition of *fall away*. Now that you have read the essay, what would you add to your definition? Look at the place in the essay where Aldrich uses the phrase. Copy down the words she uses to add to your definition.

3. Talk about these questions with your group: Does the mother want to be with her daughter at this time? Would the mother have preferred that her daughter die in a hospital? Use the text to support your opinions.

HOW IT'S WRITTEN

1. Reread the introduction. Notice how Aldrich begins her paragraph and ends her paragraph with a question. Why do you think she does this? Discuss this technique with your group.

2. The author of this essay is a poet. She has come up with an unusual way of describing her daughter's dying by saying she is falling away. Think about the words or phrases you have heard for describing death and dying. Make a list in your log. Think about the words you use in your native language to describe someone dying. Write them down

and then translate them into English. Share your findings with your group. What are the similarities and differences?

TOPICS FOR WRITING

Choose one activity.

Activity A: Pick a sentence or phrase from the essay that you find particularly moving or powerful. Copy it down exactly as it's written. Be sure to use quotation marks and tell where you took the sentence from. Then use it as the beginning of something you write: a short essay, a story, a memory, a poem, or a letter.

Activity B: Aldrich writes of the importance of "small daily rituals" in helping her and her daughter get through their last days together. Write a composition, story, or poem about a time when you were going through a painful experience. Tell about the small daily rituals in your life that helped sustain you or that helped you recover afterward.

Activity C: In her essay, Aldrich tells about the hospice concept. Look back at her definition of it. Summarize what she says and write a definition of the hospice concept in your own words. What do you think about the hospice concept versus dying in a hospital? Write a short essay arguing for or against the hospice concept. Give an example from your own experience or from what you've read to support your opinion. Remember to use quotation marks to show sentences or phrases you have taken from the reading.

Activity D: Tell the true story of what you experienced when someone close to you died. Include the cause of death and the experience of the person dying. Try to describe the person's appearance in sickness and in health. Include the last thing you remember doing for or saying to this person. What was the last thing this person said or did? Try to be brave the way Aldrich was; share the pain by using images or similes to help your readers understand what the experience was like for you.

AFTER WRITING

1. Read your writing aloud to your group. After each person reads, write a note to that person about how the piece made you feel.

2. Sometimes when writers try to explain painful subjects, they say

things like "there are no words to describe this." Or they might say "it hurt" or "it was sad" rather than trying to describe their feelings. Reread your writing or your partner's writing to see if you used phrases like these. Consider how you might revise your writing to more fully express your painful feelings, as Julia Aldrich did.

3. Revise your piece.

About All the Readings in This Unit

PREPARING FOR WRITING

1. Reread all the entries in your reading log for this unit.

2. With the class, list some *issues* that arise around the concept of be-coming/the true self, especially issues that are related to some of the readings from this unit. Make a list of generalizations about those issues. (See p. 59 for an explanation of issues and generalizations.)

3. Choose one generalization. Write it at the top of a page. Under the generalization, list all the reasons and examples you can think of that prove it is true, including something you read in this unit and some-thing you wrote.

WRITING

Write a composition about your generalization. Support your ideas by referring to one or more of the readings in this unit and your writing about those readings. You may be able to include parts of something you have al-ready written. Write the piece for someone who has not read this book.

AFTER WRITING

1. Exchange papers with others in your group. Readers should write down the main idea of each composition and then list all the support-ing information they see. They should also suggest ways the writers might make their points more powerfully.

2. Read your readers' comments. Circle the ideas you might be able to use in revising your piece.

3. Revise your writing.

4. Write in your log about *how* you wrote this composition. For example, how did you get ideas? Did the Preparing for Writing activities help you? How did you feel after you reread what you had written earlier in the unit? Did your group's suggestions help you see your writing dif-ferently?

Extra Readings

Hope Emerges As Key to Success in Life
Daniel Goleman

Psychologist Daniel Goleman writes regularly for the New York Times. *He has published many articles on stress, meditation, and relaxation and has edited and co-edited a number of books on psychology including* Mind Body Medicine: How to Use Your Mind for Better Health.

Psychologists are finding that hope plays a surprisingly potent role in giving people a measurable advantage in realms as diverse as academic achievement, bearing up in onerous jobs and coping with tragic illness. And, by contrast, the loss of hope is turning out to be a stronger sign that a person may commit suicide than other factors long thought to be more likely risks.

"Hope has proven a powerful predictor of outcome in every study we've done so far," said Dr. Charles R. Snyder, a psychologist at the University of Kansas who has devised a scale to assess how much hope a person has.

For example, in research with 3,920 college students, Dr. Snyder and his colleagues found that the level of hope among freshmen at the beginning of their first semester was a more accurate predictor of their college grades than were their S.A.T. scores or their grade point averages in high school, the two measures most commonly used to predict college performance. The study was reported in part in the November issue of The Journal of Personality and Social Psychology.

"Students with high hope set themselves higher goals and know how to work to attain them," Dr. Snyder said. "When you compare students of equivalent intellectual aptitude and past academic achievements, what sets them apart is hope."

In devising a way to assess hope scientifically, Dr. Snyder went beyond the simple notion that hope is merely the sense that everything will turn out all right. "That notion is not concrete enough, and it blurs two key components of hope," Dr. Snyder said. "Having hope means believing you have both the will and the way to accomplish your goals, whatever they may be."

Despite the folk wisdom that "where there's a will there's a way," Dr. Snyder has found that the two are not necessarily connected. In a study of more than 7,000 men and women from 18 to 70 years old, Dr. Snyder discovered that only about 40 percent of people are hopeful in the technical sense of believing they typically have the energy and means to accomplish their goals, whatever those might be.

The study found that about 20 percent of the people believed in their ability to find the means to attain their goals, but said they had little will to do so. Another 20 percent have the opposite pattern, saying they had the energy to motivate themselves but little confidence that they would find the means.

The rest had little hope at all, reporting that they typically had neither the will nor the way.

"It's not enough just to have the wish for something," said Dr. Snyder. "You need the means, too. On the other hand, all the skills to solve a problem won't help if you don't have the willpower to do it."

TRAITS AMONG THE HOPEFUL

Dr. Snyder found that people with high levels of hope share several attributes:

- Unlike people who are low in hope, they turn to friends for advice on how to achieve their goals.
- They tell themselves they can succeed at what they need to do.
- Even in a tight spot, they tell themselves things will get better as time goes on.
- They are flexible enough to find different ways to get to their goals.
- If hope for one goal fades, they aim for another. "Those low in hope tend to become fixated on one goal, and persist even when they find themselves blocked," Dr. Snyder said. "They just stay at it and get frustrated."
- They show an ability to break a formidable task into specific, achievable chunks. "People low in hope see only the large goal, and not the small steps to it along the way," Dr. Snyder said. . . .

People who get a high score on the hope scale "have had as many hard times as those with low scores, but have learned to think about it in a hopeful way, seeing a setback as a challenge, not a failure," Dr. Snyder said.

NURTURING A BRIGHTER OUTLOOK

He and his colleagues are trying to design programs to help children develop the ways of thinking found in hopeful people. "They've often learned their mental habit of hopefulness from a specific person, like a friend or teacher," Dr. Snyder said.

"Hope can be nurtured," he said. Dr. Snyder has made a videotape for that purpose, showing interviews with students who are high on hope, to help freshmen better handle the stress of their first year.

Poem [2]
Langston Hughes

Langston Hughes was a writer of novels, short stories, poetry, history, biography, plays, and lyrics for opera and musical comedy. Although he was sometimes called the poet laureate of the Negro people, his works are read and loved by people all over the world. He died in 1969.

I loved my friend.
He went away from me.
There's nothing more to say.
The poem ends,
Soft as it began—
I loved my friend.

Gravy
Raymond Carver

Raymond Carver, a writer of fiction and poetry, died in 1988 at the age of 49. This poem was written shortly before he died.

No other word will do. For that's what it was. Gravy.
Gravy these past ten years.
Alive, sober, working, loving and

being loved by a good woman. Eleven years
ago he was told he had six months to live
at the rate he was going. And he was going
nowhere but down. So he changed his ways
somehow. He quit drinking! And the rest?
After that it was *all* gravy, every minute
of it, up to and including when he was told about,
well, some things that were breaking down and
building up inside his head. "Don't weep for me,"
he said to his friends. "I'm a lucky man.
I've had ten years longer than I or anyone
expected. Pure gravy. And don't forget it."

Homework
Peter Cameron

Peter Cameron grew up in Pompton Plains, New Jersey, and currently works for a land conservation agency in New York City. His short stories have appeared in many magazines and anthologies.

My dog, Keds, was sitting outside of the A&P last Thursday when he got smashed by some kid pushing a shopping cart. At first we thought he just had a broken leg, but later we found out he was bleeding inside. Every time he opened his mouth, blood would seep out like dull red words in a bad silent dream.

Every night before my sister goes to her job she washes her hair in the kitchen sink with beer and mayonnaise and eggs. Sometimes I sit at the table and watch the mixture dribble down her white back. She boils a pot of water on the stove at the same time; when she is finished with her hair, she steams her face. She wants so badly to be beautiful.

I am trying to solve complicated algebraic problems I have set for myself. Since I started cutting school last Friday, the one thing I miss is homework. Find the value for *n*. Will it be a whole number? It is never a whole number. It is always a fraction.

"Will you get me a towel?" my sister asks. She turns her face toward me and clutches her hair to the top of her head. The sprayer hose slithers into its hole next to the faucet.

I hand her a dish towel. "No," she says. "A bath towel. Don't be stupid."

In the bathroom, my mother is watering her plants. She has arranged them in the tub and turned the shower on. She sits on the toilet lid and watches. It smells like outdoors in the bathroom.

I hand my sister the towel and watch her wrap it around her head. She takes the cover off the pot of boiling water and drops lemon slices in. Then she lowers her face into the steam.

This is the problem I have set for myself:

$$\frac{245(n + 17)}{34} = 396(n - 45)$$

$$n =$$

Wednesday, I stand outside the high-school gym doors. Inside students are lined up doing calisthenics. It's snowing, and prematurely dark, and I can watch without being seen.

"Well," my father says when I get home. He is standing in the garage testing the automatic door. Every time a plane flies overhead, the door opens or closes, so my father is trying to fix it. "Have you changed your mind about school?" he asks me.

I lock my bicycle to a pole. This infuriates my father, who doesn't believe in locking things up in his own house. He pretends not to notice. I wipe the thin stripes of snow off the fenders with my middle finger. It is hard to ride a bike in the snow. This afternoon on my way home from the high school I fell off, and lay in the snowy road with my bike on top of me. It felt warm.

"We're going to get another dog," my father says.

"It's not that," I say. I wish everyone would stop talking about dogs. I can't tell how sad I really am about Keds versus how sad I am in general. If I don't keep these things separate, I feel as if I'm betraying Keds.

"Then what is it?" my father says.

"It's nothing," I say.

My father nods. He is very good about bringing things up and then letting them drop. A lot gets dropped. He presses the button on the automatic control. The door slides down its oiled tracks and falls shut. It's dark in the garage. My father presses the button again and the door opens, and we both look outside at the snow falling in the driveway, as if in those few seconds the world might have changed.

My mother has forgotten to call me for dinner, and when I confront her with this she tells me that she did but that I was sleeping. She is loading the dishwasher. My sister is standing at the counter, listening, and separating eggs for her shampoo.

"What can I get you?" my mother asks. "Would you like a meat-loaf sandwich?"

"No," I say. I open the refrigerator and survey its illuminated contents. "Could I have some eggs?"

"O.K.," my mother says. She comes and stands beside me and puts her hand on top of mine on the door handle. There are no eggs in the refrigerator. "Oh," my mother says; then, "Julie?"

"What?" my sister asks.

"Did you take the last eggs?"

"I guess so," my sister says. "I don't know."

"Forget it," I say. "I won't have eggs."

"No," my mother says. "Julie doesn't need them in her shampoo. That's not what I bought them for."

"I do," my sister says. "It's a formula. It doesn't work without the eggs. I need the protein."

"I don't want eggs," I say. "I don't want anything." I go into my bedroom.

My mother comes in and stands looking out the window. The snow has turned to rain. "You're not the only one who is unhappy about this," she says.

"About what?" I say. I am sitting on my unmade bed. If I pick up my room, my mother will make my bed: that's the deal. I didn't pick up my room this morning.

"About Keds," she says. "I'm unhappy, too. But it doesn't stop me from going to school."

"You don't go to school," I say.

"You know what I mean," my mother says. She turns around and looks at my room, and begins to pick things off the floor.

"Don't do that," I say. "Stop."

My mother drops the dirty clothes in an exaggerated gesture of defeat. She almost—almost—throws them on the floor. The way she holds her hands accentuates their emptiness. "If you're not going to go to school," she says, "the least you can do is clean your room."

In algebra word problems, a boat sails down a river while a jeep drives along the bank. Which will reach the capital first? If a plane flies at a certain speed from Boulder to Oklahoma City and then at a different speed from Oklahoma City to Detroit, how many cups of coffee can the stewardess serve, assuming she is unable to serve during the first and last ten minutes of each flight? How many times can a man ride the elevator to the top of the Empire State Building while his wife climbs the stairs, given that the woman travels one stair slower each flight? And if the man jumps up while the elevator is going down, which is moving—the man, the woman, the elevator, or the snow falling outside?

The next Monday I get up and make preparations for going to school. I can tell at the breakfast table that my mother is afraid to acknowledge them for fear it won't be true. I haven't gotten up before ten o'clock in a week.

My mother makes me French toast. I sit at the table and write the note excusing me for my absence. I am eighteen, an adult, and thus able to excuse myself from school. This is what my note says:

> Dear Mr. Kelly [my homeroom teacher]:
>   Please excuse my absence February 17–24. I was unhappy and did not feel able to attend school.
>   Sincerely,
>   Michael Pechetti

This is the exact format my mother used when she wrote my notes, only she always said, "Michael was home with a sore throat," or "Michael was home with a bad cold." The colds that prevented me from going to school were always bad colds.

My mother watches me write the note but doesn't ask to see it. I leave it on the kitchen table when I go to the bathroom, and when I come back to get it I know she has read it. She is washing the bowl she dipped the French toast into. Before, she would let Keds lick it clean. He liked eggs.

In Spanish class we are seeing a film on flamenco dancers. The screen wouldn't pull down, so it is being projected on the blackboard, which is green and cloudy with erased chalk. It looks a little like the women are sick, and dancing in Heaven. Suddenly the little phone on the wall buzzes.

Mrs. Smitts, the teacher, gets up to answer it, and then walks over to me. She puts her hand on my shoulder and leans her face close to mine. It is dark in the room. "Miguel," Mrs. Smitts whispers, "*tienes que ir a la oficina de* guidance."

"What?" I say.

She leans closer, and her hair blocks the dancers. Despite the clicking castanets and the roomful of students, there is something intimate about this moment. "*Tienes que ir a la oficina de* guidance," she repeats slowly. Then, "You must go to the guidance office. Now. *Vaya.*"

My guidance counselor, Mrs. Dietrich, used to be a history teacher, but she couldn't take it anymore, so she was moved into guidance. On her immaculate desk is a calendar blotter with "LUNCH" written across the middle of every box, including Saturday and Sunday. The only other things on her desk are an empty photo cube and my letter to Mr. Kelly. I sit down, and she shows me the letter as if I haven't yet read it. I reread it.

"Did you write this?" she asks.

I nod affirmatively. I can tell Mrs. Dietrich is especially nervous about this interview. Our meetings are always charged with tension. At the last one, when I was selecting my second-semester courses, she started to laugh hysterically when I said I wanted to take Boys' Home Ec. Now every time I see her in the halls she stops me and asks how I'm doing in Boys' Home Ec. It's the only course of mine she remembers.

I hand the note back to her and say, "I wrote it this morning," as if this clarifies things.

"This morning?"

"At breakfast," I say.

"Do you think this is an acceptable excuse?" Mrs. Dietrich asks. "For missing more than a week of school?"

"I'm sure it isn't," I say.

"Then why did you write it?"

Because it is the truth, I start to say. It is. But somehow I know that saying this will make me more unhappy. It might make me cry. "I've been doing homework," I say.

"That's fine," Mrs. Dietrich says, "but it's not the point. The point is, to graduate you have to attend school for a hundred and eighty days, or have legitimate excuses for the days you've missed. That's the point. Do you want to graduate?"

"Yes," I say.

"Of course you do," Mrs. Dietrich says.

She crumples my note and tries to throw it into the wastepaper basket but misses. We both look for a second at the note lying on the floor, and then I get up and throw it away. The only other thing in her wastepaper basket is a banana peel. I can picture her eating a banana in her tiny office. This, too, makes me sad.

"Sit down," Mrs. Dietrich says.

I sit down.

"I understand your dog died. Do you want to talk about that?"

"No," I say.

"Is that what you're so unhappy about?" she says. "Or is it something else?"

I almost mention the banana peel in her wastebasket, but I don't. "No," I say. "It's just my dog."

Mrs. Dietrich thinks for a moment. I can tell she is embarrassed to be talking about a dead dog. She would be more comfortable if it were a parent or a sibling.

"I don't want to talk about it," I repeat.

She opens her desk drawer and takes out a pad of hall passes. She begins to write one out for me. She has beautiful handwriting. I think of her learning to write beautifully as a child and then growing up to be a guidance counselor, and this makes me unhappy.

"Mr. Neuman is willing to overlook this matter," she says. Mr. Neuman is the principal. "Of course, you will have to make up all the work you've missed. Can you do that?"

"Yes," I say.

Mrs. Dietrich tears the pass from the pad and hands it to me. Our hands touch. "You'll get over this," she says. "Believe me, you will."

My sister works until midnight at the Photo-Matica. It's a tiny booth in the middle of the A&P parking lot. People drive up and leave their film and come back the next day for the pictures. My sister wears a uniform that makes her look like a counterperson in a fast-food restaurant. Sometimes at night when I'm sick of being at home I walk downtown and sit in the booth with her.

There's a machine in the booth that looks like a printing press, only snapshots ride down a conveyor belt and fall into a bin and then disappear. The machine gives the illusion that your photographs are being developed on the spot. It's a fake. The same fifty photographs roll through over and over, and my sister says nobody notices, because everyone in town is taking the same pictures. She opens up the envelopes and looks at them.

Before I go into the booth, I buy cigarettes in the A&P. It is open twenty-four hours a day, and I love it late at night. It is big and bright and empty. The checkout girl sits on her counter swinging her legs. The Muzak plays "If Ever I Would Leave You." Before I buy the cigarettes, I walk up and down the aisles. Everything looks good to eat, and the things that aren't edible look good in their own way. The detergent aisle is colorful and clean-smelling.

My sister is listening to the radio and polishing her nails when I get to the booth. It is almost time to close.

"I hear you went to school today," she says.

"Yeah."

"How was it?" she asks. She looks at her fingernails, which are so long it's frightening.

"It was O.K.," I say. "We made chili dogs in Home Ec."

"So are you over it all?"

I look at the pictures riding down the conveyor belt. I know the order practically by heart: graduation, graduation, birthday, mountains, baby, baby, new car, bride, bride and groom, house. . . . "I guess so," I say.

"Good," says my sister. "It was getting to be a little much." She puts her tiny brush back in the bottle, capping it. She shows me her nails. They're an odd brown shade. "Cinnamon," she says. "It's an earth color." She looks out into the parking lot. A boy is collecting the abandoned shopping carts, forming a long silver train, which he noses back toward the store. I can tell he is singing by the way his mouth moves.

"That's where we found Keds," my sister says, pointing to the Salvation Army bin.

When I went out to buy cigarettes, Keds would follow me. I hung out down here at night before he died. I was unhappy then, too. That's what no one understands. I named him Keds because he was all white with big black feet and it looked as if he had high-top sneakers on. My mother wanted to name him Bootie. Bootie is a cat's name. It's a dumb name for a dog.

"It's a good thing you weren't here when we found him," my sister says. "You would have gone crazy."

I'm not really listening. It's all nonsense. I'm working on a new problem: Find the value for n such that n plus everything else in your life makes you feel all right. What would n equal? Solve for n.

A Changing World

We must act together as a united people for the birth of a new world.

NELSON MANDELA

1. Read the title of this unit. In your reading log, freewrite for a few minutes about how the world is changing.

2. Look at the photograph and read the quotation. Freewrite for a few more minutes.

3. Reread what you wrote and number the different ideas you wrote about. Summarize your ideas and tell them to a partner. Then write down one connection between what you wrote and what your partner wrote.

   Share your ideas with your group.

BEFORE READING

1. Read the title, the introductory information, and the first two sentences of the essay. Then, freewrite for a few minutes about what you expect Michael Dorris to say about Father's Day. Share your thoughts with your partner and then with the class.

2. Read the essay.

Father's Day
Michael Dorris

Michael Dorris, anthropologist, novelist, and nonfiction writer, has written essays on many topics. This selection is from a piece he wrote for National Public Radio in June of 1989. (Father's Day is in June.)

My father, a career army officer, was twenty-seven when he was killed. . . .

. . . I was a few months old the last time he saw me, and a single photograph of me in his arms is the only hard evidence that we ever met. . . .

There was a children's book in the 1950s—perhaps it still exists—titled *The Happy Family*, and it was a piece of work. Dad toiled at the office, Mom baked in the kitchen, and brother and sister always had neighborhood friends sleeping over. The prototype of "Leave It to Beaver" and "Father Knows Best," this little text reflects a midcentury standard, a brightly illustrated reproach to my own unorthodox household, but luckily that wasn't the way I heard it. As read to me by my Aunt Marion—her acid delivery was laced with sarcasm and punctuated with many a sidelong glance—it turned into hilarious irony.

Compassionate and generous, irreverent, simultaneously opinionated and open-minded, iron-willed and ever optimistic, my aunt was the one who pitched a baseball with me in the early summer evenings, who took me horseback riding, who sat by my bed when I was ill. A fierce, lifelong Democrat—a precinct captain even—she helped me find my first jobs and arranged among her friends at work for my escorts to the father-son dinners that closed each sports season. When the time came, she prevailed upon the elderly man next door to teach me how to shave.

"Daddy" Tingle, as he was known to his own children and grandchildren, was a man of many talents. He could spit tobacco juice over the low roof of his garage, gum a sharpened mumbly-peg twig from the ground even without his false teeth, and produce, from the Bourbon Stockyards where he worked, the jewel-like cornea of a cow's eye—but he wasn't much of a shaver. After his instruction, neither am I.

Aunt Marion, on the other hand, was a font of information and influence. When I was fifteen, on a series of tempestuous Sunday mornings at a deserted River Road park, she gave me lessons in how to drive a stick shift. A great believer in the efficacy of the *World Book Encyclopedia*—the major literary purchase of my childhood—she insisted that I confirm any vague belief by looking it up. To the then-popular tune of "You, You, You," she counted my laps in the Crescent Hill pool while I practiced for a life-saving certificate. Operating on the assumption that anything out of the ordinary was probably good for me, she once offered to mortgage the house so that I could afford to go to Mali as a volunteer participant in Operation Crossroads Africa. She paid for my first Smith-Corona typewriter in thirty-six $4-a-week installments.

For over sixty years Aunt Marion was never without steady employment: telegraph operator for Western Union, budget officer for the city of Louisville, "new girl" at a small savings and loan (when, after twenty-five years in a patronage job, the Democrats lost the mayor's race), executive secretary for a nationally renowned attorney.

Being Aunt Marion, she didn't and doesn't give herself much credit. Unless dragged to center stage, she stands at the periphery in snapshots, minimizes her contributions. Every June for forty years I've sent her a Father's Day card.

AFTER READING

1. Reread the text, annotating it. Underline significant words and phrases, make notes in the margins, write questions in the margins, and so on. (See Appendix B.3, pp. 233 and 235, for an explanation and example of annotating.) Exchange books with a classmate and talk about what you marked and why. Tell the class some of the points you thought were important.

2. With your partner, list the things Dorris's Aunt Marion did for him that inspire him to send her a Father's Day card every June. Notice especially the unorthodox (nontraditional) things she did.

HOW I READ IT

Talk with the class about how annotating helped you understand the essay.

HOW IT'S WRITTEN

1. With a partner, choose two or three of the important details Dorris uses to give readers a picture (an image) of Aunt Marion. Does Dorris follow the advice in Appendix E, pp. 241–244, about being specific and about showing instead of telling? Discuss this with your partner.

2. Summarize your discussion for the class.

TOPICS FOR WRITING

Choose one activity.

Activity A: In the second paragraph of this essay, Dorris refers to his "unorthodox household." Write a composition with the title "An Unorthodox Household," in which you describe a family or household that does not fit the usual definition of family. Include specific details.

Activity B: Write a *reminiscence* (a story from your past experience) about someone who was important to you while you were growing up. This might be someone who was like a parent to you, a close friend, or a teacher. Include details about specific things the person did for you. You may want to list these details before you begin writing. (See Appendix A.3, pp. 225–227, for an explanation and example of making a list.)

Activity C: In your opinion, can people other than parents do a good job of raising children? (For example, can aunts be like fathers and uncles be like mothers? Or, can fathers be like mothers and mothers be like fathers?) Write about this. Support your point of view with examples from your own experience or from what you have seen in other families. Include specific details.

AFTER WRITING

1. Photocopy your piece. Then exchange papers with a partner. Annotate one another's writing. Include a comment about how your partner used details.

2. Read your partner's annotations. Circle any comments that give you ideas for improving your piece. Revise your piece.

3. Write in your log about how your partner's annotations helped you (or did not help you) revise your writing.

BEFORE READING

1. Read the title and introductory information. Discuss with your partner what you think the title means.
2. Read the article.

New York Finds Typical Family Being Redefined
Sam Roberts

This excerpt is taken from an article that appeared in the New York Times *in October of 1992. The article is a partial analysis of the 1990 census.*

The traditional American family has declined so far in New York City that married couples living with their own children now constitute only one in six households.

The trend is neither new nor peculiar to New York. But a new analysis of the 1990 census has found that the typical family has been radically redefined.

The share of married couples living with their own children in the city declined from 19.2 percent of all households in 1980 to less than 17 percent in 1990. Among the nation's major cities, it appeared that the percentage of so-called traditional families was lower only in San Francisco.

BEYOND IMMEDIATE FAMILIES

During the last decade, one phenomenon has contributed mightily to the change: the share of New Yorkers living with aunts, uncles, grandparents and other relatives beyond their immediate families rose by 27 percent, or more than 300,000. As a result of family breakups, the rise in foster care, unaffordable housing and an influx of immigrants with extended families, the number of persons in family households living with other relatives soared from 1.1 million in 1980 to more than 1.4 million a decade later. Of all households, they accounted for 20 percent, up from about 16 percent 10 years earlier. . . .

Fully one in four whites do not live in family households at all—a re-flection of the growing number of elderly people who live alone, of unrelated roommates living together to share costs, and, perhaps, of gay and lesbian couples, whom the Census Bureau does not recognize as a separate category.

And one in five households are headed by a woman with no husband present. Female-headed households account for 8 percent of white and of Asian households, 32 percent among blacks and 31 percent among His-panic people. . . .

AFTER READING

1. Reread the article, making a double entry in your log as you read. On the left side of a page, write down three or four points made in the article. On the right side, write your feelings, thoughts, opinions, questions, and so on. (You may want to refer to Appendix B.2, pp. 230–232, to refresh your memory on doing a double-entry notebook.)

2. Exchange logs with a partner. Write a response to your partner's entry (on the next page of his or her notebook). When you are both fin-ished, read and talk about your responses.

3. Use the Reporter's Formula (who, what, where, when, how, and why) to write a one- or two-sentence summary of the article. (See Unit 2, p. 107 for details on how to do this.)

   Read your summary to your group.

HOW I READ IT

1. What was difficult about reading this article? What was easy? What helped you understand it? Freewrite answers to these questions.

2. Share the main points of your writing with the class.

TOPICS FOR WRITING

Choose one activity.

Activity A: In the article, Roberts says that the typical family has been radically redefined. Write an essay explaining this phenomenon. (You might include Dorris's family as one example of a family that does not fit the typical definition.)

Activity B: Read "Family Man," found on p. 215 in the Extra Readings section for this unit. In this essay, Roger L. Welsch says he is still trying to figure out what a family is. He contrasts his family (him, his wife, and his child) with the Omaha tribe's much wider notion of family. What is a typical family in your native culture? Define family as your culture understands it for someone who does not know. Give specific facts and examples to explain what you say.

Activity C: Think of an ancestor in your family whom you never knew but whom your parents or grandparents have told you about. Imagine something about the life and personality of the person and what the world was like then. You might get ideas from an old letter or photograph. Write about one event in the life of the person that either happened or could have happened. For example, you might write about the person's son going off to a war, the person getting married, or selling the farm and moving to the city. Tell about the event in a way that helps the reader understand the person and his or her world.

AFTER WRITING

1. Reread your piece and write a double-entry response to it. (See After Reading, question 1, p. 159, for information on double-entry responses.)

2. Give your piece and your double-entry response to a partner. Read each other's piece and the double-entry writing and write a response to both.

3. Circle anything in your partner's responses that gives you ideas for revising. Find two or three things in your piece you want to change. Number them and, on another paper, list the changes you will make. Then revise your piece.

4. Talk with the class about how the preceding tasks helped you (or did not help you) revise your writing. Write about this in your log for a few minutes.

BEFORE READING

1. The word *power* has several meanings. What comes to mind when you hear the word? Freewrite for three minutes in your reading log.
   Share what you wrote with a partner. Talk about any similarities and differences between what you and your partner wrote.

2. Read the title and introductory information. How do you expect the word *power* to be used in this passage? Read the passage.

Power
Donald McCaig

Donald McCaig and his wife, Anne, operate a sheep farm in the mountains of western Virginia. This passage is from a book called An American Homestead, *which describes life on their farm.*

As I write this, our power's been out twenty-four hours. It's not unusual. Every month or two, some natural calamity knocks lines down in the Virginia highlands, and it sometimes takes a week before it comes back on.

It's not too bad. We've got springs where we can draw water, our cookstove uses gas, and we heat with wood. The biggest problem is the freezers, which we swaddle in space blankets and down sleeping bags so they don't thaw.

The best of no electricity is the quiet. No hum of refrigerator motors, no whoosh as the gas water heater ignites, no whine of the water pump. Our farmhouse is an old log house, and for a hundred years, people must have sat in this kitchen talking quietly with no sound louder than the songbirds outside, the crackle of the fire, maybe the solemn tick of a mantel clock. News was what your neighbor told you. Right now, our news is that the electric co-op trucks have been seen just down the road in Williamsville.

It wasn't until 1948 the REA put electricity down our valley, and first place farmers wanted it was the barn—for the electric milking machine. When power did come into the house, they'd string a line across the ceiling until it stopped and dangled, bare bulb, right above the farmer's favorite reading chair.

The electricity people promised to relieve the farm family of drudgery. With no clothes to scrub or kerosene lamps to clean or water to tote, everybody could lean back and take it easy. If you ask the old people how it was before the electricity, they'll talk about quilting bees and homecomings and how they used to come calling on a Sunday afternoon. Nobody seems to remember the drudgery.

Without electricity, it gets dark in the house very early. We read by candle or kerosene lamp; the TV sits mute in the corner. Tonight I think I'll bring out a deck of cards. Perhaps Anne and I can play cribbage, or hearts, or pinochle, or bezique.

AFTER READING

1. Was the word *power* used in the way you expected or in a different way? Share your thoughts with a partner.

2. Choose one activity.

   Activity A: Reread the text, underline the ideas that strike you, and then write for five minutes in your reading log about any idea that especially interests you.
   Share your writing with your group.

   Activity B: What is McCaig's attitude toward electricity? Reread the essay to find out. Mark positive attitudes toward electricity with a plus (+) and negative attitudes with a minus (−).
   Share your findings with your group.

HOW IT'S WRITTEN

Reread paragraph three. Notice the details McCaig uses to support the first sentence of that paragraph. Make a list of the details that appeal to the sense of hearing. Are these details effective in showing how McCaig feels about the quietness when there is no electricity? Talk about this with your group.

TOPICS FOR WRITING

Choose one activity.

Activity A: Think of a time in your life when you had to do without a kind of modern technology you had become used to. Write about the effect that had on your daily life. Try to include details that appeal to one of the senses.

Activity B: Write a story, real or imaginary, about a power outage. Try to include details that appeal to one of the senses.

Activity C: Make a list of the kinds of technology that helped you at work or school today. Choose one thing on your list. First, describe in writing what your workplace or school is like *with* that technology. Then, describe in writing what it would be like at work or school *without* that technology. Try to include details that appeal to one of the senses.

AFTER WRITING

1. Exchange papers with a classmate. Write a response to your classmate's writing.

   a. What do you like best about the piece?

   b. What details are especially effective?

   c. What would you like to know more about or what is not clear to you?

2. Read your classmate's responses to your writing. Find two or three things you want to change in your piece. Revise your piece.

3. In your log, write for a few minutes about *how* you wrote this composition. (See Appendix D, pp. 238–239, for more explanation and examples.)

***

BEFORE READING

1. Skim the piece: Read the title, subtitle, author's name, and the first sentence of each paragraph. Note the form used for the end of the essay.

2. In your log, write one statement you think Berry will make in his essay. Share your statement with your group and then with the class. Then read the whole piece.

Against PCs
Why I'm Not Going to Buy a Computer

Wendell Berry

Wendell Berry is an essayist, novelist, and poet who often writes about preserving our land and resources.

Like almost everybody else, I am hooked to the energy corporations, which I do not admire. I hope to become less hooked to them. In my work, I try to be as little hooked to them as possible. As a farmer, I do almost all of my work with horses. As a writer, I work with a pencil or a pen and a piece of paper.

My wife types my work on a Royal standard typewriter bought new in 1956, and as good now as it was then. As she types, she sees things that are wrong, and marks them with small checks in the margins. She is my best critic because she is the one most familiar with my habitual errors and weaknesses. She also understands, sometimes better than I do, what *ought* to be said. We have, I think, a literary cottage industry that works well and pleasantly. I do not see anything wrong with it.

A number of people, by now, have told me that I could greatly improve things by buying a computer. My answer is that I am not going to do it. I have several reasons, and they are good ones.

The first is the one I mentioned at the beginning. I would hate to think that my work as a writer could not be done without a direct dependence on strip-mined coal. How could I write conscientiously against the rape of nature if I were, in the act of writing, implicated in the rape? For the same reason, it matters to me that my writing is done in the daytime, without electric light.

I do not admire the computer manufacturers a great deal more than I admire the energy industries. I have seen their advertisements, attempting to seduce struggling or failing farmers into the belief that they can solve their problems by buying yet another piece of expensive equipment. I am familiar with their propaganda campaigns that have put computers into public schools that are in need of books. That computers are expected to become as common as TV sets in "the future" does not impress me or matter to me. I do not own a TV set. I do not see that computers are bringing us one step nearer to anything that does matter to me: peace, economic justice, ecological health, political honesty, family and community stability, good work.

What would a computer cost me? More money, for one thing, than I can afford, and more than I wish to pay to people whom I do not admire. But the cost would not be just monetary. It is well understood that technological innovation always requires the discarding of the "old model"—the "old model" in this case being not just our old Royal standard, but my wife, my critic, my closest reader, my fellow worker. Thus (and I think this is typical of present-day technological innovation), what would be superseded would be not only some thing, but some body. In order to be technologically up-to-date as a writer, I would have to sacrifice an association that I am dependent upon and that I treasure.

My final and perhaps my best reason for not owning a computer is that I do not wish to fool myself. I disbelieve, and therefore strongly resent, the assertion that I or anybody else could write better or more easily with a computer than with a pencil. I do not see why I should not be as scientific about this as the next fellow: When somebody has used a computer to write work that is demonstrably better than Dante's, and when this better is demonstrably attributable to the use of a computer, then I will speak of computers with a more respectful tone of voice, though I still will not buy one.

To make myself as plain as I can, I should give my standards for technological innovation in my own work. They are as follows:

1. The new tool should be cheaper than the one it replaces.

2. It should be at least as small in scale as the one it replaces.

3. It should do work that is clearly and demonstrably better than the one it replaces.

4. It should use less energy than the one it replaces.

5. If possible, it should use some form of solar energy, such as that of the body.

6. It should be repairable by a person of ordinary intelligence, provided that he or she has the necessary tools.

7. It should be purchasable and repairable as near to home as possible.

8. It should come from a small, privately owned shop or store that will take it back for maintenance and repair.

9. It should not replace or disrupt anything good that already exists, and this includes family and community relationships.

AFTER READING

1. Make a double entry in your log: On the left side of a page, write down two or three things Berry said that surprised or interested you. On the right side, write your feelings, thoughts, opinions, associations, questions, and so on.
   Share your writing with your group.

2. With a partner, make a list of the reasons Berry gives for not wanting to buy a computer.
   Share the list with your group. Then each person in the group should take one of the reasons and explain it fully to the others.

3. At the end of the essay, Berry says, "I should give my standards for technological innovation in my own work. They are as follows: . . ." What does he mean? What is the purpose of the nine points he lists? Talk about this with your group.

4. A reader can learn a great deal about the character of a person by what the person writes. What kind of person do you think Wendell Berry is? Write a short description of him in your log. Support your impressions with references from his essay. Write for someone who has not read the essay.
   Share your writing with your group.

HOW I READ IT

1. How did skimming the piece before reading it help your reading? Talk about this with your group.

2. Share your findings with the class.

TOPICS FOR WRITING

1. Choose one activity.

   Activity A: Find one statement of Berry's that you strongly agree with or strongly disagree with. Write an essay stating your opinion and explaining why you think this way.

   Activity B: Think of a piece of modern technology that you do not wish to own. Write an essay called "Against _____: Why I Am Not Going to Buy a _____."

   Activity C: Berry's essay appeared in *Harper's* magazine. Write a letter to the magazine giving your reactions to the essay.

2. Save this piece.

3. Now read two of the letters in which readers responded to Berry's essay.

Letters
(in response to Berry's article)

Wendell Berry's essay "Against PCs" provoked many letters from readers of Harper's. *Two of those letters appear here.*

Wendell Berry provides writers enslaved by the computer with a handy alternative: Wife—a low-tech energy-saving device. Drop a pile of handwritten notes on Wife and you get back a finished manuscript, edited while it was typed. What computer can do that? Wife meets all of Berry's uncompromising standards for technological innovation: she's cheap, repairable near home, and good for the family structure. Best of all, Wife is politically correct because she breaks a writer's "direct dependence on strip-mined coal."

History teaches us that Wife can also be used to beat rugs and wash clothes by hand, thus eliminating the need for the vacuum cleaner and washing machine, two more nasty machines that threaten the act of writing.

GORDON INKELES
Miranda, Calif.

The value of a computer to a writer is that it is a tool not for generating ideas but for typing and editing words. It is cheaper than a secretary (or a wife!) and arguably more fuel-efficient. And it enables spouses who are not inclined to provide free labor more time to concentrate on *their* own work.

We should support alternatives both to coal-generated electricity and to IBM-style technocracy. But I am reluctant to entertain alternatives that presuppose the traditional subservience of one class to another. Let the PCs come and the wives and servants go seek more meaningful work.

TOBY KOOSMAN
Knoxville, Tenn.

AFTER READING

1. a. Each group of four people should choose one letter, reread it, and restate the important points the writer makes.

   b. Split your group into two pairs, and find another pair that read the other letter. Make a new group of four. Explain to the other pair what the letter you read said.

2. Work with your partner. Write one sentence that expresses the main point of each letter.

   Are the main points of the two letters similar or different? (In other words, do Inkeles and Koosman agree or disagree?) Discuss this with the class.

BEFORE READING

1. Write down one thing you would say in a reply if you were Berry. Read it to your group.

2. Read Berry's reply.

Wendell Berry Replies

The foregoing letters surprised me with the intensity of the feelings they expressed. According to the writers' testimony, there is nothing wrong with their computers; they are utterly satisfied with them and all that they stand for. My correspondents are certain that I am wrong and that I am, moreover, on the losing side, a side already relegated to the dustbin of history. And yet they grow huffy and condescending over my tiny dissent. What are they so anxious about? . . .

I am also surprised by the meanness with which two of these writers refer to my wife. In order to imply that I am a tyrant, they suggest by both direct statement and innuendo that she is subservient, characterless, and stupid— a mere "device" easily forced to provide meaningless "free labor." I understand that it is impossible to make an adequate public defense of one's private life, and so I will only point out that there are a number of kinder possibilities that my critics have disdained to imagine: that my wife may do this work because she wants to and likes to; that she may find some use and some meaning in it; that she may not work for nothing. These gentlemen obviously think themselves feminists of the most correct and principled sort, and yet they do not hesitate to stereotype and insult, on the basis of one fact, a woman they do not know. They are audacious and irresponsible gossips. . . .

Finally, it seems to me that none of my correspondents recognizes the innovativeness of my essay. If the use of a computer is a new idea, then a newer idea is not to use one.

AFTER READING

1. Did Berry say any of the things you or your group members would have said? Write in your log for a few minutes.

2. With a partner, write a summary sentence of each paragraph of Berry's reply. Compare your sentences with those of others in your group. Share your findings with the class.

3. Which writer do you agree with most, Inkeles, Koosman, or Berry? Or do you agree with none of the three? Write for ten minutes in your reading log.

    Read your writing to your group.

AFTER WRITING

1. Having read the two letters and Berry's reply, you can now reread with new eyes what you wrote for Topics for Writing. Rewrite the piece with these questions in mind:

   Should new ideas be added?

   Do you want to take out, change, or reorder ideas?

   Should you begin or end the piece in a different way?

   Do you want to rewrite the piece completely?

2. Pass your rewritten piece to others in your group. Attach a page to the paper on which group members can write a comment about your writing.

3. Write in your log about how you rewrote your piece. For example, what did you change? Why?

BEFORE READING

1. As a class make a cluster around the words *information highway*. (See Appendix A.2, pp. 224–225, for an explanation and example of clustering.) If someone does not understand a word or phrase, try to explain it to that person.

2. Read the title and subtitle of this piece. What do you think *cyberhood* means? Discuss this with the class.

3. Read the passage.

Cyberhood vs. Neighborhood
Won't You Be, Won't You Be, Please Won't You Be in My Newsgroup @ real.community.nowhere . . .

Editors, Utne Reader

> *This short passage appeared in the* Utne Reader *as an introduction to several articles about communicating via computer. It poses a question about computer communications and community. The magazine editors labeled the issue or question "cyberhood vs. neighborhood." The essay that follows this passage was one of the original articles on this topic.*

Community is one of those terms that six people in the same conversation might use differently without knowing it. What is "real" community? Must it be connected to a place or a neighborhood? Can it exist in cyberspace? Does it? Can the "gay community," or the "medical community," or the "Hispanic community" really be called such if they aren't place-based? Is a suburban housing development really a community, even if it *is* place-based? Although networking (on-line and otherwise) might lead people to turn their backs on the place they live, it can also be a real source of solace and fellowship for those who cannot connect with their next-door neighbors.

It isn't necessary to come to a final definition of what "community" means to understand that in an increasingly fragmented society, it's important for us to find ways to support one another, whether we live together or not. The debate that rages . . . is always, at bottom, about being good neighbors. . . .

AFTER READING

1. With the class, add to your definition of *cyberhood*.

2. Choose one question asked in the passage and freewrite an answer.
   Read your question and answer to your group.

3. As a group, write one or two sentences stating the main idea (kernel idea) of the passage. (See Appendix A.1, p. 223, for an explanation of kernel idea.)
   Read your sentences to the class.

4. With your partner, make a list of some of the words and phrases associated with the topic of computer communications that you learned from reading and talking about this passage. Put the words into groups that go together, or categories. Give a title to each category.

BEFORE READING

1. Read the title and introduction to this passage. Freewrite for a few minutes in your log about what you just read. Tell your group members what you wrote about.

2. With your group make a list of some of the uses of the Internet. Read your list to the class.

3. Read the passage.

Whiz Kid Anonymous
A 10-year-old's Take on the Internet

Michael Kearney

Michael Kearney was just ten years old and already a graduate of a four-year college when he wrote this essay. He is a correspondent on ABC's Mike & Maty *talk show.*

My dad has a modem, but he says I'll never get to use it, because he's worried that I'll roll up huge phone bills on the Internet. And he's right to be worried. I would be on it all day and night. I'd be in every discussion group, every special interest group, all the game groups, except maybe a few of the role-playing groups. (I'm just a little scared of them because I've heard that some of the people there are quite weird—people sitting at home wearing spinning beanies, waiting for the magic potion.)

One of the greatest things about the Internet is that no one has to know who you are. So if you're living in a really prejudiced part of town—say they don't like Hispanics or something—you could talk to them. And they don't have to know how old you are. There have been times when people my own age may not be interested in what I'm interested in, and, at the same time, people who are older than I am, who might be interested, don't always want to spend time with someone so much younger than they are. But if you are on the Internet, things like age are unimportant—or invisible, anyway, if you want them to be.

I think the Internet is going to help close gaps between different parts of the world, because people will be able to get answers for their problems, find research that's been gathered together. Even if only one person in a village has a computer and some training, they would be able to research much more, be able to find better ways to light houses and warm houses and things like that.

And just the fact that you are always talking to people from different groups and from different places will be very good for people. In the short run, it may squish social relationships a little. I mean, who will want to go over to someone's house for a cup of tea and some talk when you can just call up on the modem? But in the long run, for the whole world, it will probably be very good for social relationships. Because it is going to put people on the same level, for some of the time, at least. It will stick them all together—it will be great.

AFTER READING

1. Reread the essay, annotating it. Explain your annotations to a partner. Talk about whether Kearney mentions any of the uses of the Internet that you listed in Before Reading, question 2.

2. With your group, summarize Kearney's opinion about cyberhood as neighborhood.

3. Add to your list of words and phrases associated with the topic of computer communications (from After Reading, question 4, p. 172).

HOW IT'S WRITTEN

1. Do a descriptive outline of this essay. (See Appendix B.4, pp. 233 and 236, for details on how to do descriptive outlining.)

2. In your log, write about what you learned from doing a descriptive outline of this passage. How might you apply this technique to your own writing?

TOPICS FOR WRITING

Choose one activity.

Activity A: What makes a good neighbor? Could computer groups be considered good neighbors? What kinds of problems might you have with either real neighbors or computer "neighbors"? Write an essay giving your ideas. You might use Michael Kearney's essay as a model.

Activity B: Choose a sentence or idea from "Whiz Kid Anonymous" that you strongly agree or disagree with. Write a composition explaining your point of view. Use examples from your own experience or your observation of others to illustrate your ideas.

Activity C: Write an essay defining *community* as you understand it. Use examples to illustrate your definition.

Activity D: Write a story or essay with the title "Neighborhood."

AFTER WRITING

1. Photocopy your piece. Give it to a partner to annotate. The reader should then write one or two sentences stating the main point (kernel idea).

2. Read what your partner wrote to see if you communicated what you meant to say. Then reread your paper and find two or three things to improve. Number these. On another piece of paper, write down the changes you will make. Revise your composition.

3. Write in your log about what you changed and why.

BEFORE READING

1. In your log, freewrite for five minutes about the title of this passage. Read your writing to a partner.

2. Look through the passage. Note the breaks (marked by *). While reading, when you get to each break, stop and write down one thing that is in your mind (for example, a question, reaction, confusion, association, image, or prediction). Now read the passage.

Pockets of Paradise: The Community Garden
Editors, Seeds of Change

This essay appeared in a seed catalog for a company called Seeds of Change. This organization sells organically grown seeds, many of them traditional and unusual varieties, and supports biological diversity.

Through the ages, Paradise has been portrayed most often as a garden—and small wonder! Gardens, and gardening, are the source of so many delights: spiritual, psychological, aesthetic, creative, physical, and practical. Besides the obvious material rewards of fruits, flowers, and vegetables, the process of growing a garden offers contact with nature, teaches the essential life skills of responsibility, nurturing and commitments, and brings the satisfaction of achievement through work.

For those who garden with their neighbors, there are also enormous social rewards to be reaped. Since the early 1970s, community gardens across the country have been bringing people together to achieve common goals and create positive change. Many of these gardens are found in low-income neighborhoods of the inner city, in vacant lots previously filled with garbage; transforming these eyesores into gardens often calls for untraditional agricultural skills such as pulling tires and concrete out of the soil, or discouraging drug dealers from congregating at the site.

"Gardening is the catalyst that brings residents from behind locked doors to work together," says Georgia Ashby of Philadelphia Green, the country's largest comprehensive community gardening program and a model for others nationwide. "The gardens that begin as a place to grow flowers and relax, awaken a sense of community. . . . In some cases, this is the beginning of turning a neighborhood around." From Harlem to Los Angeles, from

Boston to Denver, people are finding that working in gardens has empowered them and revitalized their communities. City gardeners may start out just wanting to grow good food, but tending a garden frequently becomes a metaphor for tending a neighborhood. . . .

*

A VILLAGE GREEN

Perhaps the primary ingredient of improving a community is bringing together the people who live there. The garden is a meeting place for people of all races, colors, faiths and professions. "The garden acts like a village green," according to Jackie Beech Bukowsky of New York City's West Side Community Garden. "There's a diverse mix of people. If two older ladies saw some of these guys walking down the street, they'd probably cross to the other side. But in the garden, those guys will be playing a game of chess right next to them."

Melitte Buchman, from Lower East Side People Care in New York, talks about what she learned from Mrs. Moi, an elderly Chinese woman who speaks little English and has a special way of making things grow. "Mrs. Moi would put light-colored cans over her transplants and leave them there for two days. Her plants never went into transplanting shock. Now everyone in the garden does it. Our garden looks silly at transplanting time, but our plants take off."

The process of addressing issues and concerns in a community garden is often reminiscent of a traditional town meeting. Opinions are shared, differences are voiced, with the well-being of the garden providing the essential ingredient in reaching consensus. To Marty Kashuba of San Francisco's Good Prospect Garden, the garden is "a microcosm of society and life itself, a study of how people work out problems and address each other's differences." . . .

*

Thomas Jefferson wrote, "Cultivators of the earth are the most valuable citizens . . . the most vigorous, the most virtuous, and they are tied to their country and wedded to its liberty and interests by the most lasting bonds." Although today's urban landscape is far different from the one Jefferson imagined for America's future, the proliferation of community gardens means that his vision of a strong, democratic citizenry will continue to thrive. People at work in their gardens are beautifying their communities, improving their lives and reviving the democratic process. And all the while, they get to enjoy those great tomatoes, carrots, beans, melons, peppers, sunflowers and marigolds.

AFTER READING

1. Give your reading log to a partner. Read each other's responses to this essay. In your partner's log, write a short response to what your partner wrote.

2. Reread the essay, annotating it as you read. Explain your annotations to your group.

3. With your group, explain the meaning of the title of the essay. Share your explanation with the class.

HOW I READ IT

1. Freewrite about *how* you read this passage. Use the following questions as a guide:

   Was the essay easy or difficult to read? Why?

   Did you reread anything? What? Why?

   What did you do when you didn't understand something?

   Did writing when you came to a break help your understanding?

2. Share your writing with the class.

3. In your reading log, answer these questions about how you read: Are your reading strategies similar to other people's? Different? Did you learn any new reading strategies from hearing what other people said? If so, what? (You may want to read Appendix C again, p. 237, to refresh your memory of the reading process.)

HOW IT'S WRITTEN

1. Working with a partner, look at the use of quotation marks (" ") in this article. Talk about the purpose of using these marks.

2. With your partner, examine the way the writer uses quotations to support his or her ideas. Do the following:

   a. Reread the essay and make a list of the people cited (quoted). What does each one say? Write a brief summary next to each person's name. Explain why you think the writer quoted so many people.

b. Underline the words and phrases the writer uses to show readers who is being quoted in each case. Notice the different ways of introducing people.

3. Talk with the class about what you and your partner learned that you can apply to your own writing.

TOPICS FOR WRITING

Choose one activity.

Activity A: Paragraph three of this essay says: "City gardeners may start out just wanting to grow food, but tending a garden frequently becomes a metaphor for tending a neighborhood." Locate a community garden in your city and interview some of the people involved to discover the effects of their garden on the neighborhood. Think of some questions first. Take notes or tape record the interviews. Write about what you learned. Try to include some of the words of the people you interviewed to support your ideas.

Activity B: Think of an activity in your community that has drawn your community or neighborhood together. Talk with some of the people involved to find out how they think this activity has affected the neighborhood. Write an essay about the activity, and use some quotations from the people you talked with to support your ideas.

Activity C: Think about some of the differences and similarities between a physical neighborhood and a cyberhood (computer community). Make a list of these. Then write an essay comparing and contrasting these two kinds of communities. If you need more information, talk with someone who regularly communicates via computer. Try to quote this person in your composition.

AFTER WRITING

1. Read your partner's paper. Write a summary sentence of each paragraph. Then answer these questions:

a. What point is the piece making, if any?

     b. Does each paragraph concentrate on one aspect of the point?

     c. Does each paragraph help to develop the point?

     d. Does each paragraph connect with the paragraph before it?

     e. Does the last paragraph "wrap it up" in some way?

2. Read your partner's responses to your writing. Circle comments that give you ideas for revising. Revise your piece.

3. Read your revised piece to your group. Choose one composition to read to the class.

4. Write for a few minutes about *how* you wrote and revised this piece. For example, did your partner's paragraph summaries help you? Did the answers to the questions help you? How?

BEFORE READING

1. What do you do when you have a cold? Talk about this with your group.

2. Read the title and introduction to the passage. Write down two questions you hope the article will answer. Talk about your questions with your group.

3. Read the passage.

Take Two Bowls of Garlic Pasta, Then Call Me in the Morning
Or Try a Dose of Echinacea a Day

Suzanne Hamlin

> *This excerpt was taken from an article that appeared in the* New York Times. *A caption accompanying the article said, "To fight colds, some researchers suggest herbs, vitamin supplements and foods like garlic, chicken and chili peppers."*

It is 3:30 on a cold, darkening winter afternoon. Your throat begins to close; your eyes are watery; you feel faint, chilled. There is no mistaking the symptoms, no denying this mean, indiscriminate viral invasion that strikes without warning and without justice.

A cold is a conundrum waiting for a cure. In the hundreds of years that medical scientists have tried to eliminate the universal cold, they have managed only to provide a huge and confusing choice of boxed and bottled medications, none of which claim to cure but all of which promise to relieve specific cold symptoms. Worldwide sales of over-the-counter cold medications surpass $4 billion annually, with almost half of that total in the United States alone.

But a growing number of researchers are advocating the simplest and least expensive of remedies—food and its compounds. These approaches, some of which have traditionally been used to alleviate cold symptoms in other cultures, employ foods like garlic, ginger, chili peppers and citrus fruits; vitamins and minerals like vitamin C and zinc, and the extracts of edible flowers like echinacea.

Some of these substances, called phytochemicals in the laboratory, may eventually be shown to prevent colds, while others are being tested as treatments once symptoms start.

"This is a very exciting time to be in nutrition and disease research," said Dr. Barbara Levine, who is part of a group collecting data on the medical potential of both zinc and garlic.

"Where we used to look at nutritional deficiencies, now we are looking at the vitamins, minerals and phytochemicals in foods that may prevent and treat disease," said Dr. Levine, the coordinator of clinical nutrition research at the Memorial Sloan-Kettering Cancer Center and the director of nutrition research at the Strang Cancer Prevention Center of Cornell University Medical College.

Zinc, a mineral found in red meats, seafood, cereals, beans, cheese and nuts, may cut the duration of colds. In a 1992 study at Dartmouth College, 73 students who had just caught colds were monitored, with half of them receiving zinc gluconate lozenges and the other half placebo lozenges. Among those receiving zinc, 42 percent reported shorter colds and milder symptoms. . . .

Vitamin C and citrus fruits, long considered possible antidotes to colds, may help some people, too. A recent study by Dr. Elliot Dick, a professor of preventive medicine at the University of Wisconsin, concluded that vitamin C can reduce the severity of a cold. In a double-blind study involving 16 college students—half of whom took 2,000 milligrams of vitamin C daily with the rest receiving a placebo—13 caught colds when exposed to cold viruses, but the ones who had taken the vitamin C had much milder symptoms and recovered faster.

Research continues on the action of ginger and chili peppers as expectorants, which cause the sneezing and coughing that help work cold viruses out of the body.

But the most powerful of the food remedies may be garlic, the world's most popular folkloric food cure-all.

Since 1858, when Louis Pasteur discovered that garlic could kill bacteria, it has been the focus of extensive research on its possible role in preventing and treating cancer and heart disease as well as its use as an antibiotic. At a medical symposium on phytochemicals in Washington last year, Dr. Herbert Pierson, who developed the cancer preventive foods project at the National Cancer Institute, attributed garlic's power to its complex compounds, which appear to enhance the immune system.

Unlike the flu, which can cause high fever, violent headaches and debilitating stomach cramps, a common cold is usually characterized by a clogged head, runny nose, itchy eyes and mild aches and pains.

Chicken soup, or Jewish penicillin, has been prescribed for colds since Moses Maimonides (A.D. 1135–1204), a doctor, philosopher and cold researcher, began singing its praises. More recently, the Mayo Clinic and Mount Sinai Medical Center have endorsed chicken soup as a way to soothe cold symptoms and relieve congestion. No one knows what ingredient in the soup does the work, but controlled laboratory tests found that it was far more effective than hot water. . . .

Just as foods are being studied for potential healing powers, so are some edible flowers. Echinacea (pronounced eh-kih-NAY-sha) is especially popular now with people seeking relief from colds. An indigenous plant commonly called purple coneflower, it was used by American Indians, and later by immigrants, as an immune system booster and infection fighter.

When antibiotic drugs became available in the 1930's, echinacea waned and by the 1950's had disappeared from pharmacists' references. In the herbal revival of the 1970's it began a comeback and is now one of the five best-selling herbal medicines in the country, said Mark Blumenthal, the executive director of the American Botanical Council in Austin, Tex. . . .

Many medical researchers are skeptical of such supposed remedies.

"It would be highly irresponsible to recommend any remedy that had not been through a complete double-blind test," said Dr. Jack Gwaltney Jr., a professor who directs the division of epidemiology and virology at the University of Virginia School of Medicine and has been an authority on the cold virus for more than 20 years. (In a double-blind test, half a test group is given one medication, the other half is given a placebo, and neither the subjects nor the researchers know who is receiving the medication or the placebo until the testing ends.)

But advocates of alternative medicine say that the cost of the testing required by the Food and Drug Administration for new drugs can be astronomical, up to $231 million according to a recent study at Tufts University.

"No pharmaceutical company can afford to spend that kind of money to prove that a natural, herbal medicine is safe and effective," said Mr. Blumenthal of the Botanical Council. "Unless they can patent it, they will never make back their investment."

Meanwhile, if Dr. Asim Dasgupta is successful, all known cold remedies may become pharmaceutical dinosaurs. Dr. Dasgupta, a professor of microbiology and immunology at U.C.L.A., recently discovered, by accident, a molecule tucked into the genetic structure of everyday baker's yeast that may prevent cold viruses from replicating inside human cells. The yeast molecule is now under close scrutiny, but it will be at least two years before it can be tested in humans.

AFTER READING

1. Reread the article, annotating it. Explain your annotations to your group.
2. Work with a partner. Choose one activity. Be sure some people in your group choose a different activity.

    Activity A: Read the article again. Make a list of all the important ideas in the article. Under each main idea, list the facts and examples the writer uses to support that idea.

    Activity B: Newspaper articles are often a mixture of facts, opinions, and examples. Go through the article again, labeling each fact (f), opinion (o), or example (e) you find.

3. Talk to your group about what you just did.

HOW I READ IT

Talk with your group about *how* you read this article. For example, what did you do when you came to words you didn't understand? Did annotating the article help you understand its meaning? Did it help to talk about and list facts and examples, or label facts, opinions, and examples (as you did in After Reading)? How did asking questions (as you did in Before Reading) change the way you read the article?

In your log, write down a few ideas that might help you be a better reader.

HOW IT'S WRITTEN

Suzanne Hamlin interviewed science experts for this article. Discuss with your group how she integrated what they said into the article.

TOPICS FOR WRITING

Choose one activity.

Activity A: Interview someone who knows about herbal healing (for example, an older person in your family). Write down the person's exact words or tape record the interview. Write an article for your school newspaper about what plants or herbs this person recommends for one or several illnesses. If possible, include examples that show the effects of these herbs.

Activity B: Using herbs for healing is one kind of alternative medicine being practiced by many people today. What other kinds of alternative healing do you know about? Make a list of these in your reading log. Write an essay about one of the items on your list. Explain what this kind of healing is, who practices it, and what successes it has had. If possible, interview someone who practices this kind of medicine or healing. Include some of the person's words and examples in your essay.

Activity C: Near the end of this article, Ms. Hamlin quotes Dr. Jack Gwaltney, who said, "It would be highly irresponsible to recommend any remedy that had not been through a complete double-blind test." It seems that doctors disagree about the effectiveness of foods and plants in treating illnesses. What is your opinion about this kind of healing? Write an essay explaining your point of view. Try to include quotations from people you know or have read about to support what you say.

Activity D: The field of medicine is constantly changing. This article shows one way in which medicine has changed over the years. Think of another recent change in medicine (for example, heart bypass surgery, organ replacements, polio vaccine). If possible, interview someone who knows about this change or read about it to get more information. Write about the causes and results of this medical "innovation."

AFTER WRITING

1. Go over your paper carefully with a pen in your hand. Read each word aloud so that your ear can hear it, and touch each word with your pen to find errors and parts that don't sound right. Don't stop until you find at least three things to change.

2. Give your paper to a classmate. Ask for written comments on whatever you need help with. (For example, you might want your reader to label each fact, opinion, and example she or he finds, or to outline the main ideas and list the facts and examples.)

3. Read your classmate's comments. Revise your piece in any way you wish. (For example, you may want to add new ideas; clarify existing ideas; take out, change, or reorder material; begin or end in a different way; or rewrite the piece completely.)

4. Read your revised piece to your group.

5. Write about *how* you wrote this piece. What did you change when you revised and why? What helped you decide to make changes?

BEFORE READING

1. Read the title and introductory information about the passage.

2. Write down a question you would like to be answered in the passage. Share your question with your group, and make a group list of questions.

3. With the class and your instructor, write on the chalkboard the words you associate with the word *macho*. With a partner, put the words into categories, and give each category a heading (title).

4. Read the selection.

Taming Macho Ways
Elvia Alvarado

This selection is taken from the true story of Elvia Alvarado, who worked as an organizer of the peasant women in her community in Honduras for the National Congress of Rural Workers (CNTC). In the process, she evolved from passively accepting her poverty-stricken life to actively changing the conditions of her life and community. In this passage, she talks about wanting to change the way men and women treat each other.

Machismo is a historical problem. It goes back to the time of our great-grandfathers, or our great-great-grandfathers. In my mind, it's connected to the problem of drinking. Drinking is man's worst disease. When men drink, they fight with everyone. They hit their wives and children. They offend their neighbors. They lose all sense of dignity.

How are we going to stop campesinos from drinking? First of all, we know the government isn't interested in stopping it, because it's an important source of income. Every time you buy a bottle of liquor, part of that money goes to the government.

That's why the government doesn't let the campesinos make their own liquor, because the government doesn't make any money off homemade brew. So a campesino can go into town any time, day or night, spend all his money, and drink himself sick. But if he gets caught making *choruco*—that's what we call homemade spirits made from corn and sugar—they throw him in jail. The government wants the campesinos to drink, but only the liquor that they make money off of.

If we're ever going to get campesinos to stop drinking, we first have to look at why so many campesinos drink. And for that we have to look at what kind of society we have. We've built up a society that treats people like trash, a society that doesn't give people jobs, a society that doesn't give people a reason to stay sober. I think that's where this vice comes from.

I've seen what happens when campesinos organize and have a plot of land to farm. They don't have time for drinking any more, except on special occasions. They spend the day in the hot sun—plowing, planting, weeding, irrigating, cutting firewood for the house, carrying the produce to market. Most of them are very dedicated to their work and their families.

So I've noticed that once the campesinos have a purpose, once they have a way to make a living and take care of their families, they drink less. And they usually stop beating their wives, too. And I've seen that once the women get organized, they start to get their husbands in line.

I know that changing the way men and women treat each other is a long process. But if we really want to build a new society, we have to change the bad habits of the past. We can't build a new society if we are drunks, womanizers, or corrupt. No, those things have to change.

But people *can* change. I know there are many things I used to do that I don't do any more, now that I'm more educated. For example, I used to gossip and criticize other women. I used to fight over men. But I learned that gossip only destroys, it doesn't build. Criticizing my neighbors doesn't create unity. Neither does fighting over men. So I stopped doing these things.

Before, whenever I'd see the slightest thing I'd go running to my friends, "Ay, did you see so-and-so with what's-his-face?" I'd go all over town telling everyone what I saw. Now I could see a woman screwing a man in the middle of the street and I wouldn't say anything. That's her business.

If someone is in danger, then, yes, we have to get involved. For example, I heard a rumor that a landowner was out to kill one of the campesino leaders I work with. I made sure to warn the campesino so he'd be careful. That kind of rumor we tell each other—but not idle gossip.

I also used to flirt with married men, just for the fun of it and to make their wives jealous. Now I'm much more responsible, much more serious. That doesn't mean I don't joke around and have a good time. I just make it clear that we're friends.

We all have to make changes. Campesino men have to be more responsible with their women. They have to have only one woman. Because they have a hard enough time supporting one family, let alone two. Campesinos who drink have to stop drinking. And campesinos who fight with their wives have to stop fighting. Our struggle has to begin in our own homes.

AFTER READING

1. Write for a few minutes in your log what you think the passage is about and how you feel about it. Read over what you wrote, and underline the sentences that best express what you think and feel. Save this for discussion with your group.

2. As a group, look at the list of questions your group made before reading. Which can be answered by the passage? Find the sentences or paragraphs in the text that would contribute to the answers. Mark those places with the question number (1, 2, etc.).

   Then, write down the questions you and your group still have—the ones that were not answered in the passage.

3. Choose one activity.

   Activity A: If you aren't familiar with Spanish, first write down some possible definitions of *machismo* and *campesino*. Then, find out the meaning of those words from a native speaker of Spanish in the class (or a dictionary). Refine your definition.

   Activity B: The author, Elvia Alvarado, says "people *can* change" and uses herself as an example: "There are many things I used to do that I don't do any more, now that I'm more educated." With a partner, make a list of specific ways in which people may change when they become more educated.

4. Report your findings to your group.

HOW IT'S WRITTEN

1. One way of supporting a point of view in writing is to give examples from your own experience or from your observations of others. Reread the essay noticing Alvarado's use of examples. Circle each example. Put *P* next to each example that is personal and *O* next to each example that is an observation of others.

2. Talk about these questions with your group. Which kind of example does Alvarado use most often? What effect do these examples have on you as a reader?

TOPICS FOR WRITING

Choose one activity.

Activity A: Most societies have traditionally been dominated by men. But many societies have changed, and many women now have equal rights. Still, even in societies where men and women are considered equal, some traditions, behaviors, and patterns of unequal treatment persist. Write about some of the changes in your native society and about any inequalities that still exist.

Activity B: Alvarado talks about the relationship between machismo and drinking alcohol. She sees them as connected. In your experience and observations, is there a connection between drinking and male dominance? What are the traditions and customs in your native culture about drinking? Is drinking usually associated with men? Who drinks? Where, when, and how do people drink? Write an essay about this, giving examples where possible.

Activity C: Choose a sentence or paragraph from the passage that is meaningful to you. It may be an issue or topic that makes you angry or that you have experience with. Write an essay about it, telling how the issue or topic comes up in Alvarado's story and then how it relates to you. Look back at your log for ideas.

AFTER WRITING

1. Form a group with two or three other people in the class who wrote on the same topic you did. Read your papers aloud to one another. Notice the different ways in which you approached the same topic. Make a list of the differences and similarities in your papers.

2. Report to the whole class on what your group wrote about: Give a one- or two-sentence summary of each person's ideas on the topic, and note the differences and similarities in approaches.

BEFORE READING

1. Read the title and introductory information. Write down one thing you understood from what you read and how you feel about it. Share your writing with the class.
2. Read the passage.

Gays, the Military . . . and My Son

Roscoe Thorne

This statement is from testimony given by Roscoe Thorne in July 1992 at a naval hearing on his son, Tracey Thorne. Tracey, a naval aviator, had just appeared on a TV show and announced that he was a homosexual. Tracey's father did not know about his son's homosexuality until four days before the TV appearance. (The naval board voted to discharge Tracey from the Navy because of a Pentagon ruling that homosexuality is not compatible with military service.)

My name is Roscoe Thorne and I'm a surgeon. I'm not a speaker and I may become emotional because of the gravity of this situation, so I hope you will bear with me. It was twenty-five years ago that my wife went into the delivery room and I, a young physician, waited outside. The doctor came out and handed me a baby boy. I took him and held him in my hands, and I thought he was just fine. But until I heard my son testify here, I didn't realize what a great man was given to me twenty-five years ago.

Today you are here worrying about a twenty-five-year-old man who has already proven himself beyond a shadow of a doubt as a leader, as a commander, as a superb individual. I'm happy to say I'm his father and I wish I could be like him.

I want to talk a little bit about myself. I was born in the Deep South—Jackson, Mississippi. When I was about five, I had a colored friend named Jesse. Jesse lived over in colored town, and he would come over and play with me. Jesse was a lot of fun to be around. One day I was so happy to see him that I took him to my mother, and I said, "Mama, this is Jesse." My mother was a kind, good person, and she smiled down at Jesse and said, "It's nice to meet you, Jesse." Later, after Jesse left, my mama said, "Buddy, I want to teach you something." I said, "Yes, Mama." (First time I can remember her teaching me something.) She said, "Buddy, you never introduce a colored person to a white lady." I said, "Yes, Mama, I won't do that anymore."

I was being trained in Jackson, Mississippi, by my white mother, who was a good person. But that was how she was trained, and she was passing it along.

After high school, in 1950, I joined the 31st Infantry Division. It was called the Dixie Division—16,000 white-faced men. There were a few Italians, a few Jews, a few Spaniards, but there weren't any black faces. When my term of enlistment was up, I enrolled in the University of Mississippi. There weren't any colored people at "Ole Miss" in 1953. We had a cross section of the population—Greeks, Jews, Irishmen, Catholics—but there wasn't a black face there except for Blind Jim, who had a white cane and sold pencils in front of one of the buildings.

I graduated from the University of Mississippi with a pharmacy degree, and I went to practice in a corner drugstore in Jackson that was down the street from the Baptist Hospital. One afternoon I was filling prescriptions and I looked over and saw a young nurse sitting at the soda fountain. She was a registered nurse and had on a pretty white uniform, but she was a black person. My boss nudged me and said, "Roscoe, go over there and run her off." I was twenty-five years old—Tracey's age—but I had been trained. I had been prejudiced by my mother, by my school, by my United States Army, and by my college. And so I went over there and I said, "You're going to have to leave. We don't want you in here." And this young nurse looked at me—she was about my age and a registered nurse and a fine-looking human being—and tears ran down her cheeks and she left. I felt so bad. I wonder where she is today. I know she'd remember that I chased her out of the drugstore. Mississippi was no place for a young man in the 1950s.

In 1959 I went to medical school in Miami. I dissected bodies in anatomy class, and whether they were black or Oriental or Anglo-Saxon, inside they all looked the same. When they got sick and you gave them medicine, they all pretty much reacted the same way to the medicine. Then I interned at Tampa General, a segregated hospital. We had one ward for the dark colored folks and another where we kept the white people and the lighter colored. We liked to think that we gave them all the same treatment, but we didn't.

In 1964, when I was in private practice, the government said that we were going to have to desegregate our hospitals. We thought, how in the world can we do that? We'd been working on the Negroes in one place, the Orientals in another, the white patients somewhere else. How can we put them all together? It just won't work. Well, the government insisted. So we put all of these blacks, Italians, Poles, Germans, Jews, Hispanics, the homosexuals, the bisexuals, the heterosexuals together and we treated them. And things were better for it, and they still are today.

Now, I've been around long enough to know what kind of meeting this hearing is. And I want you officers to know that if you allow anything to interfere with this young man's ability to serve his country as he so ably has proven he can—if you allow that to happen—then I want each of you, when you go home tonight, to find a good friend. I want you to sit down with that friend, and I want you to tell him or her what you allowed to happen today. It'll make you feel better. You've got to be truthful with yourself. You tell that friend that you've allowed something to happen that, deep down, you don't feel is real good, and you feel bad about it. If you tell it to one person you trust, you'll feel better, and that person will have heard the truth. If one person hears the truth, then you've got a victory, and that's what America is all about. Now I'm leaving. Good-bye.

AFTER READING

1. In your reading log, write down one or two things you understood from what you read and how you feel about it.
2. Work with a partner. Draw a horizontal line across a page in your reading log. This will be a *time line*. Along the time line, mark the events in Roscoe Thorne's life in chronological order. Go back through the text and discuss each event with your partner before you place it on the time line. Where possible, use dates.
3. What is Roscoe Thorne's attitude today toward people of color? Toward homosexuals? (Give evidence from the text.) What event(s) in his life caused his attitude to change over the years? Discuss this with your group.

HOW I READ IT

1. Think about the time line you made in After Reading, question 1. How did it help you understand what you read? Would a time line have helped your understanding of something else you have read recently? Explain.
2. Share your observations with the class.

HOW IT'S WRITTEN

1. Working with a partner, number the paragraphs. Then, quickly reread the essay to find the parts that tell a story about Roscoe Thorne's life. Mark those paragraphs with brackets [ ].

2. Talk with your partner about Thorne's purpose in telling his story. What effect did it have on you?

3. Summarize your discussions for the class.

TOPICS FOR WRITING

Choose one activity.

Activity A: In the seventh paragraph, Thorne refers to a law passed in 1964 that required hospitals to desegregate. Interview someone who lived in the United States at the time of the passage of the 1960's civil rights laws. Find out what changes that person witnessed (for example, changes in education, or housing, or hospitals) and how those changes affected him or her. Use the person's story as part of an essay.

Activity B: Think of situations in your present community, in your native country, or in this country that you think are unjust. (Look at a newspaper or talk with your group for ideas.) Make a list and then select one situation. Imagine that you have been asked to give testimony on this issue. Write a speech that will convince an audience of your point of view. You may want to use your own experience to support your argument.

Activity C: In the last paragraph, Thorne asks the officers at the hearing to go home and tell a friend about the bad thing they allowed to happen that day. He says, "You've got to be truthful to yourself." Write about a time when you let something happen that you did not feel good about afterward, perhaps a time when you were not truthful with yourself. Tell it like a story. (You might use part of Roscoe Thorne's story as a model.)

AFTER WRITING

1. Exchange papers with someone in the class whom you have never shared your writing with. Respond in any way you wish to that person's paper.

2. Report to your group about what you learned from that person, especially anything that might be useful to other group members.

BEFORE READING

1. Read the title. What picture comes to mind? Draw it in your reading log. Explain your drawing to a partner.

2. Read the essay.

Buzzard
Bailey White

This essay appears in a book called Mama Makes Up Her Mind and Other Dangers of Southern Living. Ms. *White teaches first grade in south Georgia.*

There was something in the road. I drove closer to it. It was a buzzard eating a dead armadillo. I got closer. It was a big buzzard. And I'd never seen a buzzard's tail feathers so bleached and pale.

That buzzard better move, I thought. I'd never had to slow down for a buzzard before. They always lope out of the way. I got closer.

The buzzard turned his head and looked at me. He stood up on his big yellow legs. His head was snow white. His eyes were gold. He wasn't a buzzard. He was a bald eagle.

Then, not until after I had brought the car to a full stop, he spread his wings and with a slow swoop lifted himself into the air. He turned his head and gave me a long look through the car windshield with his level yellow eyes. Then he slowly wheeled up into the sky until he was just a black dot against the blue.

I turned the car off. I thought about that glare he had given me: What are *you* doing here? it had said. When I got started again, I drove slower and felt smaller. I think it does us all good to get looked at like that now and then by a wild animal.

AFTER READING

1. Freewrite or draw for a few minutes in your log about what you just read. Share your work with your group.

2. As a group, find one sentence in the text that expresses White's main point. Where is this sentence located?

HOW IT'S WRITTEN

1. Work with a partner. Choose one activity.

   Activity A: Look at the first three paragraphs of the essay. Notice the short, simple sentences. Compare the sentences in the first three paragraphs with the sentences in paragraphs four and five. Why do you think White chose to use short sentences in the first part of the essay? What effect do they have on the reader?

   Activity B: Talk about how White uses a personal story to make a point. Which part of the essay is a story? Which part is her opinion or main point? What effect does that order have on the reader? How would this essay be different if White had stated her main point at the beginning instead of at the end? (You may want to read about beginnings and endings in Appendix E, pp. 240–241.)

2. Summarize your discussions for the class.

TOPICS FOR WRITING

Choose one activity.

Activity A: White said she drove slower and felt smaller after her encounter with the bald eagle. Write about a similar experience you have had with nature. Tell what happened to you and how it made you feel. Use White's story as a model, making a generalization or point at the end of your essay.

Activity B: The bald eagle is an endangered species. What other endangered species do you know about? Write an essay about one endangered species. Tell where the species lives, why it is endangered, and what could (or should) be done to save it. Use the library to find out more about this animal or plant, if you need more information. In your writing, try to convince readers of your point of view.

Activity C: Write a composition in any form (poem, story, essay, and so on) using the name of an animal or plant as the title.

AFTER WRITING

1. Go over your paper carefully with a pen in your hand. Read each word aloud so that your ear can hear it, and touch each word with your pen to find errors and parts that don't sound right. Don't stop until you find at least three things to change.

2. Exchange papers with a classmate. Ask your reader to write one or two questions about your piece.

3. Revise your writing if you wish.

BEFORE READING

1. With your group, read this list of facts about what is happening to the earth today:

   It takes an entire forest—over 500,000 trees—to supply Americans with their Sunday newspapers every week.

   Over a billion people could be fed by the grain and soybeans eaten by U.S. livestock every year.

   The junk mail Americans receive in one day could produce enough energy to heat 250,000 homes.

   Each year, 27 million acres of tropical rainforests are destroyed. That's an area the size of Ohio, and translates to 74,000 acres per day . . . 3,000 acres per hour . . . 50 acres per minute.

   Americans produce enough "styrofoam" cups every year to circle the earth 436 times.

   These facts were taken from a book entitled *Fifty Simple Things You Can Do to Save the Earth*. As a group, suggest one thing people could do to help conserve resources in two of the situations described above. Share your suggestions with the class.

2. Read the introduction to "The Brave Little Parrot." With your group, talk about what connections you see between the preceding list and Martin's idea that the world is "burning."

3. Read the story.

The Brave Little Parrot
Rafe Martin

Rafe Martin is an award-winning author and storyteller. He has been featured at many of the most prestigious storytelling events around the country and has performed as far away as Japan. His work has received several Parents Choice Gold Awards, several ALA Noble Book Awards, the IRA Teachers Choice Award, the Golden Sower Award, the Georgia State Picture Award, as well as many others. He is often featured in Time, Newsweek, *and* USA Today.

Once a little parrot lived happily in a beautiful forest. But one day without warning, lightning flashed, thunder crashed, and a dead tree burst into flames. Sparks, carried on the rising wind, began to leap from branch to branch and tree to tree.

The little parrot smelled the smoke. "Fire!" she cried. "Run to the river!" Flapping her wings, rising higher and higher, she flew toward the safety of the river's far shore. After all, she was a bird and could fly away.

But as she flew, she could see that many animals were already surrounded by the flames and could not escape. Suddenly a desperate idea, a way to save them, came to her.

Darting to the river, she dipped herself in the water. Then she flew back over the now-raging fire. Thick smoke coiled up, filling the sky. Walls of flame shot up, now on one side, now on the other. Pillars of fire leapt before her. Twisting and turning through a mad maze of flame, the little parrot flew bravely on.

Having reached the heart of the burning forest, the little parrot shook her wings. And the few tiny drops of water that still clung to her feathers tumbled like jewels down into the flames and vanished with a hiss.

Then the little parrot flew back through the flames and smoke to the river. Once more she dipped herself in the cool water and flew back over the burning forest. Once more she shook her wings, and a few drops of water tumbled like jewels into the flames. *Hisssss.*

Back and forth she flew, time and time again from the river to the forest, from the forest to the river. Her feathers became charred. Her feet and claws were scorched. Her lungs ached. Her eyes burned. Her mind spun as dizzily as a spinning spark. Still the little parrot flew on.

At that moment some of the blissful gods floating overhead in their cloud palaces of ivory and gold happened to look down and see the little parrot flying among the flames. They pointed at her with their perfect hands. Between mouthfuls of honied foods, they exclaimed, "Look at that foolish bird! She's trying to put out a raging forest fire with a few sprinkles of water! How absurd!" They laughed.

But one of those gods, strangely moved, changed himself into a golden eagle and flew down, down toward the little parrot's fiery path.

The little parrot was just nearing the flames again, when a great eagle with eyes like molten gold appeared at her side. "Go back, little bird!" said the eagle in a solemn and majestic voice. "Your task is hopeless. A few drops of water can't put out a forest fire. Cease now, and save yourself before it is too late."

But the little parrot continued to fly on through the smoke and flames. She could hear the great eagle flying above her as the heat grew fiercer. He called out, "Stop, foolish little parrot! Stop! Save yourself!"

"I didn't need some great, shining eagle," coughed the little parrot, "to tell me that. My own mother, the dear bird, could have told me the same thing long ago. Advice! I don't need advice. I just"—cough, cough—"need someone to help!"

Rising higher, the eagle, who was a god, watched the little parrot flying through the flames. High above he could see his own kind, those carefree gods, still laughing and talking even as many animals cried out in pain and fear far below. He grew ashamed of the gods' carefree life, and a single desire was kindled in his heart.

"God though I am," he exclaimed, "how I wish I could be just like that little parrot. Flying on, brave and alone, risking all to help—what a rare and marvelous thing! What a wonderful little bird!"

Moved by these new feelings, the great eagle began to weep. Stream after stream of sparkling tears began pouring from his eyes. Wave upon wave they fell, washing down like a torrent of rain upon the fire, upon the forest, upon the animals and the little parrot herself.

Where those cooling tears fell, the flames shrank down and died. Smoke still curled up from the scorched earth, yet new life was already boldly pushing forth—shoots, stems, blossoms, and leaves. Green grass sprang up from among the still-glowing cinders.

Where the eagle's teardrops sparkled on the little parrot's wings, new feathers now grew: red feathers, green feathers, yellow feathers too. Such bright colors! Such a pretty bird!

The animals looked at one another in amazement. They were whole and well. Not one had been harmed. Up above in the clear blue sky they could see their brave friend, the little parrot, looping and soaring in delight. When all hope was gone, somehow she had saved them.

"Hurray!" they cried. "Hurray for the brave little parrot and for this sudden, miraculous rain!"

AFTER READING

1. Choose one activity.

   Activity A: Freewrite in your log for a few minutes about what you just read.
   Read your writing to your group.

   Activity B: Write answers to these questions: What do you understand or see in what you read? How do you feel about this? What do you associate with your understanding?
   Read your writing to your group.

2. What do you think the message of this story is? Do you get a clue from the introduction? Talk about this with your group.

HOW IT'S WRITTEN

1. With a partner, read the story aloud, alternating paragraphs.

2. Work with a partner. Choose one activity.

> **Activity A:** In the introduction, Martin says that storytelling is a way to change things in ways we might never guess. What effect do you think this story could have on listeners? How might it change them? Would the effect be different if Martin had chosen to present his message through a written essay or newspaper article instead of through an oral fable? What is the value of fables? (A fable is a story that has a message or lesson and often uses animals that speak and act as human beings.)
>
> Talk about these questions with your partner.

> **Activity B:** Reread the story, looking for figures of speech that show comparison, such as similes and metaphors. Underline them. (See Unit 1, p. 24, for examples of *similes* and *metaphors*.) Then look for strong active verbs. Circle those that describe an action so that you can see exactly how it happened. For example, when you read *thick smoke coiled up*, you can imagine a spiral of smoke moving upward. (See Unit 2, p. 132, for a discussion of strong active verbs.)
>
> How did Martin help the listener (or reader) understand the story by using these kinds of details and images? Talk about this with your partner.

3. Share your findings with the class.

TOPICS FOR WRITING

Choose one activity.

Activity A: In the introduction to "The Brave Little Parrot," Martin says: "Small deeds, done wholeheartedly, may have the potential to change everything." Write about a small deed that changed things. Begin your essay with Martin's quotation and use your story to prove and illustrate his idea. Try to include strong active verbs or figures of speech to show comparison.

Activity B: Think of a fable or tale that was told to you as a child or that you have heard or read as an adult. Write the story as though you are going to tell it at a National Storytelling Festival. Try to include strong active verbs or figures of speech to show comparison. Begin with an introduction, as Rafe Martin did, telling something about the origin of the story and its message.

Activity C: Think of an environmental problem you have heard or read about (for example, the cutting of rain forests, the disappearance of whales or songbirds, an oil spill). Use the library to find more information about the problem you chose. Write a composition explaining the problem and suggesting some solutions.

AFTER WRITING

1. Give your paper to a classmate. Ask your reader for feedback on two or three things.

2. Read your classmate's responses. Circle any ideas you may be able to use in revising. Revise your paper.

3. Write about *how* you wrote this piece. For example, how did you decide which topic to write about? What did you do first, second, and so on? Did your reader's responses help you revise? If so, how? What did you change? Why?

   Talk about your writing process with your group.

BEFORE READING

1. Read the introductory information to "The Future Is Yours (Still)." Then read the first sentence of each paragraph of the essay.

2. Write down one thing you understood from what you read. Share your writing with the class. Then read the passage.

The Future Is Yours (Still)
Abbie Hoffman

Serving as his own lawyer, Abbie Hoffman presented a closing argument in a district court in Massachusetts on April 15, 1987. He and eleven others were on trial for trespassing while protesting the recruiting of students by the CIA (Central Intelligence Agency) at the University of Massachusetts. The group was acquitted. This is part of Hoffman's statement.

When I was growing up in Worcester, Massachusetts, my father was very proud of democracy. He often took me to town-hall meetings in Clinton, Athol, and Hudson. He would say, See how the people participate, see how they participate in decisions that affect their lives—that's democracy. I grew up with the idea that democracy is not something you believe in, or a place you hang your hat, but it's something you do. You participate. If you stop doing it, democracy crumbles and falls apart. It was very sad to read last month that the New England town-hall meetings are dying off, and, in a large sense, the spirit of this trial is that grass-roots participation in democracy must not die. If matters such as we have been discussing here are left only to be discussed behind closed-door hearings in Washington, then we would cease to have a government of the people.

You travel around this country, and no matter where you go, people say, Don't waste your time, nothing changes, you can't fight the powers that be— no one can. You hear it a lot from young people. I hear it from my own kids: Daddy, you're so quaint to believe in hope. Kids today live with awful nightmares: AIDS will wipe us out; the polar ice cap will melt; the nuclear bomb will go off at any minute. Even the best tend to believe we are hopeless to affect matters. It's no wonder teenage suicide is at a record level. Young people are detached from history, the planet, and, most important, the future. I maintain to you that this detachment from the future, the lack of hope, and the high suicide rate among youth are connected. . . .

Thomas Paine, the most outspoken and farsighted of the leaders of the American Revolution, wrote long ago:

> Every age and generation must be as free to act for itself, in all cases, as the ages and generations which preceded it. Man has no property in man, neither has any generation a property in the generations which are to follow.

Thomas Paine was talking about this spring day in this courtroom. A verdict of not guilty will say, When our country is right, keep it right; but when it is wrong, right those wrongs. A verdict of not guilty will say to the University of Massachusetts that these demonstrators are reaffirming their rights as citizens who acted with justification. A verdict of not guilty will say what Thomas Paine said: Young people, don't give up hope. If you participate, the future is yours. Thank you.

AFTER READING

1. Reread the passage and do one of these activities:

   a. Annotate the passage. In your log, summarize your annotations or write a reaction to what you read.

   b. Make a double entry in your log.

   Share your writing with your group.

2. As a group, write one sentence summarizing Hoffman's main point. Discuss this sentence with the class.

TOPICS FOR WRITING

Choose one activity.

Activity A: Hoffman said, "Young people, don't give up hope. If you participate, the future is yours." But he also reported that many young people say, "Don't waste your time, nothing changes." Have you seen young people make changes in the world around them? Do you agree with Hoffman that young people can—and should—try to make positive changes in their society? Explain your opinion in writing, using your own experience and what you have seen and read to illustrate what you say.

Activity B: Hoffman and his colleagues protested against something they thought was wrong. Do you know of other people, either in this country or in other countries, who have done that? What were they protesting? How effective were the protests? Is "demonstrating" a good way to make change? Explain your opinion in writing, using your own experience and what you have seen and read to illustrate what you say.

Activity C: Think of a situation in your school, city, or country that you think is wrong. Make a list of ways in which you could let people know your ideas. Choose three or four of these ways, and write a composition describing and discussing them. Write this for someone who really wants to know how to go about suggesting a change.

AFTER WRITING

1. Attach a blank page to your paper. Pass the paper around so that one or two of your group members can write comments.

2. Read your readers' comments. Then read your writing to someone from another group.

BEFORE READING

1. The title of this unit is "A Changing World." How do you think this poem will relate to that theme? Freewrite for a few minutes about this. Read your writing to a partner.

2. Read the poem. Then read it aloud to your partner.

Keeping Quiet
Pablo Neruda

Pablo Neruda was a Chilean poet and activist. He was described as a political poet and a fiery poet of love. He died in 1973.

And now we will count to twelve
and we will all keep still . . .

For once on the face of the earth
let's not speak in any language;
let's stop for one second,
and not move our arms so much.

It would be an exotic moment
without rush, without engines,
we would all be together
in a sudden strangeness.

Fishermen in the cold sea
would not harm whales
and the man gathering salt
would look at his hurt hands.

Those who prepare green wars,
wars with gas, wars with fire,
victory with no survivors,
would put on clean clothes
and walk about with their brothers
in the shade, doing nothing.

What I want should not be confused
with total inactivity.

(Life is what it is about;
I want no truck with death.)

If we were not so singleminded
about keeping our lives moving,
and for once could do nothing,
perhaps a huge silence
might interrupt this sadness
of never understanding ourselves
and of threatening ourselves with death.

Perhaps the earth can teach us
as when everything seems dead
and later proves to be alive.

Now I'll count up to twelve,
and you keep quiet and I will go.

AFTER READING

1. Write a sentence in your reading log that summarizes the meaning of the poem as you understand it. Compare it with what another person wrote.

2. Underline all of the activities that Neruda says would change if we all kept still. Discuss what you underlined with a partner.

3. Think of two more activities that would change if we kept quiet— one activity normally done by women and another normally done by men. Write these activities in your log.
    Read what you wrote to your group.

HOW I READ IT

Did reading the poem aloud help your understanding and appreciation of it? How does reading something aloud help one hear a writer's voice? Free-write for a few minutes in your log about this question.

TOPICS FOR WRITING

Choose one activity.

Activity A: Write another verse to Neruda's poem. Add it in the middle of the poem immediately following verse five, after the words "doing nothing."

Activity B: Pick a line from the poem and use it to begin a piece of your own writing. Write in any form (a poem, a story, an essay, or something else).

Activity C: Have you ever wanted to say to people "Just stop. Be quiet. Calm down." What kind of situation comes to mind? Do people keep quiet after you ask them to? Or do you find you have to go off to a quiet place and sit by yourself in silence? Does that bring you quietness and peace? Tell about these times and what you recommend. Imagine you are writing a letter of advice that will appear in a newspaper.

Activity D: Which writers or people in the readings in this unit do you think would be in favor of Neruda's idea? Who would be opposed? Make two lists. Then choose two people (one from each list) and write about the similarities and differences between them.

AFTER WRITING

1. Read your piece aloud to your group. Ask listeners what they understood and what they liked best about your writing. Ask for one suggestion to make your writing better.

2. Revise your piece.

BEFORE READING

1. With the class, make a cluster around the words *twenty-first century*. Talk about how some of your words and phrases are connected to the theme of this unit, "A Changing World."

2. Read the passage. As you read, pause for a minute after each paragraph to let an image come to your mind.

Entering the Twenty-first Century
Thich Nhat Hanh

Thich Nhat Hanh was born in Vietnam in 1926, and he left home as a teenager to become a Zen Buddhist monk. He has taught at several universities and was nominated by Martin Luther King, Jr., for the Nobel Peace Prize. Since 1966, he has lived in exile in France, where he writes, teaches, gardens, and helps refugees worldwide. This essay is taken from his book entitled Peace Is Every Step.

The word "policy" is very much in use these days. There seems to be a policy for just about everything. I have heard that the so-called developed nations are contemplating a garbage policy to send their trash on huge barges to the Third World.

I think that we need a "policy" for dealing with our suffering. We do not want to condone it, but we need to find a way to make use of our suffering, for our good and for the good of others. There has been so much suffering in the twentieth century: two world wars, concentration camps in Europe, the killing fields of Cambodia, refugees from Vietnam, Central America, and elsewhere fleeing their countries with no place to land. We need to articulate a policy for these kinds of garbage also. We need to use the suffering of the twentieth century as compost, so that together we can create flowers for the twenty-first century.

When we see photographs and programs about the atrocities of the Nazis, the gas chambers and the camps, we feel afraid. We may say, "I didn't do it; they did it." But if we had been there, we may have done the same thing, or we may have been too cowardly to stop it, as was the case for so many. We have to put all these things into our compost pile to fertilize the ground. In Germany today, the young people have a kind of complex that they are somehow responsible for the suffering. It is important that these young people and the generation responsible for the war begin anew, and together create a path of mindfulness so that our children in the next century can avoid repeating the same mistakes. The flower of tolerance to see and appreciate cultural diversity is one flower we can cultivate for the children of the twenty-first century. Another flower is the truth of suffering—there has been so much unnecessary suffering in our century. If we are willing to work together and learn together, we can all benefit from the mistakes of our time, and, seeing with the eyes of compassion and understanding, we can offer the next century a beautiful garden and a clear path.

Take the hand of your child and invite her to go out and sit with you on the grass. The two of you may want to contemplate the green grass, the little flowers that grow among the grasses, and the sky. Breathing and smiling together—that is peace education. If we know how to appreciate these beautiful things, we will not have to search for anything else. Peace is available in every moment, in every breath, in every step. . . .

AFTER READING

1. Choose one activity.

    Activity A: Write for a few minutes in your log about what you read. What did you understand? How do you feel about what you understood? What associations come to mind?
       Look over what you wrote and underline any sentences or phrases you like. Read these to your group.

    Activity B: Write a double-entry response as you reread the essay. (See Appendix B.2, pp. 230–232, for more explanation and examples of double entries.)
       Look over what you wrote and underline any sentences or phrases you like. Read these to your group.

2. With a partner, write down two or three questions you have about what the author says. Talk about these questions with your group.

3. With your group, write a one-sentence summary of the kernel idea of each paragraph. Read your four sentences to the class.

HOW I READ IT

Freewrite about how you read (and reread) this essay. For example, how did pausing after each paragraph to let an image come to your mind affect your reading? Did writing in your log (in After Reading, question 1) help you understand the essay? Did asking questions about the text and trying to answer them help? Did summarizing the idea of each paragraph help? What was useful? Not so useful? Why?

HOW IT'S WRITTEN

1. The author uses the metaphor of a garden in this essay by using words like *compost* and *flower*. With a partner, find and circle all the words that can be associated with a garden.

   Talk with your group about how this metaphor helps you appreciate and understand the author's ideas.

2. Find one sentence in the essay that you like or that you find especially expressive or meaningful. Copy the sentence on the left side of a page in your log. On the right side of the same page, write about why you like the sentence or what makes the sentence well written.

   Read what you wrote to your group.

3. Discuss your findings with the class.

TOPICS FOR WRITING

Choose one activity.

Activity A: Thich Nhat Hanh says, in the third paragraph, "The flower of tolerance to see and appreciate cultural diversity is one flower we can cultivate for the children of the twenty-first century." Do you agree that we need to help our children develop the tolerance to see and appreciate cultural diversity? Explain your point of view, writing to convince a reader of your opinion. Think of one or two authors of the readings in this unit who you think would agree with you and, if appropriate, quote them (or restate some of their ideas) in your essay.

Activity B: Read the titles of all the readings in this unit. Then, look in your log for ideas you could include in an essay called "Entering the

Twenty-first Century" or "Peace Education." Pick one of the titles. Write the essay. If appropriate, quote one or two authors of the readings in the unit. (You may also want to read some of the Extra Readings at the end of this unit before you write the essay.)

Activity C: Write about anything this essay suggests to you.

AFTER WRITING

1. Go over your paper carefully with a pen in your hand. Read each word aloud so that your ear can hear it, and touch each word with your pen to find errors and parts that don't sound right. Continue checking your paper until you find at least three things to change.

2. Give your paper to at least two other people. Ask for written comments on whatever you want help with. Each reader should also find one sentence they like or find especially well written and explain why.

3. Read your classmate's comments on your piece. Revise your piece in any way you wish. (For example, you may want to add or clarify ideas; take out, change, or reorder material; begin or end in a different way; or rewrite the piece completely.)

4. Read your revised piece to your group. As a group, choose one piece to read to the class.

5. Look back in your log at all the writing you did about *how* you wrote. How has your writing process changed? For example, what do you do now to get started on a composition? To make your writing clearer? How are these things different from what you used to do? Discuss this with the class.

About All the Readings in This Unit

PREPARING FOR WRITING

1. Reread all of the entries in your reading log for this unit.

2. With the class, list some *issues* that arise around the concept of a changing world. Make a list of generalizations about those issues. (See p. 59 for an explanation of issues and generalizations.)

3. Choose one generalization. Write it at the top of a page. Under the generalization, list all the reasons and examples you can think of that prove it is true, including something you read in this unit and something you wrote.

WRITING

Write a composition about your generalization. You may want to include an introduction in which you discuss an assumption that you are going to disprove in your composition. Support your ideas by referring to one or more of the readings in this unit. You may also want to include some writing you did for this unit.

AFTER WRITING

1. When you finish, go over your paper with a pen in hand. Read each word aloud so that you can hear it, and touch each word with your pen. This proofreading technique will help you to find errors and things that don't sound right. Don't stop until you find at least three things to change. Fix them.

2. Give your piece of writing to two different people to read. Each person should write a response to your composition, answering the following questions:

   a. What do you think the main point is?

   b. What do you like about the piece (form or content or both)?

   c. What do you think should be added?

3. Read your readers' responses. Revise your piece.

4. Reread what you wrote for After Writing, question 5, p. 212, or look back in your log at all the writing you have done about *how* you wrote. Did you write this piece any differently from the way you wrote the last piece? Other pieces in this unit? Write about this in your log.

Haiku
Teishitsu

The haiku, *a seventeen-syllable verse form, has been used by Japanese poets for hundreds of years. A haiku is not a complete poem as we know it; rather, it suggests a picture that readers are expected to fill in from their own imaginations.*

Icicles and water
   Old differences dissolved . . .
Drip down together

Family Man
Three Is the Loneliest Number

Roger L. Welsch

Folklorist Roger L. Welsch lives on a tree farm in Dannebrog, Nebraska. One of his books, Touching the Fire: Buffalo Dancers, the Sky Bundle, and Other Tales, *explores rites, objects, and places sacred to Native Americans.*

A lot of fuss has been made during the past year about the importance of family values, and little agreement has been reached on what exactly those values should be. As usual, I'm a word or two behind things because I am still trying to sort out what a family is. Political moralists long for the good old days of June, Ward, Wally, and the Beaver. But that vision is in reality far too puny.

The lesson came home to me in vivid fashion twenty-six years ago when my first wife gave birth to our son. A couple of days after we welcomed Chris into the world, I drove to the hospital and went to the front desk. The nurse went to get my wife and son and brought them to me at the hospital door. "There you are, Mr. Welsch," she said, handing me five diapers, a bottle, a sample box of formula, a blanket, my wife, and a baby. "Goodbye and good luck."

A few weeks earlier I had bought a used car from Weird Wally. Wally is weird but he can be down-to-earth when he has to be: "I need to see your insurance papers, driver's license, and loan agreement." To get those three documents required a written exam, a driving test, proof of identification, a photograph, and a demonstration of financial responsibility. It took me days to get the stuff together. When they hand over a car to you, they want lots of evidence that you have some idea what you are doing. A baby? "There you are, Mr. Welsch. Goodbye and good luck."

That was only the beginning—for both the baby and the automobile. Two or three times a day my wife called my mother, her aunts, friends, and neighbors to find out how to run this little mechanism we called Chris. "What's it mean when he spits up clear stuff and cries with little short blasts like 'Wahn wahn wahn'?" Two or three times a week I called my father, my pals, and the guy at the filling station to find out how to run this mechanism I called "that damned Ford." "What's it mean when it makes clunking sounds in the rear wheels like 'Wunk wunk wunk'?"

Forget single mothers. Here we were, the ideal American family, and still we were woefully understaffed. Generally, throughout a good part of the world a family includes at least a husband, a wife, their children, and the surviving grandparents. That's the way it was in the United States, too, until fairly recently. If that tradition hadn't faded, my mother and father and my wife's father would have been living with us—available to serve as built-in baby sitters, cooks, mechanics, therapists, and, as we later needed, chaperons and marriage counselors. The concept of family held by those who consider themselves defenders of "family values" turns out to be a radical departure from tradition.

Even the old-fashioned family arrangement—parents, children, and surviving grandparents—is a trimmed down version of the Ur-family. Within my foster culture, the Omaha tribe of eastern Nebraska, a family is much wider. I once asked a niece of my Omaha brother, Buddy Gilpin, "Where is Buddy?"

"Dad is in Lincoln," she said.

Okay, so her dad is in Lincoln, I thought. What about Buddy? I tried again. "But where is Buddy?"

She looked at me curiously and tried again, "Dad is in Lincoln."

Then it dawned on me. Within traditional Omaha culture, when a man died, his brother married the widow—a crucial economic and cultural safety net in a society where a woman alone was in peril. Similarly, when a woman died, her sister married the widower—to keep house, support the hunting, provide food, make hunting tools and clothing, and care for his children, who otherwise would have no one. Thus, your mother's sisters were potential mothers for you, while your father's brothers were potential fathers—and that is how they are labeled in the Omaha kinship system. My brother Buddy, this woman's "uncle" in standard American terms, was in her world and mind, her father, just as surely as her biological father.

Within Omaha culture, kinship terms are also used honorifically whenever a kinlike relationship is established. For example, Omaha children, even adults, frequently move from one biological family unit to another for any number of reasons. A family with economic problems might ask another family to take children for a year or so until things get better, or a child who shows a talent for singing may be sent to live for a while with a family noted for its repertoire of Helushka songs. As a result, members of the host family are viewed as kin. I once sent a child of mine to live with Comanche friends because they kept horses, my daughter loved horses, she was having a lot of problems, and we all thought a summer with the Comanches and their horses would help. So off she went—not as a gesture of despair but of love. My daughter now has a Comanche uncle and aunt and cousins.

Among the Omahas several people were especially kind in guiding me through my efforts to understand the ways of the tribe. They weren't just friendly—they took chances for me, they stood beside me in important ceremonial trials, they loved me, and I certainly loved them. So I wound up with an Aunt Elizabeth, Uncle Clyde, Cousin Dennis, Cousin Ago, among others. And they are as close to me as those biological brothers and sisters of my German father and mother I call "aunt" and "uncle."

And that isn't all there is to an Omaha family. I was adopted by Buddy Gilpin as his brother in 1967, during a long evening of solemn, yet joyful ritual on the Omaha reservation near Macy, Nebraska. In receiving my Omaha name I not only acquired a brother but entered the roster of the Wind Clan.

The following week I was at another Omaha celebration, and when the singers began the song called "The Half-Breed Dance," I rose to dance. My Omaha friends had always made a fuss about making me get up and dance "The Half-Breed Dance" because they said I ate so much corn soup and frybread and spent so much time among them, that by ingestion and association, I had become a half-breed. This time, however, my friends rushed to pull me back to my seat. I could no longer dance "The Half-Breed Dance," they explained, because I was no longer a half-breed. Or a white man. The adoption ceremony was not merely a gesture. In the minds of my friends, I had become an Omaha, a part of The Family, and therefore I had a whole bunch of relatives I didn't even know about.

In fact, nearly everyone I know in the Omaha tribe calls me "uncle" or "cousin" or "nephew." Old men of high station call me "uncle." Children call me "nephew." People I've never seen before call me "Dad." I might just as well go ahead and say that the entire Omaha tribe of 5,000 souls is my family.

Of course, here at the farm there is my family of my wife and child, but we three are a pretty lonely tribe, out here in the world all by ourselves. So, even though I live 150 miles from the Omaha reservation, I find a lot of comfort in knowing that all of those relatives of mine are out there whenever I need them.

And surely, surely, one of them has to be a good auto mechanic.

Need We Say More?

Average Hours per Week Spent by Eighth Graders on Various Activities

U.S. Department of Education

This graph appeared in a national teachers' magazine in 1992.

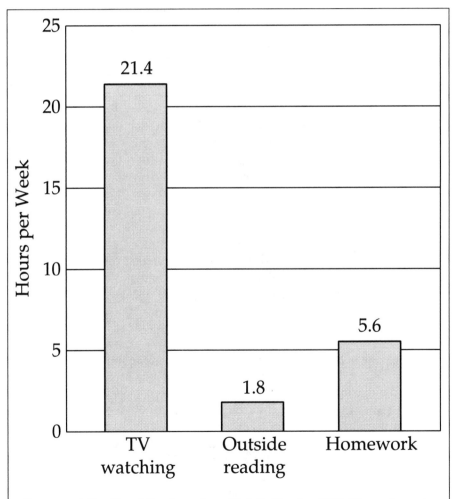

Source: *A Profile of the American Eighth Grader*, U.S. Department of Education, National Environmental Laboratories: 88, Base Year.

How Flowers Changed the World
Loren Eiseley

This passage is from The Immense Journey, *Loren Eiseley's book about the evolution of life on the planet Earth, which began millions of years before humans appeared. Loren Eiseley is an anthropologist.*

Once upon a time there were no flowers at all.

A little while ago—about one hundred million years, as the geologist estimates time in the history of our four-billion-year-old planet—flowers were not to be found anywhere on the five continents. Wherever one might have looked, from the poles to the equator, one would have seen only the cold dark monotonous green of a world whose plant life possessed no other color.

Somewhere, just a short time before the close of the Age of Reptiles, there occurred a soundless, violent explosion. It lasted millions of years, but it was an explosion, nevertheless. It marked the emergence of the angiosperms—the flowering plants. Even the great evolutionist, Charles Darwin, called them "an abominable mystery," because they appeared so suddenly and spread so fast.

Flowers changed the face of the planet. Without them, the world we know—even man himself—would never have existed. Francis Thompson, the English poet, once wrote that one could not pluck a flower without troubling a star. Intuitively he had sensed like a naturalist the enormous interlinked complexity of life. Today we know that the appearance of the flowers contained also the equally mystifying emergence of man. . . .

A high metabolic rate and the maintenance of a constant body temperature are supreme achievements in the evolution of life. They enable an animal to escape, within broad limits, from the overheating or the chilling of its immediate surroundings, and at the same time to maintain a peak mental efficiency. Creatures without a high metabolic rate are slaves to weather. Insects in the first frosts of autumn all run down like little clocks. Yet if you pick one up and breathe warmly upon it, it will begin to move about once more. . . .

A high metabolic rate, however, means a heavy intake of energy in order to sustain body warmth and efficiency. It is for this reason that even some of these later warm-blooded mammals existing in our day have learned to descend into a slower, unconscious rate of living during the winter months when food may be difficult to obtain. On a slightly higher plane they are following the procedure of the cold-blooded frog sleeping in the mud at the bottom of a frozen pond.

The agile brain of the warm-blooded birds and mammals demands a high oxygen consumption and food in concentrated forms, or the creatures cannot long sustain themselves. It was the rise of the flowering plants that provided that energy and changed the nature of the living world. Their appearance parallels in a quite surprising manner the rise of the birds and mammals.

The Earth Community
Thomas Berry

Thomas Berry, a Catholic priest, has studied and written about many fields, including the biological sciences, astronomy, physics, Asian culture, Native American traditions, economics, and especially, ecology. He writes here of the Earth, the changes taking place on the planet, and the care we need to give it. This passage is part of an essay that appeared in a book called The Dream of the Earth.

It is important that we be mindful of the earth, the planet out of which we are born and by which we are nourished, guided, healed—the planet, however, which we have abused to a considerable degree in these past two centuries of industrial exploitation. This exploitation has reached such extremes that presently it appears that some hundreds of thousands of species will be extinguished before the end of the century. . . .

In our times . . . human cunning has mastered the deep mysteries of the earth at a level far beyond the capacities of earlier peoples. We can break the mountains apart; we can drain the rivers and flood the valleys. We can turn the most luxuriant forests into throwaway paper products. We can tear apart the great grass cover of the western plains and pour toxic chemicals into the soil and pesticides onto the fields until the soil is dead and blows away in the wind. We can pollute the air with acids, the rivers with sewage, the seas with oil. . . . We can invent computers capable of processing ten million calculations per second. And why? To increase the volume and the speed with which we move natural resources through the consumer economy to the junk pile or the waste heap. Our managerial skills are measured by the competence manifested in accelerating this process. If in these activities the topography of the planet is damaged, if the environment is made inhospitable for a multitude of living species, then so be it. We are, supposedly, creating a technological wonderworld. . . .

Extinction is a difficult concept to grasp. It is an eternal concept. It's not at all like the killing of individual lifeforms that can be renewed through normal processes of reproduction. Nor is it simply diminishing numbers. Nor is it damage that can somehow be remedied or for which some substitute can be found. Nor is it something that simply affects our own generation. Nor is it something that could be remedied by some supernatural power. It is rather an absolute and final act for which there is no remedy on earth or in heaven. A species once extinct is gone forever. The passenger pigeon is gone and will never return. So, too, the Carolina parakeet. However many generations succeed us in coming centuries, none of them will ever see a passenger pigeon in flight or any of the other living forms that we extinguish. . . .

Not only are we bringing about the extinction of life on such a vast scale, we are also making the land and the air and the sea so toxic that the very conditions of life are being destroyed. As regards basic natural resources, not only are the nonrenewable resources being used up in a frenzy of processing, consuming, and disposing, but we are also ruining much of our renewable resources, such as the very soil itself on which terrestrial life depends. . . .

The change that is taking place on the earth and in our minds is one of the greatest changes ever to take place in human affairs, perhaps *the* greatest, since what we are talking about is not simply another historical change or cultural modification, but a change of geological and biological as well as psychological order of magnitude. We are changing the earth on a scale comparable only to the changes in the structure of the earth and of life that took place during some hundreds of millions of years of earth development.

While such an order of magnitude can produce a paralysis of thought and action, it can, we hope, also awaken in us a sense of what is happening, the scale on which things are happening, and move us to a program of reinhabiting the earth in a truly human manner. It could awaken in us an awareness of our need for all the living companions we have here on our homeland planet. To lose any of these splendid companions is to diminish our own lives.

To learn how to live graciously together would make us worthy of this unique, beautiful, blue planet that evolved in its present splendor over some billions of years, a planet that we should give over to our children with the assurance that this great community of the living will lavish upon them the care that it has bestowed so abundantly upon ourselves.

Gathering Ideas

1. FREEWRITING

Freewriting is one way of responding to what you read. It is also a way of unlocking ideas for writing.

Freewriting is writing without stopping for a certain period of time about a reading, topic, or question. When ideas stop coming, you simply write, "I can't think of anything to write" until a new idea comes into your mind. When freewriting, you should not be critical. Don't worry about things like spelling, grammar, or punctuation. Don't worry if ideas seem out of order or unrelated. Once you start freewriting, you just keep on writing until the time is up.

Figure 1 on page 224 shows the freewriting of one person about the sentence "When one door closes, another opens."

After you freewrite, you may want to write one sentence that summarizes or states the most important thing you said in your writing. We call this important idea the *kernel*, the nucleus or core, of what you wanted to say.

Once you have a kernel sentence, you can freewrite about that sentence, and so on, until you get tired or until you think you've exhausted the subject. Or you can stop after one freewrite and read over what you've written. This will help you to discover what you think and feel about a reading, topic, or question and to get ideas for more writing.

LOOPING

If you don't have much time and you have to come up with an idea on a specific topic for a writing assignment, you can try *looping*. Looping combines freewriting and kernel sentences. It is useful for finding your ideas on a given topic without losing a lot of time.

To do looping, you need a topic, even if it's nonspecific and broad. Put the topic at the top of a page. Then freewrite without stopping for five to ten minutes on the topic. Before starting, decide on the amount of time you

Figure 1

I like the image of going through doors in life: closing doors and leaving behind (inside?) certain things, people, ideas, places, securities—But by moving away or out of a certain time or phase in your life, you move to something else. I guess she also means new opportunities come—the image of "open doors" has a feeling of new scenery, new ideas, new risks and challenges, new friends, job, home, and so on. It's exciting to think about looking behind different doors to see what might be ahead.

can spend, and check the clock or set a timer. Stop when the time is up. Read over what you have written, and determine the main thing you seem to be talking about, the most important thing. Don't summarize. Pick out the main thing you want to say, and write a sentence stating that. It doesn't have to be what you wrote the most about. It can be something you like or even something you didn't quite say but want to. It is like a kernel sentence.

Now do another loop, using the sentence you wrote at the end of the first loop as the first sentence of the second loop. Time yourself again. Stop when the time is up. Read what you wrote. What was the main idea in what you just wrote? Write a sentence about it. Use that second sentence to start your third loop. Repeat the process one more time so that you have three loops. By this time, you will probably find that you have an idea you can develop into a longer piece of writing.

2. CLUSTERING

Clustering or *making a map* can be done before you read, after you read, or before you write. It's one way of gathering ideas about a topic.

Clustering can be done with a group or by yourself. When it's done with the class, the instructor (or a student) starts by writing a topic in the middle of the chalkboard. Students then suggest words or phrases they associate with the topic, and the instructor writes them on the board around the topic. If the instructor or other students don't understand the relationship between the words suggested and the topic, the speaker explains it. You'll find that doing clustering with a group will often make you think of associations you might not think of on your own.

To cluster on your own, you start by writing a topic in the middle of a page in your reading log. Then you let your mind move out from the central topic in different directions. You quickly write down any word or idea that comes to you, sometimes connecting it to the previous word with a line.

When a different idea comes to your mind, one unrelated to a previous word, you begin a new branch off the main topic. When you're finished, your page will have a design or a map of all your ideas.

Clustering allows the mind to bring forth ideas and thought patterns you might not see if you were simply writing. Because you splash down thoughts spontaneously, without judging their logic or appropriateness, you can often come up with new and creative ideas and relationships.

Figure 2 shows one class's cluster (map) around the title "Sometimes Home Is Not Really Home."

Figure 2

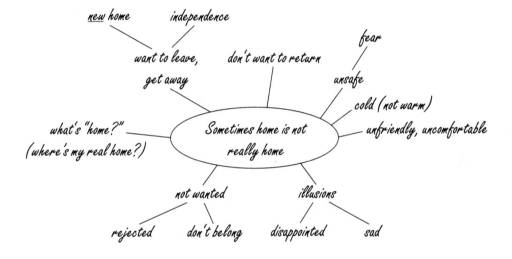

3. MAKING A LIST

Making a list can sometimes help you collect your ideas on a topic. You start by writing the topic at the top of your paper; underneath it, you list whatever words or phrases come to you. Just as with clustering or freewriting, it's important to let your mind flow without interruption, without being critical of what you put down. In other words, don't reject any idea that comes to mind. You will have a chance to select later. When you run out of ideas on the topic, you stop writing. Figure 3 on page 226 shows one person's list about a place.

Brainstorming a list can also be done with a group or the class. One person records all the ideas other students suggest in response to a topic.

Figure 3

Places

    72nd & Broadway
    Fairway
    W. 72nd St. entrance
        to Central Park
    the Boat Basin
    * *construction on Columbus*
        Ave.

Columbus & W. 75th St. 9:20 a.m. Friday morning

Sights	*Sounds*	*Smells*	*Feelings*
men digging	*chug-chug*	*perfumes*	*busyness*
backhoe	*squeal of M7 brakes*	*exhaust*	*energy*
man sweeping loose dirt	*back-up ding-ding*	*fresh breezes*	*waves of action as*
billows of sand dust	*pounding machine*		*lights change*
people hailing cabs	*footsteps*		*rush*
pedestrians	*horns*		*displeasure on*
woman with stroller	*cars accelerating*		*faces at*
backpacks	*birds in tree chirping*		*sounds—*
truck with rolls of			*wincing*
newsprint			*people carrying on*
flashing WALK/			
DON'T WALK			
clear skies-sunlight			
MET PAYS blimp			

Group brainstorming is a good way to generate a lot of ideas on a topic. Often someone else's idea can prompt a new idea from you, one you might not have thought of on your own.

    Once you have a list of ideas, it's easy to read them over, pick out those that are most closely related to the topic, and cross out those that aren't suitable. If you wish, you can put the remaining ideas into categories or groups, or you can draw arrows connecting things that go together. You may find that one idea can be a heading for one of your categories. Or you might find that one idea is a good central focus for what you want to write about. You may even want to make another list, using one of the ideas on your original list as the new topic.

Making a list of events in a story, for example, can also help you put things in the order in which they happened or the order in which you want to present them. Then, when you start writing the story, you have a guide for what to write about next.

Getting Started
Robert M. Pirsig

In this excerpt from Zen and the Art of Motorcycle Maintenance *by Robert M. Pirsig, Chris's father gives him advice on how to use a list to help him start a letter to his mother.*

This road keeps on winding down through this canyon. Early morning patches of sun are around us everywhere. The cycle hums through the cold air and mountain pines and we pass a small sign that says a breakfast place is a mile ahead.

"Are you hungry?" I shout.

"Yes!" Chris shouts back.

Soon a second sign saying CABINS with an arrow under it points off to the left. We slow down, turn and follow a dirt road until it reaches some varnished log cabins under some trees. We pull the cycle under a tree, shut off the ignition and gas and walk inside the main lodge. The wooden floors have a nice clomp under the cycle boots. We sit down at a tableclothed table and order eggs, hot cakes, maple syrup, milk, sausages and orange juice. That cold wind has worked up an appetite.

"I want to write a letter to Mom," Chris says.

That sounds good to me. I go to the desk and get some of the lodge stationery. I bring it to Chris and give him my pen. That brisk morning air has given him some energy too. He puts the paper in front of him, grabs the pen in a heavy grip and then concentrates on the blank paper for a while.

He looks up. "What day is it?"

I tell him. He nods and writes it down.

Then I see him write, "Dear Mom:"

Then he stares at the paper for a while.

Then he looks up. "What should I say?"

I start to grin. I should have him write for an hour about one side of a coin. I've sometimes thought of him as a student but not as a rhetoric student.

We're interrupted by the hot cakes and I tell him to put the letter to one side and I'll help him afterward.

When we are done I sit smoking with a leaden feeling from the hot cakes and the eggs and everything and notice through the window that under the pines outside the ground is in patches of shadow and sunlight.

Chris brings out the paper again. "Now help me," he says.

"Okay," I say. I tell him getting stuck is the commonest trouble of all. Usually, I say, your mind gets stuck when you're trying to do too many things at once. What you have to do is try not to force words to come. That just gets you more stuck. What you have to do now is separate out the things and do them one at a time. You're trying to think of what to *say* and what to say *first* at the same time and that's too hard. So separate them out. Just make a list of all the things you want to say in any old order. Then later we'll figure out the right order.

"Like what things?" he asks.

"Well, what do you want to tell her?"

"About the trip."

"What things about the trip?"

He thinks for a while. "About the mountain we climbed."

"Okay, write that down," I say.

He does.

Then I see him write down another item, then another, while I finish my cigarette and coffee. He goes through three sheets of paper, listing things he wants to say.

"Save those," I tell him, "and we'll work on them later."

"I'll never get all this into one letter," he says.

He sees me laugh and frowns.

I say, "Just pick out the best things." Then we head outside and onto the motorcycle again.

4. CUBING

Cubing is a good way to look at a person, an object, a feeling, or an idea from six different perspectives. Like a cube, the writing you do while cubing has six sides (see Figure 4 on the following page). You should write quickly, spending three to five minutes on each side of your cube.

Figure 4

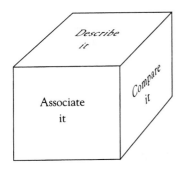
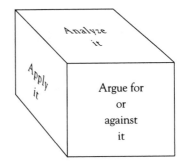

Here's what you do on each side of your cube:

1. *Describe it:* What does it look like? What are its characteristics? What are the first things you notice about it?

2. *Compare it:* What is it similar to? What is it different from?

3. *Associate it:* What does it remind you of? How does it connect with your individual life, with the life of your family or community?

4. *Analyze it:* Look deeper. What is it really made of? How does it work?

5. *Apply it:* What is it used for? Who uses it?

6. *Argue for it or against it:* Is it a good thing or a bad one? Explain why.

When you are finished, read what you wrote. Put a star beside one or two of the six small pieces of writing that seem the most powerful or the most interesting to you or that you would like to develop further. Freewrite about them again.

Responding to Readings

1. RESPONSE QUESTIONS

Rather than writing freely in response to a reading, you may sometimes want guidance. These three questions in this order are a useful guide:

1. What did you perceive (notice, remember) in what you read? What did you understand the reading to be about?

2. How do you feel about what you understood or saw? What is your opinion of what you read (or of one part of what you read)?

3. What associations flow from your thoughts and feelings? What does the reading remind you of in your own life, in the lives of people you know, or in other pieces you have read?

Figure 5 on the following page shows the answers one person wrote to these three questions after reading "Sometimes Home Is Not Really Home."

2. DOUBLE-ENTRY NOTEBOOK

A *double-entry notebook* is a special reading log. It allows you to note points in your reading that interest you and then to talk with yourself about them. Here is how it works.

Draw a line down the middle of one page of your notebook. As you read a passage or after you finish reading it, on the left side of your notebook page, jot down interesting or important words, phrases, sentences, ideas, points, details, and the like. You can write down the exact words as they appear in the text (*quote*), you can say the ideas in your own words (*paraphrase*), or you can *summarize*, in your own words, important or interesting ideas or main events from the passage. Then, on the right side of your notebook page, write your own comments about the material you put on the left side. You

Figure 5

1. What do you understand?

   Maggie Mok went to visit her "real home" in Mainland China, but she didn't feel at all at home there. In fact, she felt so much like a stranger that she returned to Hong Kong, her birthplace, sooner than she had planned.

2. How do you feel about what you understand?

   I feel sad for Maggie Mok. She felt so out of place in that village that she had been so eager to visit and to feel "at home" in. I suppose I could say she should have known this would happen, but when you have a dream like that, it's hard to be realistic.

3. What do you associate with your understanding?

   I'm going to visit my hometown this summer, the town I lived in until I was 18 years old. I wonder how I'll feel, especially when I see my old house. I know I'll feel sad, with some longing for those days and being with my parents there again. But maybe I'll be happy not to be living there, in that small town, anymore. Will anyone in the town remember me? recognize me?

---

can question; react; express confusion; connect; relate to other reading or your own experience; make observations about your reading process; express your feelings, thoughts, and ideas; and so on.

Left Side	**Right Side**
interesting/important	your comments:
quotes/paraphrases:	ideas
words	questions
phrases	reactions
sentences	confusions
ideas	connections
points	feelings
details	thoughts

Figure 6 on page 232 shows what one person wrote in her double-entry notebook after reading "A Walk to the Jetty."

She first copied a sentence from the story on the left side of her notebook page. On the right side of the page, she wrote several kinds of comments:

Question ("Why did she repeat that so many times?")

Figure 6

A Walk to the Jetty

"I never wanted to lie in my bed again"	*Why did she repeat that so many times? I guess to tell the reader exactly how she felt, to emphasize that idea.*
	I've never felt that way, that I can think of. I guess I'm more cautious about making changes in my life than Annie John was.
description of her room: *prizes I had won in school* *old thermos* *shells* *washstand* *beautiful basin of white enamel with blooming red hibiscus painted at the bottom and an urn that matched*	*I like how these details help me see the room and tell me what's important to Annie. I can just picture that beautiful white basin—I could draw it, it's so clear to me.*

Answer to her question ("I guess to tell the reader exactly how she felt. . . .")

Reaction ("I've never felt that way. . . .")

On the left side of the page, the reader then listed items Kincaid had included in a description of her room. On the right side of the page, she commented on how those details made her feel.

Another reader, of course, would note different things and have different reactions to the story simply because each reader's knowledge and experience are unique. The value of writing your *own* understanding and your *own* comments about what you read is that it helps you enrich your reading by relating to it personally. In other words, there is no right answer; you notice what's important to *you*, and you react and respond from *yourself*.

Further enrichment can come when you share your notebooks with other readers. Reading (and then talking about) other people's interpretations of a piece of writing will broaden your understanding of it. Other readers' reactions and associations help you see the text in new ways. For these reasons, this book often asks you to share your notebook entries with other students, usually in small groups.

TRIPLE-ENTRY NOTEBOOK

Instead of talking aloud to someone about your double-entry responses, you can have a "conversation in writing" in a triple-entry notebook. Here's how it works.

Do a double-entry response on a left-hand page of your notebook. Pass your notebook to another person. This person reads your double entry and writes a response on the right-hand page of your notebook.

Figure 7 on page 234 shows an example of a triple-entry notebook. Columns 1 and 2 contain one person's double-entry response to "On Turning Fifty." Column 3 shows a second person's response to what the first person wrote.

3. ANNOTATING

Annotating is a way of reading with a pencil in hand. As you read, you mark up the text in any way that makes sense to you:

Underline, circle, or bracket important or interesting words, phrases, and sentences.

Draw arrows to connect related ideas.

Write comments and questions in the margins.

Number points.

Make any other markings that are meaningful to you.

Don't be shy about making marks on the text! If you don't want to write directly on the text, you can write on a photocopy or make the same kinds of notes in your notebook.

Most people who annotate read a text several times and make more annotations each time they read it. Rereading helps them see things in a new way and with fresh understanding.

Figure 8 on page 235 shows one person's annotations on "The Colorings of Childhood."

4. DESCRIPTIVE OUTLINING

The goal of the descriptive outline is to help you see a piece of writing more clearly and objectively. Descriptive outlining is a tool for revision and should be done between two drafts of a piece of writing.

Figure 7

"My thoughts were so powerful I had to write them down in order to move them outside my body, in order to manage them, to transform painful feelings into marks on a paper."	Can writing about strong feelings help me "manage" them? Does writing make things less painful? If so, I should be doing more writing!	I don't know that writing makes things *less* painful but it may help by putting the pain on paper.
"I thought I would live my mother's life. I suppose all girls do."	When I was a girl, I'm not sure that I thought this way. For example, I couldn't imagine myself ever married, and I didn't think I would enjoy doing some of the things my mother did that I really enjoy now——like gardening and baking bread.	Do you enjoy being married, too? As for me, I'm more like my father and wanted to be like him.
"I too am passionate about my work."	Me too!	I'm not. I'm passionate about what I'd like to do, but not what I do.

Figure 8

The Colorings of Childhood

Five or six years ago, when my older sister revealed to the rest of our family her intention of marrying her boyfriend, from Ghana, I remember that my reaction, as a nervous and somewhat <u>protective</u> younger brother, was something like "Well, that's fine for them—I just wonder about the children." I'm not sure what I was wondering, exactly, but it no doubt had to do with the <u>thorny</u> questions of race and identity, of having parents of different complexions, and a child, presumably, of some intermediate shade, and what that would mean for a child growing up here, in the United States of America.

that question again—I've heard it before

difficult?

main point?

*

I had no idea, at the time, that I, too, would one day marry an African, or that soon thereafter we would have a child, or that I would hear my own <u>apprehensions</u> of several years before echoed in the words of one of my wife's friends. [She was a white American of a classic liberal mold—wearer of Guatemalan shawls, befriender of Africans, espouser of worthy causes—]but she was made uneasy by the thought of Njoki, her friend from Kenya, marrying me, a white person. She first asked Njoki what my "politics" were and, having been assured that they were okay, went on to say, "Well, I'm sure he's a very nice person, but before you get married I just hope you'll think about the children."

he doesn't like her—distances her by the way he describes

*

I recognized in her remarks the shadow of my own, but when it is one's own marriage that is being worried about, one's children, not yet conceived, one tends to <u>ponder</u> such comments more closely. But this time, too, I was the uncle of two handsome, happy boys, Ghanian-American, who, as far as I could tell, were <u>suffering no side</u> effects for having parents of different colors. Njoki, too was displeased.

he's like her though

think about?

*

"What is she trying to say, exactly—that *my* child will be disadvantaged because he looks like me?" my wife asked. "So what does she think about me? Does she think *I'm* disadvantaged because I'm African?"

235

* * *

Set up your descriptive outline this way:

Main idea:_____
    Paragraph 1 says: _____
              does: _____
    Paragraph 2 says: _____
              does: _____
    Paragraph 3 says: _____
              does: _____

For *main idea*, write the main idea of the composition, either as it is stated by the writer or in your own words.

For what each paragraph *says*, write a one-sentence summary of the paragraph.

For what each paragraph *does*, explain the function of the paragraph in the composition. That is, what does the writer intend each paragraph to accomplish? A paragraph can do many things. It can present an idea, give an example, give a reason, argue logically; it can analyze; it can explain; it can list and catalog objects, events, scenes, or problems; it can tell a story; it can describe a person, place, or thing; it can compare; it can conclude. Paragraphs analyze, describe, and argue in order to help defend or explain the main point of the composition. When you tell what a paragraph *does*, you are telling how it develops the main idea.

DESCRIPTIVE OUTLINING EXAMPLE

"My Way or Theirs?" from *Raising Children* by Liu Zongren

Main idea (Paragraph 1): A Chinese woman told the writer, who was spending two years in the United States, to observe how much freedom American parents gave their children to make choices about things to buy.

Paragraph 2 says: Chinese parents help their children choose things to buy. If the child chooses something the Chinese parent doesn't think is right for the child, the parent will most likely refuse to buy it.

Paragraph 2 does: Shows the Chinese way by giving a typical example of how a Chinese parent acts with his or her child in a store.

Paragraph 3 says: The writer likes the American way because it fosters independence in children. He plans to adopt this practice with his children when he returns to China.

Paragraph 3 does: Compares and contrasts the Chinese and American ways. The writer draws a conclusion from his observations. He ends with a look to the future and change.

The Reading Process
(How We Read)

A number of times in this book, you'll be asked to reflect on *how* you read a passage, that is, on your reading process. Becoming aware of the reading strategies you already use and learning some new ones from your classmates and from the activities in this book will help you to become a better, more fluent reader.

In response to the How I Read It activity on p. 16, students in one class described a variety of strategies they used when reading "Going to America." These were some of the strategies they mentioned.

It was difficult because of the vocabulary, so I read it quickly the first time, and then slowly the second time. I tried to figure out the meaning of the hard words from the sentences around them.

I read it slowly and tried to understand the meaning of every word.

I underlined words I didn't know and then later, at home, looked them up in the dictionary.

I didn't use a dictionary because it would take too long.

When I couldn't understand a word, I looked at the rest of the sentence and the paragraph to see if I could get the meaning from the context.

I reread parts I didn't understand.

I skipped things and words I didn't understand.

I asked questions. Then sometimes, when I read more of the story, I could answer my questions.

It was hard because of the mother's story. I don't know the history. I had to try to figure that out.

I read it two or three times. I understood it better then.

The Writing Process
(How We Write)

In this book, you'll be asked to reflect on *how* you wrote your composition, that is, on your writing process. Your writing process is a complex activity, like playing soccer or dancing. You can develop it by learning and practicing certain skills and strategies. For example, you can learn ways of getting started, like freewriting or clustering; you can sharpen your observation skills; you can write faster and longer, and do rewriting and editing. You can learn new strategies by reflecting on what you do as you write and by watching or talking to other people about how they write.

Here are some examples of what several students said about *how* they wrote on the Topics for Writing, p. 17, after reading "Going to America." In After Writing, question 4, p. 18, they were told: "Write in your log about *how* you wrote this composition (your process of writing)." Their responses give you an idea of their writing process.

> First, I started doing freewriting to build up my idea. . . . I wrote it three times: First I took out the freewriting that I did. Then I checked which sentences I could keep, the ideas, many details, and so on. That was my first draft. Then I rewrote it because I thought about new words, new sentences, and I had to add more paragraphs. And the final draft, that is the one I am giving to you. That I think is perfect and well done.

> I decided to write about Topic B, about the cross my grandmother gave me when I came to America. . . . When I faced this topic I thought about it for two or three minutes . . . going back to the past and . . . to the present. I tried to remember how I felt at different times when the cross helped me. I kept writing for 20 minutes. I wrote it twice, the second time I just . . . cut certain things. I did not change it. And then in the morning I reread it again and that's that.

I chose Topic A because I have a photograph of my family at my sister's wedding, and I wanted to write about that. I wrote my composition two times, the first one here in the classroom, but I was not sure about some words and I changed some things. I added many things the second time. I had an idea here but I didn't know how to write it in English and wrote it in Spanish and I translated it at home.

I wrote my composition about raising adolescents in the U.S. I took around two hours because I rewrote it two times. I changed a lot of words and tried to organize my ideas and the meaning of each word.

It takes a long time to learn to write. Don't get impatient, but be reflective and watchful. Try to add strategies like the ones that these student writers used to your own writing process. The more you can do this, the more prepared you will be to meet future writing assignments.

Suggestions on Writing
(Beginnings, Endings, Being Specific, Showing Instead of Telling)

In the pieces that follow, three professional writers give their ideas on story beginnings and endings, being specific, and the importance of showing instead of telling. We think you will find these hints useful in improving your writing.

Beginnings
Christina Baldwin

I tell writing students that the beginning of a story is like the threshold of a doorway: You want the reader to feel confident enough in the imagined world so that s/he will step into the story's reality without hesitating.

Endings
Elizabeth Cowan

MAKE THE MOST OF YOUR CONCLUSION

Like the introduction, the conclusion must be "concocted." It is not organically contained in the thesis as the middle of an essay is, so it has to come entirely out of your head.

As with introductions, many writers fail to make the most of conclusions. Yet if your paper fizzles out at the end, the reader may forget what you said the minute he finishes reading it. Having come this far, you should want to make sure your reader doesn't end with a "Ho hum! So what?" So make the most of your conclusion.

ESSAY CONCLUSIONS

The ending of your paper ought to do three things:

1. Remind your readers of what you have said.
2. Give your readers at least one new thing to think about.
3. Provide a gentle completing of the paper so that your readers are not left hanging in the air.

Be Specific
Natalie Goldberg

Be specific. Don't say "fruit." Tell what kind of fruit—"It is a pomegranate." Give things the dignity of their names. Just as with human beings, it is rude to say, "Hey, girl, get in line." That "girl" has a name. (As a matter of fact, if she's at least twenty years old, she's a woman, not a "girl" at all.) Things, too, have names. It is much better to say "the geranium in the window" than "the flower in the window." "Geranium"—that one word gives us a much more specific picture. It penetrates more deeply into the beingness of that flower. It immediately gives us the scene by the window—red petals, green circular leaves, all straining toward sunlight.

About ten years ago I decided I had to learn the names of plants and flowers in my environment. I bought a book on them and walked down the tree-lined streets of Boulder, examining leaf, bark, and seed, trying to match them up with their descriptions and names in the book. Maple, elm, oak, locust. I usually tried to cheat by asking people working in their yards the names of the flowers and trees growing there. I was amazed how few people had any idea of the names of the live beings inhabiting their little plot of land.

When we know the name of something, it brings us closer to the ground. It takes the blur out of our mind; it connects us to the earth. If I walk down the street and see "dogwood," "forsythia," I feel more friendly toward the environment. I am noticing what is around me and can name it. It makes me more awake.

If you read the poems of William Carlos Williams, you will see how specific he is about plants, trees, flowers—chicory, daisy, locust, poplar, quince, primrose, black-eyed Susan, lilacs—each has its own integrity. Williams says, "Write what's in front of your nose." It's good for us to know what is in front of our nose. Not just "daisy," but how the flower is in the season we are looking at it—"The dayseye hugging the earth/in August . . . brownedged,/ green and pointed scales/armor his yellow." Continue to hone your awareness: to the name, to the month, to the day, and finally to the moment.

Williams also says: "No idea, but in things." Study what is "in front of your nose." By saying "geranium" instead of "flower," you are penetrating more deeply into the present and being there. The closer we can get to what's in front of our nose, the more it can teach us everything. "To see the World in a Grain of Sand, and a heaven in a Wild Flower . . ."

In writing groups and classes too, it is good to quickly learn the names of all the other group members. It helps to ground you in the group and make you more attentive to each other's work.

Learn the names of everything: birds, cheese, tractors, cars, buildings. A writer is all at once everything—an architect, French cook, farmer—and at the same time, a writer is none of these things.

Don't Tell, but Show
Natalie Goldberg

There's an old adage in writing: "Don't tell, but show." What does this actually mean? It means don't tell us about anger (or any of those big words like honesty, truth, hate, love, sorrow, life, justice, etc.); show us what made you angry. We will read it and feel angry. Don't tell readers what to feel. Show them the situation, and that feeling will awaken in them.

Writing is not psychology. We do not talk "about" feelings. Instead the writer feels and through her words awakens those feelings in the reader. The writer takes the reader's hand and guides him through the valley of sorrow and joy without ever having to mention those words.

When you are present at the birth of a child you may find yourself weeping and singing. Describe what you see: the mother's face, the rush of energy when the baby finally enters the world after many attempts, the husband breathing with his wife, applying a wet washcloth to her forehead. The reader will understand without your ever having to discuss the nature of life.

When you write, stay in direct connection with the senses and what you are writing about. If you are writing from first thoughts—the way your mind first flashes on something before second and third thoughts take over and comment, criticize, and evaluate—you won't have to worry. First thoughts are the mind reflecting experiences—as close as a human being can get in words to the sunset, the birth, the bobby pin, the crocus. We can't always stay with first thoughts, but it is good to know about them. They can easily teach us how to step out of the way and use words like a mirror to reflect the pictures.

As soon as I hear the word *about* in someone's writing, it is an automatic alarm. "This story is about life." Skip that line and go willy-nilly right into life in your writing. Naturally, when we do practice writing in our notebooks, we might write a general line: "I want to write about my grandmother" or "This is a story about success." That's fine. Don't castigate yourself for writing it; don't get critical and mix up the creator and editor. Simply write it, note it, and drop to a deeper level and enter the story and take us into it.

Some general statements are sometimes very appropriate. Just make sure to back each one with a concrete picture. Even if you are writing an essay, it makes the work so much more lively. Oh, if only Kant or Descartes had followed these instructions. "I think, therefore I am"—I think about bubble gum, horse racing, barbecue, and the stock market; therefore, I know I exist in America in the twentieth century. Go ahead, take Kant's *Prolegomena to*

Any Future Metaphysic and get it to show what he is telling. We would all be a lot happier.

Several years ago I wrote down a story that someone had told me. My friends said it was boring. I couldn't understand their reaction; I loved the story. What I realize now is that I wrote "about" the story, secondhand. I didn't enter it and make friends with it. I was outside it; therefore, I couldn't take anyone else into it. This does not mean you can't write about something you did not actually experience firsthand; only make sure that you breathe life into it. Otherwise it is two times removed and you are not present.

Appendix F

After Writing

Each After Writing section has two types of activities: sharing your writing and giving feedback (or responding) to your classmates' writing, and reflecting on how you wrote (your writing process). (Reflecting on your writing process is discussed in Appendix D. Look there for examples and discussion.)

You will be asked to *share your writing* with your classmates, either by exchanging papers and reading silently or by reading your piece aloud. After you read or listen to your classmates' writing, you will be asked to *give a response or feedback* based on questions or guidelines provided. Sometimes this is done in a group, sometimes with a partner, and occasionally you may be asked to give yourself feedback on your own writing.

The questions in the After Writing sections are about things any reader or listener can respond to concerning a piece of writing. They are not technical. That is, you are not expected to give feedback as an editor or a teacher. You don't have to give suggestions for revision or make corrections. Simply be yourself as an active reader or listener, and say something to the writer. Use the questions as guidelines.

Here are a few examples of the kinds of questions you will be asked to respond to in After Writing:

What do you like about the composition?

What do you understand about it?

What details stand out for you, the reader?

What point does this piece make?

How could this piece of writing be improved?

What examples does the writer include?

Do the examples illustrate the writer's point?

How does the writer develop the point (idea)?

Some of the terms used in these After Writing questions may not be familiar to you at first. If you don't understand certain terms, discuss them with your instructor and classmates. Try to use the words as you think they should be used. They will become clearer as you go along. Remember, there are no right or wrong answers.

A few terms used frequently in the After Writing questions are defined here briefly. The reading passages throughout the book contain many examples of each term. If you discuss these terms with your instructor and classmates, look back at some of the readings for examples.

point: central idea; what the writer is trying to say; the message; the lesson; may be implied or stated explicitly.

example: a story, an experience, or other specifics used to illustrate a point.

detail: a bit of added information, often sensory (visual, auditory, related to touch or feeling, etc.).

development: how the writer starts, builds, and concludes an idea or a point throughout a piece of writing.

Acknowledgments (continued from page iv)

Judy Scales-Trent, "On Turning Fifty," from *Lifenotes: Personal Writings by Contemporary Black Women* by Patricia Bell-Scott. Copyright © 1994 by Judy Scales-Trent. Reprinted by permission of Patricia Bell-Scott and W. W. Norton & Company, Inc.

Aurora Levins Morales, "Child of the Americas," from *Getting Home Alive* by Aurora Levins Morales. Copyright © 1986 by Aurora Levins Morales and Rosario Morales. Reprinted by permission of Firebrand Books, Ithaca, New York.

Liu Zongren, "My Way or Theirs?" Copyright © 1988 by Liu Zongren. Reprinted by permission of China Books & Periodicals, Inc., 2929 24th Street, San Francisco, CA 94110. Phone: 415/282-2994, fax: 415/282-0994, catalog available.

Linda Hogan, "The Sacred Seed of the Medicine Tree: Can Indian Identity Survive?" First appeared in *Northern Lights* magazine, spring 1990. Reprinted by permission of Northern Lights, Box 8084, Missoula, Montana 59807.

Armando Socarras Ramírez, "Stowaway." Reprinted with permission from the January 1979 *Reader's Digest.* Copyright © 1969 by The Reader's Digest Assn., Inc.

Julia Alvarez, "Snow," from *How the Garcia Girls Lost Their Accent.* Copyright © 1991 by Julia Alvarez. Published by Plume, an imprint of New American Library, a division of Penguin USA, New York. First published in hardcover by Algonquin Books of Chapel Hill. Reprinted by permission.

Yeghia Aslanian, "A Story of Conflicts," from *Hudson River Review*, a Manhattan community journal (EDN 27/December 1987). Reprinted by permission of the author.

Evelyn C. Rosser, "Chocolate Tears and Dreams," from *Lifenotes: Personal Writings by Contemporary Black Women* by Patricia Bell-Scott. Copyright © 1994 by Evelyn C. Rosser. Reprinted by permission of Patricia Bell-Scott and W. W. Norton and Company, Inc.

Tess Gallagher, "I Stop Writing the Poem." Copyright © 1992 by Graywolf Press. Reprinted from *Moon Crossing Bridge* with the permission of Graywolf Press, Saint Paul, Minnesota.

Gloria Steinem, "Believing in the True Self," from *Revolution from Within* by Gloria Steinem. Copyright © 1992 by Gloria Steinem. Reprinted by permission of Little, Brown and Company.

Russell Baker, "Becoming a Writer," from *Growing Up* by Russell Baker. Copyright © 1982. Used with permission of Congdon & Weed, Inc., and Contemporary Books, Chicago.

Becky Birtha, "Johnnieruth," from *Lover's Choice* (Seal Press, Seattle). Copyright © 1987 by Becky Birtha. Reprinted with permission of the publisher.

Lucille Clifton, "homage to my hips." Copyright © 1980 by Lucille Clifton. First appeared in *two-headed woman*, published by The University of Massachusetts Press. Reprinted by permission of Curtis Brown Ltd.

Luis J. Rodriguez, "Rekindling the Warrior," from *Utne Reader* (July/August 1994). Copyright © 1994 by Luis J. Rodriguez. Reprinted with permission of the author.

Cherylene Lee, "Safe," from *Charlie Chan is Dead: An Anthology of Contemporary Asian-American Fiction*, Jessica Hagedorn, ed. Viking Penguin (1993) pp. 204–214. Reprinted by permission of the author.

Dorothy Allison, "I'm Working on My Charm," from *Trash* by Dorothy Allison. Copyright © 1988 by Dorothy Allison. Reprinted by permission of Firebrand Books, Ithaca, New York.

Leticia Fuentes, "My First Job." Reprinted by permission of the author.

Dana Milbank, "New-Collar Work," from *The Wall Street Journal* (September 9, 1992) pp. A3, A8. Reprinted by permission of The Wall Street Journal. Copyright © 1992 Dow Jones & Company, Inc. All rights reserved worldwide.

Studs Terkel, "The Bread Shop: Interview with Kay Stepkin, Director of the Bakery Cooperative" from *Working* by Studs Terkel. Copyright © 1972, 1974 by Studs Terkel. Reprinted by permission of Pantheon Books, a division of Random House, Inc.

Susan Ovelette Kobasa, "A Scale of Stresses," from *American Health Partners*, September 1984, p. 87. Copyright © 1984 by Susan Ovelette Kobasa. Reprinted by permission of American Health Magazine.

Jane Brody, "It's O.K. to Cry," from *The New York Times*, February 22, 1984. Copyright © 1984 by The New York Times Company. Reprinted by permission.

Claire Braz-Valentine, "Going Through the House," from *Breaking Up Is Hard to Do*, ed. Amber Coverdale Sumrall. Published by The Crossing Press, Freedom, California 95019 (1994). 800-777-1048. Reprinted by permission of the author.

Julia Aldrich, "Falling Away, Here at Home," from *The New York Times*, April 26, 1987. Copyright © 1987 by The New York Times Company. Reprinted by permission.

Daniel Goleman, "Hope Emerges As Key to Success in Life," from *The New York Times*, December 24, 1991. Copyright © 1991 by The New York Times Company. Reprinted by permission.

Langston Hughes, "Poem [2]," from *The Dream Keeper and Other Poems* by Langston Hughes. Copyright © 1932 by Alfred A. Knopf, Inc., and renewed 1960 by Langston Hughes. Reprinted by permission of the publisher and Harold Ober Associates, Incorporated.

Raymond Carver, "Gravy," from *Fires* by Raymond Carver. Copyright © 1983. Reprinted by permission of Capra Press, Santa Barbara, CA.

Peter Cameron, "Homework," from *One Way or Another* by Peter Cameron. Copyright © 1986 by the author. First appeared in *The New Yorker.* Reprinted by permission of the author.

Michael Dorris, "Father's Day," from *Paper Trail* by Michael Dorris. Copyright © 1994 by Michael Dorris. Reprinted by permission of HarperCollins Publishers, Inc.

Sam Roberts, "New York Finds Typical Family Being Redefined," from *The New York Times*, October 20, 1992. Copyright © 1992 by The New York Times Company. Reprinted by permission.

Donald McCaig, "Power," pages 145–146 from *An American Homeplace* by Donald McCaig. Copyright © 1992 by Donald McCaig. Reprinted by permission of Crown Publishers, Inc., and Knox Burger Assoc.

Wendell Berry, "Against PCs: Why I'm Not Going to Buy a Computer" and "Letters" excerpted from *What Are People For?* Copyright © 1990 by Wendell Berry. Reprinted by permission of North Point Press, a division of Farrar, Straus and Giroux, Inc., and Random House UK.

Joshua Glenn, "Cyberhood vs. Neighborhood." Editor's note, *Utne Reader.* #68, March/April 1995. Copyright © Utne Reader.

Michael Kearney, "Whiz Kid Anonymous." Reprinted in *Utne Reader* #68, March/April 1995. Originally from *Net Guide*, CMP Media, 600 Community Drive, Manhasset, N.Y. 11030.

"Pockets of Paradise: The Community Garden." This article is an excerpt of one which first appeared in the 1995 *Seeds of Change* catalog, P. O. Box 15700, Sante Fe, New Mexico 87506-5700. Reprinted by permission.

Suzanne Hamlin, "Take Two Bowls of Garlic Pasta, Then Call Me in the Morning," from *The New York Times.* Copyright © by The New York Times Company. Reprinted by permission.

Elvia Alvarado, "Taming Macho Ways," pages 54–56 from *Don't Be Afraid Gringo: A Honduran Woman Speaks from the Heart, the Story of Elvira Alvarado,* translated by Medea Benjamin. Copyright © 1987. Reprinted by permission of the Institute for Food and Development Policy.

Roscoe Thorne, "Gays, the Military . . . and My Son." Copyright © 1993 by *Harper's Magazine.* All rights reserved. Reproduced from the April issue by special permission.

Bailey White, "Buzzard," pages 156–157 from *Mama Makes Up Her Mind: And Other Dangers of Southern Living.* Copyright © 1993 by Bailey White. Reprinted by permission of Addison-Wesley Publishing Company, Inc.

Rafe Martin, "The Brave Little Parrot," from *More Best-Loved Stories Told at the National Storytelling Festival,* collected and edited by the National Storytelling Association (NSA), P. O. Box 309, Jonesborough, Tenn. 37659. Copyright © 1992 by NSA. Reprinted by permission of the author and National Storytelling Press. This is the text of the story the way he actually *tells* it. His picture book version of the story will be published by G. P. Putnam's Sons (1996).

Abbie Hoffman, "The Future Is Yours (Still)." Copyright © 1987 by *Harper's Magazine.* All rights reserved. Reproduced from the July issue by special permission.

Pablo Neruda, "Keeping Quiet," from *Extravagaria* by Pablo Neruda. Translation copyright © 1974 by Alistair Reid. Reprinted by permission of Farrar, Straus & Giroux, Inc., and Jonathan Cape Ltd. London.

Thich Nhat Hanh, "Entering the Twenty-first Century," from *Peace Is Every Step* by Thich Nhat Hahn. Copyright © 1991 by Thich Nhat Hanh. Used by permission of Bantam Books, a division of Bantam Doubleday Dell Publishing Group, Inc.

Teishitsu, "Haiku," from *The Four Seasons: Japanese Haiku.* Copyright © 1958. Reprinted by permission of Peter Pauper Press.

Roger L. Welsch, "Family Man: Three Is the Loneliest Number," from *Natural History* magazine, November 1992. Copyright © 1992 by the American Museum of Natural History. Reprinted with the permission of the Museum of Natural History.

Loren Eiseley, "How Flowers Changed the World," from *The Immense Journey* by Loren Eiseley. Copyright © 1957 by Loren Eiseley. Reprinted by permission of Crown Publishers, Inc.

Thomas Berry, "The Earth Community," from *The Dream of the Earth* by Thomas Berry. Copyright © 1988 by Thomas Berry. Reprinted by the permission of Sierra Club Books.

Illustration Credits

Page xx, © Deborah Kahn Kalas, Stock, Boston, 1988.

Page 12, Courtesy of Nicholas Gage.

Page 76, Courtesy of the United Nations.

Page 114, Courtesy of National Aeronautics and Space Administration.

Index

"Against PCs" (Berry), 164–66
Aldrich, Julia, 135–37
Allison, Dorothy, 103–104
Alvarado, Elvia, 187–88
Alvarez, Julia, 70–71
"Ancestral Origins" (Leigh), 27
Annotating, 47, 98, 155, 157, 174, 175, 178, 184, 204, 233
Aslanian, Yeghia, 71–73
Associating, 4, 9, 41, 122, 174, 187, 211

Baker, Russell, 81–83
Baldwin, Christina, 240
Becoming a Writer (Baker), 81–83
Beginnings, 10, 33, 196, 240
"Believing in the True Self" (Steinem), 78–79
Bernard, Claude, 1
Berry, Thomas, 221–22
Berry, Wendell, 164–66, 169
Birtha, Becky, 85–89
Brainstorming, 225
"Brave Little Parrot, The" (Martin), 198–200
Braz-Valentine, Claire, 129–31
"Bread Shop, The" (Terkel), 114–16
Brody, Jane, 124–26
"Buzzard" (White), 195

Cameron, Peter, 144–50
Carver, Raymond, 143–44
Categorizing, 7, 34, 132, 172, 187
"Child of the Americas" (Morales), 56–57
"Chocolate Tears and Dreams" (Rosser), 73–74
Clifton, Lucille, 93
Clustering, 4, 5, 43, 96, 171, 209, 224–25
"Colorings of Childhood, The" (Updike), 45–47, 235
Conclusions. *See* endings

Context clues, 24, 42
Cowan, Elizabeth, 241
Cubing, 25, 228–29
"Cyberhood vs. Neighborhood" (Editors, *Utne Reader*), 171

Descriptive outline, 5–6, 40, 174
Descriptive outlining, 6, 40, 48, 174, 233, 236
Descriptive writing, 6
Detail, 246
Development, 246
Dorris, Michael, 154–155
Double-entry notebook, 23, 83, 159, 160, 166, 204, 210, 230–32

"Earth Community, The" (Berry), 221–22
Ecclesiastes 3:1–8, 42
"Education of Berenice Belizaire, The" (Klein), 30–32
Eiseley, Loren, 220–21
Emerson, Ralph Waldo, 77
Emotions, expression of, in writing, 9, 16, 53, 55, 104, 105, 116, 133, 189
Endings, 10, 33, 196, 241
"Entering the Twenty-first Century" (Hanh), 209–10
Examples, 189, 246

"Falling Away, Here at Home" (Aldrich), 135–37
"Family Man" (Welsch), 215–18
"Father's Day" (Dorris), 154–55
Feedback, 6, 10, 17, 18, 58, 91, 94–95, 202, 245
Figures of speech, 24–25, 201
  metaphors, 24–25, 57, 201, 211
  similes, 24, 201
"First Day, The" (Jones), 7–9
Fodor, Denis, 66–69

249

Freewriting, 1, 2, 7, 16, 36, 38, 39, 43, 45,
    50, 77, 79, 81, 98, 100, 101, 108, 117,
    124, 129, 131, 137, 153, 154, 159,
    161, 172, 173, 176, 178, 195, 200,
    206, 207, 211, 223
  clustering, 4, 5, 43, 96, 171, 209, 224–25
  cubing, 25, 228–29
  listing, 5–7, 9, 19, 59, 78, 83, 94, 99,
    100, 101, 103, 104, 106, 107–9, 112,
    118, 122, 124, 127, 128, 132, 134,
    137, 140, 155, 156, 160, 162, 163,
    166, 172, 173, 174, 184, 187, 194,
    205, 208, 213, 225–27
  looping, 223–24
  mapping, 224–25
Fuentes, Leticia, 106–7
"Future Is Yours (Still), The" (Hoffman),
    203–4

Gage, Nicholas, 11–16
Gallagher, Tess, 74
"Gays, the Military . . . and My Son" (Ros-
    coe), 191–93
Generalizations, 59, 140, 213
Gnostic Gospels, 78, 80
"Going Through the House" (Braz-
    Valentine), 129–31
"Going to America" (Gage), 11–16
Goldberg, Natalie, 241–44
Goleman, Daniel, 141–43
"Gravy" (Carver), 143–44

Haiku (Teishitsu), 215
Hamlin, Suzanne, 181–83
Hanh, Thich Nhat, 209–10
Hoffman, Abbie, 203–4
Hogan, Linda, 64–65
"homage to my hips" (Clifton), 93
"Homework" (Cameron), 144–50
"Hope Emerges As Key to Success in Life"
    (Goleman), 141–43
"How Flowers Changed the World" (Eise-
    ley), 220–21
Hughes, Langston, 143

Idea gathering, 43, 44, 102
  clustering, 4, 5, 43, 96, 171, 209, 224–25
  cubing, 25, 228–29
  listing, 5–7, 9, 19, 59, 78, 83, 94, 99,
    100, 101, 103, 104, 106, 107–9, 112,
    118, 122, 124, 127, 128, 132, 134,
    137, 140, 155, 156, 160, 162, 163,
    166, 172, 173, 174, 184, 187, 194,
    205, 208, 213, 225–27
  looping, 223–24
Images, 133
"I'm Working on My Charm" (Allison),
    103–4
Interviewing, 23, 25, 33, 40, 80, 99, 108,
    109, 112, 179, 184–85, 194
Issues, 59, 140, 213
"I Stop Writing the Poem" (Gallagher), 74
"It's O.K. to Cry" (Brody), 124–26

Jesus, 78
"Johnnieruth" (Birtha), 85–89
Jones, Edward P., 7–9

Kearney, Michael, 173–174
"Keeping Quiet" (Neruda), 206–7
Kernel idea, 36, 172, 175, 210, 223
Kernel sentence, 43, 223, 224
Kincaid, Jamaica, 19–23
Klein, Joe, 30–32
Kobasa, Susan Ovelette, 119–120
Kutner, Lawrence, 34–36

Lee, Cherylene, 100–101
Leigh, Michelle Dominique, 27
Letters (in response to Berry's article), 167–
    68
Listing, 5–7, 9, 19, 59, 78, 83, 94, 99, 100,
    101, 103, 104, 106, 107–9, 112, 118,
    122, 124, 127, 128, 132, 134, 137,
    140, 155, 156, 160, 162, 163, 166,
    172, 173, 174, 184, 187, 194, 205,
    208, 213, 225–27
Looping, 223–24

McCaig, Donald, 161–62
Mandela, Nelson, 153
Mapping, 224–25. See also clustering
Martin, Rafe, 198–200
Metaphors, 24–25, 57, 201, 211
Milbank, Dana, 110–11
Misconceptions, 36, 37
"Misconceptions with Roots in the Old
    Days" (Kutner), 34–36

Mok, Maggie, 4
Morales, Aurora Levins, 56–57
"My First Job" (Fuentes), 106–7
My Way or Theirs? (Zongren), 61–64

Nearing, Helen, 2
"Need We Say More?" (U.S. Department of Education), 219
Neruda, Pablo, 206–7
"New-Collar Work" (Milbank), 110–11
News stories, 23
"New York Finds Typical Family Being Redefined" (Roberts), 158–59
Notebook
  double-entry, 23, 83, 159, 160, 166, 204, 210, 230–32
  triple-entry, 53, 233

"On Turning Fifty" (Scales-Trent), 50–53

Pagels, Elaine, 78
Paragraphs, functions of, 5–6, 40, 41, 48, 236
Parallel structure, 79
Paraphrasing, 230
Pirsig, Robert M., 227–28
"Pockets of Paradise: The Community Garden" (Editors, *Seeds of Change*), 176–77
"Poem [2]" (Hughes), 143
Poetry
  features associated with, 43, 57, 132
  reading, 42–43, 57, 131, 207
  writing, 43–44, 57–58, 132–33, 208
Point, 246
"Power" (McCaig), 161–62
Proofreading, 59, 128, 185, 197, 212, 213

Quotation marks, use of, 178–79
Quote, 230

Ramirez, Armando, 66–69
Reading
  activities after, 3, 4–5, 9, 16, 23, 27, 32, 36, 39, 42–43, 47–48, 53, 57, 79, 83, 90, 93–94, 98, 101, 104, 107, 111–12, 116–17, 121–22, 126, 131, 137, 155, 159, 162, 166, 168, 169–70, 172, 174, 178, 184, 189, 193, 195, 198, 204, 207, 210
  activities before, 1, 2, 4, 7, 11, 18, 30, 34, 38, 42, 45, 50, 56, 78, 81, 85, 93, 96, 100, 103, 110, 114, 119, 124, 129, 135, 154, 158, 161, 164, 169, 171, 173, 176, 181, 187, 191, 195, 198, 203, 206, 209
  responding to, 230–36
  strategies for, 5, 9–10, 16–17, 24, 39–40, 43, 98, 117, 122, 131, 156, 159, 166, 178, 184, 193, 207, 211, 237
Reading log, 2–6, 9, 11, 16, 17, 23–28, 30, 32, 38, 39, 41–44, 53, 58, 59, 60, 77–80, 83, 84, 90, 92, 93, 95, 98, 102, 105, 118, 122, 123, 131, 135, 137, 140, 153, 157, 159–64, 166, 169, 170, 173–76, 178, 184, 185, 189, 193, 195, 200, 207, 210–14
Reddy, John, 66–69
Rekindling the Warrior (Rodriguez), 96–98
Reminiscence, 156
Reporter's Formula, 107, 108, 112, 159
Research findings, 36
Response questions, 5, 230
Roberts, Sam, 158–59
Rodriguez, Luis J., 96–98
Rosser, Evelyn C., 73–74

"Sacred Seed of the Medicine Tree, The" (Hogan), 64–65
"Safe" (Lee), 100–101
Sayings, 3
"Scale of Stresses, A" (Kobasa), 119–120
Scales-Trent, Judy, 50–53
Showing, 243–44
Similes, 24, 201
"Snow" (Alvarez), 70–71
"Sometimes Home Is Not Really Home" (Mok), 4
Specifying, 156, 241–42
Steinem, Gloria, 78–79
Stepkin, Kay, 114–116
Stevenson, Robert Louis, 28
"Story of Conflicts, A" (Aslanian), 71–73
"Stowaway" (Ramirez), 66–69
Stresses, scale of, 120–21
Summarizing, 16, 36, 41, 48, 57, 77, 80, 84, 90, 93, 112–113, 127, 128, 138, 153,

Summarizing (*continued*)
    156, 169, 174, 179, 190, 194, 196,
    204, 207, 210, 211, 230

"Take Two Bowls of Garlic Pasta, Then
    Call Me in the Morning" (Hamlin),
    181–83
"Taming Macho Ways" (Alvarado), 187–
    88
Teishitsu, 215
Terkel, Studs, 114–16
Thorne, Roscoe, 191–93
Time line, 193
Triple-entry notebook, 53, 233

Updike, David, 45–47, 235

Verbs, 132, 133
Vocabulary skills, 24, 57, 114, 119, 132,
    133, 135, 137, 161, 162, 171, 174,
    187, 189, 211

"Walk to the Jetty, The" (Kincaid), 19–23
Welsch, Roger L., 215–18
"When One Door Opens" (Nearing), 2
White, Bailey, 195
"Whiz Kid Anonymous" (Kearney),
    173–74

Writing, 59, 140, 213
    activities after, 3, 6, 10, 18, 26, 29, 33,
        37, 41, 44, 49, 55, 58, 59–60, 80, 84,
        91–92, 94–95, 99, 102, 105, 109, 113,
        118, 123, 128, 133, 138–39, 140, 157,
        160, 163, 170, 175, 179–80, 185–86,
        190, 194, 196, 202, 205, 208, 212,
        213–14, 245–46
    preparing for, 59, 140, 213
    strategies for, 5–6, 17, 18, 24–25, 28, 32–
        33, 40, 43, 48, 53–54, 57, 79, 83, 90–
        91, 101, 104, 107, 112, 122–23, 126–
        27, 132, 137–38, 156, 162–63, 174,
        178–79, 184, 189, 193–94, 196, 201,
        211, 238–39
    topics for, 3, 6, 10, 17–18, 25, 28–29, 33,
        36–37, 40–41, 43–44, 48–49, 54–55,
        57–58, 59, 79–80, 84, 91, 94, 98–99,
        102, 104–5, 108–9, 112–13, 117–18,
        123, 127, 132–33, 134, 138, 156, 159–
        60, 162, 167, 174–75, 179, 184–85,
        190, 194, 196, 201–2, 204–5, 208,
        211–12

Zen and the Art of Motorcycle Maintenance
    (Pirsig), 227–28
Zongren, Liu, 61–64